MASTERING
PUBLIC
ADMINISTRATION

CHATHAM HOUSE SERIES ON CHANGE IN AMERICAN POLITICS

SERIES EDITOR: Aaron Wildavsky
University of California, Berkeley

MASTERING PUBLIC ADMINISTRATION

From Max Weber to Dwight Waldo

BRIAN R. FRY
University of South Carolina

CHATHAM HOUSE PUBLISHERS
SEVEN BRIDGES PRESS, LLC
NEW YORK • LONDON

MASTERING PUBLIC ADMINISTRATION
From Max Weber to Dwight Waldo

Chatham House Publishers, Inc.
135 Fifth Avenue, 9th Floor, New York, NY 10010-7101

Copyright © 1998 by Chatham House Publishers

Publisher: Edward Artinian
Cover design: Quentin Fiore
Composition: Bang, Motley, Olufsen
Printing and Binding: R.R. Donnelley & Sons Company

Library of Congress Cataloging-in-Publication Data

Fry, Brian R. 1939–
   Mastering public administration / Brian R. Fry
     p.   cm. — [Chatham House series on change in
American politics]
   Includes index.
   ISBN 0-934540-56-X
   1. Public administration—history.   I. Title.   II. Series.
JF1341.F78   1989
350'.0009—dc19   89-624
                                                          CIP

Manufactured in the United States of America
10   9   8   7   6

*To my wife Lois and my son Mark,
who give meaning to my life and
inspiration to my work*

Contents

Preface

Those of us who study and teach public administration often refer to the ideas of authors who have made significant contributions to the field. Yet we seldom have the opportunity to trace the genesis of those ideas, explore the broader context of the writings of the authors, or come to know much about the authors to whose ideas we so frequently refer. This book is intended to provide such a background for those with a shared interest in public administration. For me, the task has been a labor of love, though not without its hardships and frustration. Writing this book has afforded me the opportunity to explore, in some depth, the ideas and lives of people for whom I have had the deepest respect, but, in most cases, comparatively casual acquaintance.

I have, of course, incurred a number of debts of gratitude in this endeavor. A seminar taught by Robert Walker at Stanford University exposed me to the fascination of examining intensively the works of leading authors in public administration. Paul Van Riper gave a careful, and often critical, reading of several of the chapters and some valuable advice about the overall plan of the project. Becky Deaton and Lori Joye provided invaluable secretarial and typing assistance as well as unflagging good spirits under often adverse circumstances. I have benefited beyond this project from the careful editorial attention and suggestions of Marlene Ellin. I am thankful to the support and faith of my wife Lois and my son Mark who never seemed to doubt that a book would eventually emerge from this elongated process. Finally, and most obviously, I am deeply indebted to the authors whose works are reviewed in this volume. I will be content if this modest effort has even a small fraction of the impact and influence of the works that inspired it.

MASTERING
PUBLIC
ADMINISTRATION

Introduction

The intellectual genesis of this book is probably not unusual. The idea arose from a casual request by a colleague for a single reference that would summarize the work and significance of Frederick Taylor and the Scientific Management movement. I was hard pressed to render appropriate advice. General textbooks typically deal with the subject too briefly. Books on the specific subject are too long. Excerpts in readers are not comprehensive. What my colleague wanted was a single source of manageable length that would summarize, in a fairly comprehensive manner, the works and contributions of a major author in the field of public administration. In this book I intend to provide such a source for a collection of leading authors in the field.

A key to the success of this effort is the authors chosen for inclusion. It should be noted at the outset that the book is not meant to be a treatise on the current status of the field of public administration. It is more concerned with origins and how we got where we are than with current status. Consequently, I focus on authors who were pioneers in public administration and whose work largely shaped the current contours of the field. These authors are Max Weber, Frederick Taylor, Luther Gulick, Mary Parker Follett, Elton Mayo, Chester Barnard, Herbert Simon, and Dwight Waldo. The diversity of these authors reflects the diversity of the field of public administration. Several disciplines are represented, with Gulick, Simon, and Waldo trained in political science; Mayo in psychology; Follett in English, political economy, and history; Weber in economics and law; Barnard in economics; and Taylor in mechanical engineering. The level of education also varies, ranging from Barnard, who never received an undergraduate degree, through Weber, Gulick, Simon, and Waldo, who earned Ph.D.s. Follett had an undergraduate degree, and Taylor and Mayo held masters' degrees. They are almost evenly split between academics and practitioners, though there is substantial overlap in those categories. Taylor, Barnard, and Follett were primarily practitioners; Mayo, Weber, Simon, and Waldo are, or were, basically academicians. Gulick has a legitimate claim to membership in both groups.

Perhaps the significance of these authors is best revealed by placing them in the context of the history of the study of public administration

1

in the United States. There are at least three broadly identifiable approaches in that study—the Classical approach, the Behavioral approach, and the Administration-as-Politics approach. Representatives of each approach are included among the authors treated in this volume.

The beginning of the self-conscious study of public administration in the United States is usually traced to Woodrow Wilson's 1887 essay "The Study of Administration." Though the direct impact of his ideas is in some doubt, Wilson's definition of the field expressed in that essay was widely accepted during the Classical period. Writing in response to an age of widespread governmental corruption and in the spirit of the reform movement, Wilson argued that administration should be separated from political and policy concerns. According to Wilson, public administration should be concerned solely with the "detailed and systematic execution of public law."[1] As for political officials and politics, they should set the tasks for administration, but not be "suffered to manipulate its offices."[2] Given this separation of administration from politics, Wilson suggested that the task of the public administrator was not significantly different from that of any administrator: the selection of appropriate means to accomplish given ends.

Based on the preceding postulates, Wilson called for the development of a science of administration, the objective of which should be the discovery of general principles to guide administrators in the efficient performance of their duties. The principles were to be based on systematic and empirical investigations performed on a comparative basis. The call for comparative analysis entailed the examination of administrative techniques successfully employed in other settings—for example, in other political and constitutional systems or in the private sector—and a determination of the applicability of those techniques to the practice of public administration in the United States. Wilson was particularly adamant in asserting that there is no difference between public and private administration. In Wilson's words, "The field of administration is a field of business. It is removed from the hurry and strife of politics. . . . It is a part of political life only as methods of a countinghouse are a part of the life of society; only as machinery is part of the manufactured product."[3]

Wilson's separation of politics from administration, his proposed search for a science of administration, and his assertion that business techniques are applicable in the public sector all became a part of the dominant image of public administration in the Classical period. Policy and political matters were conceptually divorced from administrative matters with efficiency in execution seen as the legitimate area of concern for students and practitioners of public administration. Scientific procedures were espoused, if not fully adopted. And many of the techniques suggested to improve the efficiency of public-sector operations were based on private-sector practices.

Two major groups in the Classical period were the Scientific Management movement and what March and Simon refer to as the *Departmentalists.*[4] Together they formed what was considered the "administrative theory" of the day. Scientific Management, founded by Frederick Taylor, focused on the performance of routine and repetitive physical tasks. The objective of Scientific Management was to discover the basic principles of motion involved in the performance of physical tasks and then to determine the "one best way" of performing any task. The primary tool of analysis in this endeavor was the time-and-motion study. Though its analyses were conducted largely in the private sector, Scientific Management attracted a large number of enthusiasts in the public sector.

The Departmentalist approach formed a logical complement to the Scientific Management movement and is represented in this volume by the works of Luther Gulick. Whereas the primary focus of Scientific Management was the performance of physical tasks, that of the Departmentalists was the formal organizational structure. Accordingly, while the basic tool of analysis of Scientific Management was the time-and-motion study, that of the Departmentalists was the formal organization chart. The general problem addressed by the Departmentalists was the identification of the tasks necessary to accomplish an organizational objective and the grouping and coordination of those tasks in a way that would maximize organizational efficiency. The lexicon of the Departmentalists is familiar. Terms such as *chain of command, span of control,* and *line and staff* are common fare even for those acquainted only peripherally with the literature on organizations. The principles educed by the Departmentalists are equally familiar, if now in a state of some disrepute. Principles such as authority should be commensurate with responsibility, there should be unity of command in the organization, and the chain of command should not be circumvented have become deeply ingrained in our administrative culture. The Departmentalists, as had Scientific Management, sought to establish a science of administration equally applicable in the public and private sectors. They differed from Scientific Management, however, in that their analyses were not as systematic as those of Scientific Management. Moreover, the Departmentalists attempted to derive specific applications from preordained general principles rather than rely on generalizations built inductively from an accumulation of specific observations as had Scientific Management.

The combination of the definition of the field as proposed by Wilson and the Scientific Management and Departmentalist prescriptions for organizational management and structure (relying heavily on hierarchy as a primary mechanism for control and coordination) constituted the core of the Classical approach to public administration. Max Weber's work, too, should at least be mentioned in regard to the Classical approach. Though his work defies either precise classification or delimitation, Weber is related to the Classical approach in two basic ways. First, Weber takes the same position as the Classical authors on the appropriate relationship between the politician and the administrator. For Weber, the bureaucrat should be the neutral servant of his political masters, which is precisely the position embodied in the Classical politics-administration dichotomy. Second, Weber's formulation of the ideal-type bureaucracy is perhaps the most famous summary statement of those attributes and bears a close resemblance to the kind of organization widely prescribed in the Classical approach. Despite those similarities, it would be a mistake to suggest that Weber's influence was limited to the Classical approach. His influence has been pervasive. Weber's support for a value-free social science and his sociological interests are related to similar concerns in the Behavioral approach. His concern with power relationships in society is similar to the basic focus of the Administration-as-Politics approach.

A caveat is probably in order here. Though I have referred to a logical progression and a correlation of ideas, it is often difficult to draw causal linkages among those ideas. Wilson expressed concerns and proposed formulations widely accepted in the Classical approach. But there is little evidence that Wilson's essay was widely known among the authors of the Classical period.[5] There is a direct relationship between the Scientific Management and Departmentalist approaches. Taylor's ideas were widespread and frequently cited in the Departmentalist literature. It is likely that few, if any, of the authors of the Classical approach had read Weber. His writings did not become well known in the United States until some time later. Nevertheless, Weber did know of the Scientific Management movement, and he traveled in the United States; it is possible that some of his later works may have been influenced by these contacts.

Though the Classical approach was dominant in the United States before 1940, it did not go unchallenged. In this period, the seeds were sown for the subsequent flowering of the Behavioral approach. The Behavioral approach defies brief definition. Fesler ascribes the following characteristics to the Behavioral approach: It entails the study of actual behavior, usually with the individual as the preferred unit of analysis; it is multidisciplinary in focus; it calls for "rigor" in the use of scientific procedures; and it proscribes prescription (i.e., it is primarily descriptive in intent). As the word is employed here, *Behavioralism* incorporates a diversity of perspectives, including the Human Relations movement,

4

Simon's model of decision making, organizational humanism, and contingency theory.[6] The Behavioral approach was not much concerned with the Classical definition of the field of public administration. As had the Classical authors, the Behavioralists sought an organization theory that, it was assumed, would be applicable in both public and private settings. The political environment was more ignored than conceptually separated as it had been in the Classical approach. Simon, one of the few students of public administration who identified himself with the Behavioral approach, did suggest that the fact-value dichotomy be substituted for the politics-administration dichotomy, but this was generally viewed at the time as simply another twofold division of the administrative world closely akin to that of politics-administration dichotomy in intent, if not entirely in substance.[7] The major thrust of the Behavioral approach was organization structure and management, not definition of the field, and here the differences from the Classical approach are substantial.

The Behavioral approach sought to modify, though seldom to eliminate, the hierarchical organizational structures so ardently espoused by Classical authors. This was thought to be necessary to appeal to a wider range of human needs and thus effectively motivate man in the organization. Accordingly, the Behavioral approach supported a number of changes in organizational structure and process. Whereas the Classical approach emphasized executive decision-making responsibilities, the Behavioral approach argued for more participatory decision-making procedures. Supervision under the Classical approach was to be basically "production-oriented" while the Behavioral approach supported a more "employee-oriented" style of supervision. The Classical approach (particularly Scientific Management) preached the benefits of specialization, but the Behavioral approach counseled job enlargement (i.e., expanding the range of work functions performed) to give employees more of a sense of satisfaction from the performance of their tasks. The Classical approach urged a restricted span of control to ensure close supervision. The Behavioral approach suggested a wider span of control to prevent close supervision and allow sufficient latitude for the expression of self-initiative and self-control on the part of the worker. The Classical authors demanded centralization in the name of control and coordination. The Behavioral authors insisted on decentralization to give more members of the organization a greater sense of control over their own destinies.

These contrasts in managerial style were derived, in large part, from more fundamental conceptual differences between the two approaches. The approaches differ most basically in their notions about the relationship between man and the organization. In the Classical approach, there was what might be called a "mechanical view" of man in the organization. It was assumed that man was involved only segmentally in the organization (i.e., work was only one of many interests and not necessarily the primary interest), and the member of the organization sought instrumental rewards that could be used to obtain basic satisfactions elsewhere. Given this conceptualization of the relationship between man and the organization and assuming that money is the primary instrumental reward, it was felt that man's behavior in the organization could be controlled by the judicious manipulation of monetary incentives.

The Behavioralists construct a substantially different scenario. For the Behavioralists, man's behavior is more variable (less manipulable) than had been presumed by Classical authors. In part, this is because man is, or should be, more totally involved in the organization and should expect intrinsic, rather than merely instrumental, rewards from the organizational experience. These social and psychological rewards extend beyond money and are less easily manipulated than are monetary incentives. Moreover, there are forces affecting man's behavior in the organization that are either beyond the control of the organization or at least more difficult for the organization to control. Internal to the organization are informal groups, a major focus of analysis for the Behavioral approach, which often elude organizational control but act as major determinants of individual behavior. Beyond the organization lie a variety of social forces that influence behavior in the organization but are likely to escape organizational control.

All of this means, according to the Behavioralists, that the organization must learn to respond to a wider range of human needs if it is effectively to motivate man in the organization, let alone control his behavior. Organization man may be malleable, but he is not necessarily compliant. The organization cannot simply assume obedience to its directives, it must actively seek the consent and compliance of its participants. Indeed, the question of how best to secure compliance is a major theme, perhaps the central theme, of the Behavioral literature.

There were also some major differences between the Classical and Behavioral approaches in the methods employed to realize the common ambition of constructing a science of administration. The Classical approach, as has been mentioned, was largely deductive and normative in its emphasis. The Behavioral approach, in contrast, was more inductive and descriptive in emphasis. The Behavioral approach pursued much of its research in the logical-positivist tradition stressing the operationalization of concepts, the use of systematic techniques of analysis in the testing of hypotheses, and generalization based on an accumulation of empirical findings. Normative attributions about organizations were not so much abandoned as deferred pending the acquisition of more descriptive information.[8] It was maintained that we should not try to prescribe how organizations should operate (normative analysis) until we know more about how they actually operate (descriptive analysis).

The works of Mary Parker Follett, Elton Mayo, and Chester Barnard are all integral to this developing challenge to the Classical organizational paradigm and precursors to the development of the Behavioral approach. Follett's work was the earliest of these, and her work anticipated by more than two decades some of the central themes of the Behavioral period. Most prominent among them were Follett's ideas about the nature of authority in the organization. In contrast to the Classical literature, which maintained that coordination flows from the exercise of authority and that authority resides in the apex of the organizational pyramid, Follett argues the authority flows from coordination and that authority is neither supreme nor is it delegated. Instead, authority is pluralistic (i.e., it exists at many points in the organization), and it is "cumulative" (i.e., it arises from below instead of descending from above). Moreover, Follett argues that authority is exercised increasingly on the basis of the objective demands of the situation rather than personal and arbitrary mandates. Finally, Follett contends that authority is not a final moment of decision embodied in a command, but a reciprocally conditioned relationship among hierarchical superiors and subordinates in a series of interactions that precede, and determine, final choice.

Mayo's famous research at the Hawthorne Plant of the Western Electric Company in the late 1920s and early 1930s laid much of the conceptual and empirical foundation for the Behavioral approach. Indeed, this research led directly to the Human Relations movement, a major component of the Behavioral approach. Mayo's research focused on social and psychological factors in human behavior in the organization with particular emphasis on informal group activity. Mayo asserts that informal groups develop within the organization in response to needs and expectations not effectively served by the formal organization and adopt norms of behavior that are not necessarily the same as those of the organization. Moreover, these informal groups, which are nowhere described in the organization chart, exert significant influence on individual behavior in the organization. Mayo contends that management must learn to deal with these groups, and to respond to the needs and expectations expressed therein, in order to achieve the objectives of the organization. By directing attention to the social and psychological aspects of organizational behavior, the Western Electric researches set the stage for a continuing empirical investigation of the relationship between changes in the organization (with particular emphasis on style of supervision), worker satisfaction, and productivity as emphasis shifted to precisely those elements of human feelings, passions, and sentiments that were largely either avoided or ignored in the Classical literature on organizations.

Barnard provides a conceptualization of the organization supportive of both Follett's ideas on authority and Mayo's assertion that subordinate needs, as they perceive them, must be satisfied to achieve organizational effectiveness. Barnard asserts that the organization is a system of exchange in which each participant makes contributions in return for inducements offered by the organization. Both organizational inducements and individual contributions are subjectively evaluated by each participant, and an individual's participation will continue only as long as the participant perceives that the value of the inducements received from the organization exceeds the value of the contributions required by the organization. Why, then, should the organization pay attention to subordinate needs as they themselves see them? Because each subordinate subjectively evaluates the balance of contributions required and inducements received, and will terminate his association with the organization if these expectations and needs are not being met. This view of the organization prompts Barnard to formulate a concept of authority in a manner generally consistent with that of Follett. Barnard defines authority as "the character of a communication (order) in a formal organization by virtue of which it is accepted by a contributor to or 'member' of the organization as governing the action he contributes."[9] In short, authority lies in the consent of the governed. As such, it resides in a relationship between a superior and a subordinate, not in a position, and it is exercised only on acceptance of a directive, not on its issuance. By so defining authority, Barnard emphasizes the role of subordinate and the importance of compliance.

If Follett, Mayo, and Barnard were precursors of the Behavioral movement, Simon was an important part of the movement itself. Simon's distinctive contribution was to shift the focus of analysis to decision making in the organization. More specifically, Simon argued that the science of administration should be founded on the factual premises of administrative decision making. In examining decision making, Simon sought to reconcile the rational-choice model of economic theory (and at least implicit in Classical administrative theory) with the emergent findings on human behavior in the organization. In Simon's hands the image of man is transformed from the "lightning quick" and omniscient calculator of the economics literature into an empirically more realistic image of a decision maker limited in cognitive and analytical abilities who chooses alternatives that are likely to be merely satisfactory rather than optimal.

This revised view of the decision maker is relevant to the organization in that the organization must devise ways to cope with the probable limits on rationality in human decision making. The primary

8

organizational strategy for dealing with human decision-making frailties is to devise appropriate decision premises so that organizationally rational decisions can be made despite the likelihood of individually nonrational processes. This means that the organization should alert the individual to decision situations (by structuring stimuli in the organizational environment) and provide decision rules that can be mechanically applied to render an organizationally correct outcome.

This returns Simon to the central theme of the Behavioral approach—the problem of compliance. The problem is simply translated from a question of authority in general to a question of getting the subordinate to recognize and apply the appropriate decision rule. This Simon sees as largely a problem of providing appropriate inducements so that individuals will respond in the desired manner.

As was the case with the Classical authors, there are both interesting relationships, and a lack thereof, among these authors and between these authors and those of the Classical approach. Follett was known, but not extensively cited, by the authors considered here. One of her pieces did appear in the famous *Papers on the Science of Administration*. Mayo was similarly included in the *Papers*. Interestingly enough, Mayo considered his work to be more a complement to, than a substitute for, the Classical formulation. As Mayo put it, there are three dimensions to management: the application of science and technical skill (the primary emphasis of Scientific Management), the systematic ordering of operations (the primary emphasis of the Departmentalists), and the organization of teamwork and cooperation. Mayo sought to redress what he perceived to be an imbalance in previous works by stressing the problem of securing teamwork and cooperation. Though the relationship between Mayo's work and that of Barnard seems obvious, Barnard denies that Mayo had any influence on his ideas about the organization. In contrast, the relationship between Barnard and Simon is both present and acknowledged. Simon relies heavily on Barnard's conceptualization of the organization as a system of exchange. There are also some intriguing relationships between Simon and the Classical authors, especially with those in the Scientific Management movement. In particular, Simon's continuing stress on hierarchical control and coordination, here exercised through the formulation and induced application of decision rules, would appear to be more closely akin to the Classical stance than that of his Behavioral brethren.

The ideas of this set of authors have also had substantial impact on their successors, or contemporaries, in the Behavioral approach. The Human Relations movement was a direct outgrowth of research at the Western Electric Company. This movement sought ways of restructuring the organization and revamping managerial styles to become more responsive to a wider range of social and psychological needs in the organization. A related, but more negative, approach focused on bureaucratic organizations and their dysfunctional consequences and is exemplified by the writings of authors such as Robert Merton, Philip Selznick, and Peter Blau. Combined, these approaches pronounced a need for change and stimulated a search for alternatives to the hierarchical structures so warmly embraced in the Classical literature.

The Human Relations approach, in turn, prompted its own reaction as we move into the more contemporary literature. One response addressed the empirical difficulties encountered by the Human Relations approach in the attempt to sort out the relationships among organizational characteristics, worker satisfaction, and productivity. To state the matter briefly, it was found that the suggested changes in the organization did not, as had been expected, always lead to higher levels of satisfaction, nor were higher levels of satisfaction always associated with increased productivity. The response to these empirical difficulties came in the form of the Contingency approach. Contingency theory suggests that the Human Relations approach made the same mistake as had the Classical authors in assuming that there is one best way of managing all organizations. The Contingency approach suggests that management is a relative and adaptive process and that the appropriate style is contingent on a number of organizational considerations. The task assumed by the Contingency approach is to stipulate the conditions under which a particular approach is likely to be successful.

A second response to Human Relations has been what has been called *organizational humanism*. Based originally on the conceptual apparatus of humanist psychologist Abraham Maslow, organizational humanism is more concerned with the morality of the Human Relations movement than its empirical difficulties. Here it is argued that the Human Relations approach, as was the Classical approach, is simply concerned with raising productivity. The only difference, it is argued, is that whereas the Classical approach relied primarily on command, the Human Relations approach employs more sophisticated forms of psychological manipulation. Organizational humanism attempts to establish the intrinsic value of the satisfaction of human needs in the organization, rather than view it simply as a means for increasing productivity.

The second major challenge to the Classical paradigm came in the form of the Administration-as-Politics approach, and in combination with the Behavioral approach questioned every fundamental premise of the Classical perspective. Whereas the basic difference between the Classical and Behavioral approaches concerns the way organizations should be structured and managed, the basic difference between the Classical approach and the Administration-as-Politics approach lies in their differing definitions of the field of public administration. In direct contrast to the Classical approach, the Administration-as-Politics approach maintains that it is impossible, and undesirable, to separate politics from administration. Consequently, public administration is different from private administration with the distinguishing characteristic of public administration being the political milieu in which the public administrator is required to operate. Moreover, this approach questions the possibility of separating facts and values. The combination of the rejection of the politics-administration dichotomy and the reservations about the fact-value dichotomy mean that the Administration-as-Politics approach considers public administration to be both art and science, and perhaps more art than science.

The politics-administration dichotomy is rejected on both empirical and normative grounds. Empirically, it is argued that even casual observation reveals that administrators are involved in political and policy concerns. An age of size and complexity requires the exercise of administrative initiative in the formulation of policy and the exercise of administrative discretion in its implementation, and both activities centrally involve the administrator in policy and political processes. Normatively, it is maintained that separating the administrator from policy and political matters deprives society of the creative input of those likely to be best informed about the programs they administer and tends to insulate the administrator from the legitimate demands of the public he is charged with serving.

With the rejection of the politics-administration dichotomy, the central challenge for the Administration-as-Politics approach is to seek a satisfactory reconciliation of the necessity of administration and the requirements of democracy. This concern manifests itself in two forms: a focus of the concept of administrative responsibility and an emphasis on the public policy process itself. The former, a focus on administrative responsibility, has concentrated on defining an appropriate role for the administrator in a pluralistic political environment. The Classical approach had stressed a role of neutrality regarding policy matters. The Administration-as-Politics approach counsels a role of policy advocacy, but with some differences about the standards on which that advocacy should be based. At first, the emphasis was on professional standards as the appropriate base. Later emphasis switched to representing clientele interests. This culminated in what has been called the *new public administration* which stressed participation both within the organization in a spiritual alliance with organizational humanism and clientele representation with the administrator charged with a special responsibility for representing those interests not adequately reflected through the formal electoral process or by elected representatives. This meant, for the most part, an obligation to represent the interests of minorities and the poor. The second development in the Administration-as-Politics approach has been an analytical interest in the processes by which policy is formulated, adopted, implemented, and evaluated. In part, this has led to increasing concern with the techniques of policy analysis, such as planning and evaluation. More generally, there has been a focus on the policy process with particular emphasis on the role of the administrator at various stages of the process.

I have included the works of Dwight Waldo in this volume, in part because they are illustrative of the concerns of the Administration-as-Politics approach, those concerns being stated most forcefully in his book *The Administrative State*. Beyond that, Waldo is widely recognized as perhaps the chief chronicler of the development of the field of public administration and one of its most astute critics.

The diversity of the field of public administration is reflected both in the selection of authors to be included in this volume and the history just recounted. There are two basic reasons for this. First, public administration is notoriously a borrowing discipline, if indeed "discipline" is the right word. It has borrowed heavily from economics, business administration, sociology, psychology, and political science and draws what cohesiveness it possesses more from its object of analysis than its intellectual parentage. The second factor promoting diversity in public administration is its sometimes unnerving tendency to be cumulative rather than substitutive in its development. In other words, the field tends simply to add new ideas to old rather than substitute the new for the old. Take the ideas of the Classical period, for example. The staying power of those ideas is attributable to both the prescriptive nature of that literature (i.e., it tells you what to do if something is wrong and focuses on factors largely under the control of the organization) and the basic truth that formal organizational structure has an important influence on behavior in organizations. As a result, many of those ideas still live, sometimes in different manifestations, such as what is now called *management science* and the new emphasis on organizational design, and sometimes in much the same incarnation as is the case with industrial engineering. The result of this cumulative development is a field whose ideas and perspectives, though often complementary, sometimes exist in a state of uneasy, internal tension.

Let me conclude this introduction with some comments on the possible uses of the book and its construction. The book can serve in a number of roles. The introductory course at both undergraduate and graduate levels is, I think, the most obvious setting for the adoption of this book. I have incorporated readings from the manuscript in an introductory course at the graduate level. This has met with a positive response, though from an admittedly biased sample. That should not be the limit of its utility, however. It would also be useful in courses on administrative/organization theory and personnel administration. Selected chapters could be useful in fields such as public policy (the Simon chapter) or collective bargaining and labor relations (Follett). Given the diversity of the authors covered, some chapters (or the entire book) may be of value in fields such as business administration and social work.

The book is not meant to be a substitute for a general textbook, nor is it a replacement for selected excerpts from the authors themselves. Each of these vehicles has a specific function to perform. The textbook places the authors in a broader context. The excerpts expose the student directly to the words and ideas of the authors and allows the instructor to emphasize particular points. I think this book is best thought of as a supplemental text and is best used in conjunction with other resources in a manner that will allow the instructor to capitalize on the comparative advantages of each of the media of presentation.

In regard to construction, a number of comments are in order. One important matter is the authors omitted from consideration. I think few would quarrel with the selection of the authors included in the book; the exclusions are likely to be more controversial. One does not have to contemplate the matter at any great length to assemble a much longer list of worthy contributors to public administration, particularly within the generous confines of the field as defined here. I can only plead limitations of time and space and signal my intent to expand the coverage if this initial effort is well received. I would welcome suggestions in this regard. Another consideration is the style used in writing the chapters. I have tried to be faithful to the style and tone of the authors in attempting to write these summaries as the authors themselves might have done. In so doing, I have attempted to segregate personal evaluations and confine them to a section on "summary and conclusions."

Finally, a word about the sequencing of the chapters. I have grouped authors according to the relationship among their ideas. Weber and Waldo serve as "bookends" for the others. Weber provides a useful beginning by placing the study and practice of public administration in the broader historical context of the processes of rationalization in society. Weber is also logically related, as noted earlier, to the works of the Classical period. The Weber chapter is followed by chapters on Frederick Taylor and Luther Gulick, representatives of the Scientific Management and Departmentalist perspectives. This is followed by chapters on Mary Parker Follett, Elton Mayo, and Chester Barnard, whose works signal the nascent stages of the Behavioral approach. Next comes Herbert Simon, who borrows heavily from the previous authors (particularly Barnard), represents some major elements of the Behavioral approach, and introduces a focus on decision making. The final chapter is on Dwight Waldo, who was chosen both to relate some features of the Administration-as-Politics approach and to provide a fitting conclusion in his review and assessment of the development of the enterprise of public administration in the United States.

Notes

1. See Woodrow Wilson, "The Study of Administration," *Political Science Quarterly* 2 (June 1887): 212. There is some controversy about whether Wilson really meant for politics/policy and administration to be separated. His statements in the article are confusing, if not contradictory, and admit of differing interpretations. My conclusion is that Wilson did intend to suggest such a separation, though with reservations.

2. Ibid., 10.

3. Ibid.

4. James C. March and Herbert A. Simon, *Organizations* (New York: Wiley, 1958), 22.

5. See Paul P. Van Riper, "The Administrative State: Wilson and the Founders—An Unorthodox View," *Public Administration Review* 43, no. 6 (November/December 1983): 478–79.

6. James W. Fesler, "Public Administration and the Social Sciences: 1946 to 1960," in *American Public Administration: Past, Present, Future*, ed. Frederick C. Mosher (University, Ala.: University of Alabama Press, 1975), 114–15.

7. There is some question about whether or not Simon should be classified as a Behavioralist. I do so for two primary reasons. First, he fits the general criteria proposed by Fesler as cited above. Second, he attempts to incorporate many of the findings of the Behavioral approach in his own work. There are some difficulties with such a classification. Most significantly, Simon has little in common with the analysis of the Human Relations movement or the organizational humanists—also classified as part of the Behavioral approach—in regard to the affective elements of organizational behavior, the importance of the satisfaction of human needs in the organization, or the appropriate organizational responses to such considerations.

8. Some have argued that normative attributions were not so much deferred as they were hidden. As we see in later chapters, a substantial portion of the Behavioral approach, particularly in the form of the Human Relations movement, has been challenged as ideologically based and involving unstated or unwarranted assumptions about the nature of man and/or his relationship with the organization. See especially the following chapters on Elton Mayo and Dwight Waldo.

9. Chester I. Barnard, *The Functions of the Executive*, 30th Anniversary ed. (Cambridge, Mass.: Harvard University Press, 1968), 163.

CHAPTER 1

Max Weber:
The Process of Rationalization

To include the works of Max Weber in a volume on the study and practice of public administration in the United States may, on its face, seem somewhat unusual. Max Weber, a German sociologist, was neither much read nor often noted in this country until considerably after the beginnings of the field of public administration as an object of self-conscious study. Moreover, administration was not the principal focus of Weber's analysis. The reason for considering Weber is that he places public administration, including public administration in the United States (of which he was quite conscious), in a broad historical context and sees the processes of public administration as part of the more general process of rationalization in Western societies. The purpose of this chapter is not to attempt to summarize Weber's works; that would be an impossible task in the space available. The scope of Weber's interests and the reach of his intellect are truly awesome. Instead, the more modest ambition is to place Weber's ideas about administration in the broader setting of his more general concerns with processes of rationalization and patterns of domination. His analysis of the social and historical context of administration and, more particularly, bureaucracy may well be Weber's distinctive contribution to the literature on public administration and probably accounts for his lasting impact on the field.

Weber clearly saw administration in general, and bureaucracy in particular, as vital to these processes. Indeed, Weber asserts that domination is exerted through administration and that legal domination requires bureaucracy for its exercise. Moreover, Weber considered bureaucracy to be the most rational and efficient form of organization yet devised by man. In this stance, Weber, who may have penned the most famous statement on bureaucracy, uses the term in a manner opposite to its common meaning, both before and after he wrote. Not only that, Weber contends that bureaucracy embodies a concept of justice familiar to Western systems of jurisprudence. In the case of bureaucracy, the "equal application of the law" is simply translated into the equal (and impersonal) application of the rule.

Despite his general admiration for bureaucracy, Weber was also aware of its flaws. As an organizational form, bureaucracy subjects the individual to an oppressive routine, limits individual freedom, and favors the "crippled personality" of the specialist. As a potential political force, bureaucracy becomes a danger when it oversteps its proper function and attempts to control the rule of law rather than be subject to it. Weber argues that the bureaucrat should stay out of politics and limit himself to the "impartial administration of his office" and that he should subordinate his personal opinion on matters of policy to his sense of duty.

There are obvious relationships between Weber and the authors of the Classical period. His call for bureaucrats to be the neutral servants of their political masters echoes Wilson's admonition that administrators should be responsible only for the efficient execution of the law. His description of the "ideal-type bureaucracy" is similar in form and process to organizations widely prescribed by the Classical authors. But to limit Weber's influence to the Classical approach alone would be misguided. His call for the construction of a value-free social science corresponds to the the ambition and stated intent, if not the accomplishment, of the Behavioral approach. His overall concern with power relationships in society is similar to the concerns of the Administration-as-Politics approach. In short, Weber's influence, although often indirect, has been pervasive in the field of public administration.

Life

Max Weber was born in Erfurt, Thuringia, Germany, on 21 April 1864. Weber's family numbered among its members a long line of persons distinguished in the professions, especially the Lutheran clergy. Weber's father, Max Weber, Sr., was a prosperous right-wing politician whose governmental posts included a seat in the Reichstag. Weber's mother, Helene Fallenstein Weber, was a cultured liberal woman of the Protestant faith and the daughter of a well-to-do official.

Weber was a sickly child, suffering from meningitis at an early age, and the object of his mother's brooding concern. As a student in his pre-university years, Weber had a recognized talent, but was perceived to lack routine industry by his teachers, who were not much impressed by this stringy young man with sloping shoulders.[1]

In 1882 Weber commenced the study of economics, philosophy, and law at the University of Heidelberg. He also began to change from a slender, withdrawn adolescent into a large, pompously virile young man. Weber joined heartily in the social life of a dueling fraternity, engaged in drinking bouts, and fell into debt. After three semesters at

Heidelberg, Weber moved to Strassburg to serve a year in the military. Here, Weber, who would later become a recognized authority on bureaucracy, suffered under what he considered to be the stupidity of barracks drill and the chicanery of junior officers. He rebelled against attempts to, in his words, "domesticate thinking beings into machines responding to commands with automatic precision."[2] On receiving his officer's commission, however, Weber learned to see the brighter side of army life.

The next year Weber resumed his studies, this time at Göttingen University in Berlin. In 1886 he took his first examination in law and subsequently took up the practice of law in Berlin. Three years later, Weber completed a Ph.D. thesis and subsequently qualified as a university teacher by writing a thesis on Roman and agrarian legal history. In 1892 Weber obtained a position teaching law in Berlin.

The following year Weber married Marianne Schnitzer, a second cousin on his father's side and reputed to be something of a beauty. She was to become one of the leading exponents of women's rights in Germany. After his marriage, Weber embarked on the life of a successful young scholar in Berlin, and his early academic years were filled with both practical studies directed at public policy issues and more scholarly works. Weber soon accepted a chair in economics at the University of Frieberg, having found economics to be more challenging than legal history, and in 1897 he became a professor of economics at Heidelberg.

Complications in Weber's life began shortly thereafter. Following his appointment at Heidelberg, Weber had a quarrel with his father. The father died shortly afterward, and Weber suffered a nervous breakdown. This forced him to suspend his regular work, and he would not resume that work for a period of approximately six years. After three and one-half years, Weber did return to a light schedule of work at Heidelberg. Although he suffered repeated setbacks, Weber published a book review in 1903, and by 1904 his writing productivity was returning to its previous level. In the same year Weber visited the United States where he delivered a paper and toured the country.

Weber spent the war years as a hospital administrator; after the war, he served as a consultant to the German Armistice Commission in Versailles and to a commission that drafted the Weimar constitution.[3] In 1918 Weber spent the summer in Vienna where he gave his first university lectures in nineteen years. He still experienced compulsive anxieties, however, and had to use opiates in order to sleep. Weber accepted an academic position in Munich in 1919, but held it only for a short time before his death from influenza at the age of fifty-six in June 1920.

Weber has been graphically described by a personal associate as follows: He was tall with heavy hair and a graying beard that covered two dueling scars obtained in his youth; he had a beautifully modulated baritone voice, eyes that were simultaneously kindly and critical, and a pug nose; he spoke in an exquisite German entirely different from his labored writing style; his face was manly, and he had a volcanic temperament coupled with occasional coarseness.[4] Weber was capable of both great impetuosity and righteous indignation. He had an ascetic drive for work and was considered by his colleagues at Heidelberg to be a difficult person with a demanding conscience and a rigidity of honor.[5]

Weber did not consider himself to be a scholar, and although he chose an academic career, he held a regular academic position for only five years. Weber was reportedly more at home on a political platform than in an academic setting. In politics, Weber was, in the context of his times, a "liberal" and a "nationalist." As a liberal, he fought against both conservatives, who sought protection for agriculture and bureaucratic control of industry, and the Marxists.[6] As a nationalist, Weber believed in force as the last argument of any policy and he developed a German tendency to "brutalize romance and to romanticize cynicism."[7] In Weber's words, "Policy making is not a moral trade, nor can it ever be."[8] As both a nationalist and a German patriot, Weber perceived the German culture to be worth preserving against the Russian menace and the rising Slavic tide. Weber even had fleeting political ambitions. He had an opportunity to be nominated for election to the National Assembly in 1918, but he refused to make any effort on his own behalf and lost the nomination.

Religion, as we see later in this chapter, played an important role in Weber's sociology, but he described himself as "religiously unmusical."[9] Although Protestantism was integral to his family, Weber rejected conventional "church" Christianity and was indifferent toward religion in general. He was apparently equally repulsed by his father's philistinism and his mother's piety. Nonetheless, Weber's writings on religion start from a Protestant viewpoint and offer the ideas generated by Protestantism as the wave of the future.[10]

Weber's Sociology

Widely acknowledged as one of the founders of modern social science, Weber conceived of sociology as a science with the objective of interpreting and understanding social conduct. Weber's own ambition was to examine the relationships between economic institutions and actions and all other social institutions and actions constituting a given social structure.[11]

Though Weber acknowledges that sociology is not confined to the study of social action, it is the main focus of his analysis. Weber viewed the world of man in society as "a world of unit social acts, ordered by the need to make choices for an always uncertain future in terms of some principle of choice which we call a value."[12] In analyzing social action, Weber hoped to go beyond statements of "lawful regularities" (the limited preoccupation of the natural sciences) to the definition of the causal and motivational forces that produce systems of action in social situations. More precisely, Weber is concerned with examining and explaining individual, purposive, rational social actions.

Weber's focus on motivated behavior means that he is interested in what he calls "meaningful" action, not merely reactive behavior. Processes that are not the results of motivations are to be considered only conditions, stimuli, or circumstances that further or hinder motivated individual action. Moreover, the affective and irrational components of human behavior are relegated to the status of "deviations" from rational behavior as Weber concentrates on "ideal type" rational behavior such as that exhibited in the formal elements of law and pure economic theory.[13] Weber's sociology thus focuses on the single deliberate action of the individual that is directed toward affecting the behavior of others. The intention of the act is primary, and the success, failure, or unanticipated consequences are of only secondary importance.

Weber asserts that individual actions fall into categories and that they can be combined into social structures. His intent is to understand the categories and structures of social actions as they have appeared in history. In classifying social actions, Weber's distinctions are based on degrees of rationality. These range from rational expediencies such as economic actions, which are the most understandable of motivated actions, through the pursuit of absolute ends and affectual actions flowing from sentiments, to instinctual behavior and traditional conduct. Weber groups social actions by their determinants and orientations. Purposive, rational conduct is determined rationally and is oriented toward discrete individual ends. Affectual conduct is both determined by, and oriented toward, feelings and emotions. Traditional conduct is determined by, and oriented toward, historical precedent. These categories of social action yield three kinds of social structure: *society*, which is based on rationally expedient social action; *association*, which is based on affective social action; and *community*, which is based on traditional social action.[14]

Weber's approach to sociology is one of the primary alternatives to a Marxist perspective, and it was clearly intended as such by the author. Weber felt that Marx had only a partial perspective on history and had unduly emphasized material interests in his analysis. In contrast, Weber argues for causal pluralism in which factors such as nationalism and ethnicity join material interests as determinants of social actions. Although Weber agrees with Marx's belief that ideas are powerless unless joined with economic interests, he denies that ideas are simply reflections of those economic interests. Weber emphasizes the autonomous role of ideas and is concerned with the relative balance between "ideal" and "material" factors in history.[15] This viewpoint is most dramatically stated, of course, in Weber's famous analysis of the relationship between Protestantism and capitalism in which Weber argues that the particular form of capitalism that arose in the West was, in large part, a product of the ideas and ethic of Protestantism. Of this, I have more to say later.

This emphasis on the importance of ideas leads Weber to distinguish between class and status and to identify the latter as the primary basis of social dynamics. According to Weber, while class is based solely on economic power, status is determined by social estimates of honor and a style of life.[16] Weber maintains that society is a composite of positively and negatively privileged status groups with the positively privileged status groups attempting to preserve their style of life through the monopolization of economic opportunities. Consequently, for every idea or value one should seek out the status group whose ideal and material interests are served. Conflicts among the divergent interests of status groups are resolved in social patterns of compliance and domination.[17]

A final distinction between Marx and Weber is the role of class struggle in their formulations. Weber does not deny the importance of class struggle, but he does reject the idea that class struggle is the central dynamic of society. Instead, Weber emphasizes the forces of rationalization and their organizational counterpart, bureaucracy. Human behavior is thus guided not only by economic interests but also by social affinity (status) and a legitimate order of authority that depends on a bureaucratic structure for its exercise.

Weber's Methodology

Weber's methodological objective is to make possible the treatment of social phenomena in a systematic and scientific manner. Although he personally contributed little to the realm of quantitative studies, Weber emphasizes the possibility of using quantitative techniques to define and explain social and cultural matters. Weber himself uses a comparative, historical approach to conduct causal analyses of social action.

A crucial aspect of Weber's methodology is his use of the "ideal type" construct. Weber believes the construction of ideal types to be essential to causal analysis, and it was part of his broader effort to codify the concepts of the social sciences. Weber asserts that two kinds of meaning can be ascribed to social behavior: a concrete meaning and a theoretical or "pure" type of subjective meaning. The problem with concrete meaning is that there is a bewildering variety of actual social phenomena each of which is complex in its own right. Consequently, most concepts in the social sciences are necessarily abstractions from reality, not "presuppositionless" descriptions, and they are not likely actually to appear in their full conceptual integrity.[18]

The ideal type is intended as a mental construct that categorizes thought and helps capture the "infinite manifoldness of reality."[19] More precisely, the ideal type is the conceptual construction of elements of reality into a logically precise combination that represents historical phenomena but that may never be found in its ideally pure form in concrete reality.

It is important to understand what Weber's ideal type is *not*. The ideal type is not a description of reality. Reality is too complex to be seized and held. It is not a hypothesis, though it can be used to generate hypotheses. Most emphatically, it is not a normative model. As Weber puts it, the ideal type "has no connection at all with value judgements and it has nothing to do with any type of perfection other than a purely logical one."[20] The ideal type is, "the pure case, never actualized, uncluttered by extraneous attributes and ambiguities."[21]

The Role of Science

Science, according to Weber, is the affair of an intellectual aristocracy and its quest the knowledge of the particular causes of social phenomena. It is not possible to analyze all social phenomena, however, Weber notes that a description of even the smallest slice of reality can never be exhaustive and that one can bring order to the confusion of reality only by concentrating on that part of reality that is interesting and significant in regard to cultural values. Accordingly, a cultural social science necessarily involves some subjective presuppositions in regard to significance.[22]

It is clear that Weber sees a crucial role for values in the development of a cultural social science. Value discussions are important in the elaboration of value axioms as one attempts to discover general, irreducible evaluations. Value discussions are important in deducing the implications of value axioms. Value discussions are important in the determination of the factual consequences of alternative courses of action insofar as necessary means or unavoidable consequences are involved. Value discussions are important in providing empirical research with problems for investigation, particularly in Weber's cultural social science. Moreover, science itself is not free from suppositions of its own that may mask value orientations.[23] Science supposes both that the rules of logic and method are valid and that the knowledge yielded is worth knowing. These suppositions are based on faith, not proof.

Nonetheless, Weber argues strongly that science must eschew value judgments and seek "ethical neutrality." By value judgments, Weber means practical evaluations of the satisfactory or unsatisfactory character of the phenomena under consideration.[24] Weber asserts that there is no way to resolve conflicts about value judgments except by acceptance of a transcendental order of values such as those prescribed by ecclesiastical dogmas. Such an acceptance, he contends, is more an intellectual sacrifice than an assertion of science. Weber asserts that science cannot tell us what we shall do, it cannot tell us how we shall live, it cannot tell us whether the world has meaning or whether it makes sense to live in such a world.[25] These matters, however important, are simply beyond the legitimate purview of science.

In particular, Weber condemns those who "feel themselves competent to enunciate their evaluations on ultimate questions 'in the name of science' in governmentally privileged lecture halls in which they are neither controlled, checked by discussion, nor subject to contradiction."[26] Weber argues that it is one thing to state facts, to determine mathematical or logical relationships, or to reveal the internal structure of cultural values. It is another to take a stand on the value of culture itself. The task of the teacher is to serve students with knowledge and scientific experiment, not to imprint values or personal political views. The teacher in the lecture hall should simply fulfill a given task in a workmanlike fashion, recognize facts and distinguish them from personal evaluations, and repress the impulse to exhibit personal tastes or other sentiments unnecessarily. Weber contends that those who seek something more than analysis and statements of fact in the classroom crave a leader, not a teacher.[27]

Processes of Rationalization

In moving from the method of sociology to its substance, Weber focuses on the concept of rationalization, which he considers to be the most general element in the philosophy of history and the constitutive element of modern Western society.[28] Weber contends that it is only in the contemporary West that science exists at a stage recognized as valid, that law is characterized by the strictly systematic forms of thought essential to rational jurisprudence, and that the trained official has become the pillar of both the modern state and economic life. Weber measures the degree of rationalization in society in two ways. Positively, rationalization is measured by the extent to which ideas gain in systematic coherence and consistency. Negatively, it is measured by the displacement of magical elements of thought. A second and related emphasis in Weber's analysis is the concept of domination. Weber maintains that the emergence of rational societies is critically dependent on the way in which domination has been exercised. Domination, for Weber, is a subset of the broader phenomenon of power. Weber defines power as the possibility of imposing one's will on the behavior of other persons despite their resistance.[29] Domination is distinguished from other exercises of power on the basis of the perceived legitimacy of its exercise; that is, for domination, it is believed that the ruler has the right to exercise power and the ruled have a duty to obey.[30] Weber describes two forms of domination: domination based on constellations of interests and domination based on authority.[31] Domination based on constellations of interests is found in religious and economic associations, whereas domination based on authority is found in legal and bureaucratic relationships.

Domination Based on Constellations of Interests

The first form of domination based on constellations of interests is religion. Weber's sociology of religion contains three major themes: an explanation of the distinguishing features of Western civilization; an analysis of the relationship between social stratification and religious ideas; and an examination of the effects of religious ideas on economic activities. Underlying all of this is Weber's central theme of the rationalization of the processes of domination, which, for religion, comes in a movement from magicians to priests who attempt to protect their positions by systematizing established beliefs. Weber identifies domination within each religion with a particular status group of religious leaders. For Confucianism, that status group is governmental officials with a literary education; for Hinduism, it is a hereditary caste of expert advisers (Brahmins); for Judaism, it is intellectuals trained in ritual and literature; and for Christianity, it is the urban bourgeoisie. Nevertheless, Weber did not argue that religion is simply a function of the ideal, material, or political interests of a particular status group. Instead, the church stands for a universalism of grace and for the ethical sufficiency of all who are enrolled under its institutional authority. Moreover, as is the case with all bureaucracies, there is a democratic tendency in religions as they become bureaucratized that fights against status privileges, an argument to which I return in discussing bureaucratic organizations.[32]

Weber's analysis of Christianity focuses primarily on the Protestant sects and their relationship to capitalism. His interest in the development of capitalism is derived both from his perception that capitalism has been a pervasive and unifying theme in modern history and from a desire to respond to Marx's concept of historical materialism. Weber's examination of the relationship between Protestantism and capitalism, and his assertion that causality flows in that direction, is an excellent example of both Weber's emphasis on ideas, as opposed to material interests, and his historical, comparative approach to causal analysis. Weber did not posit a simple cause-effect relationship between Protestantism and capitalism, however, nor did he consider the Protestant ethic to be the sole cause of capitalism. Weber emphasizes that social dynamics require a pluralistic analysis and that capitalism should be seen as the result of a specific combination of political, economic, and religious factors, not just the religious factor.

In discussing the relationship between Protestantism and capitalism, Weber employs a rather special perspective on modern capitalism. Modern capitalism, according to Weber, presupposes the existence of a number of conditions: that there is private ownership of the means of production; that formally free labor exists; that a limited government allows the market to operate relatively freely; and that a system of finances exists, particularly a money economy.[33] Modern capitalism is characterized by the following attributes:

1. The calculation of capital is made in terms of money.
2. Everything is done in terms of balances.
3. Calculation underlies every act of partners to a transaction.
4. Economic action is adapted to a comparison of money income with money expenses.[34]

Weber believes that capitalism represents the highest stage of rationality in economic behavior. By "rational," Weber means an economic system based, not on custom or tradition, but on a systematic and deliberate adjustment of economic means to attain pecuniary profit.[35] The rationality of modern capitalism is of a special type, however. The rationality of capitalism is "formal" and is measured by the extent to which quantitative calculation is both technically possible and actually applied. In contrast, "substantive" economic rationality involves the adequacy of the provision of goods and services.[36] Weber asserts that the two concepts of economic rationality are always in conflict and that the formal rationality of money accounting and capitalism has no direct relationship to substantive considerations concerning the provision and distribution of goods and services.

A primary question for Weber, and one that joins his interests in religion and economics, is the source of the particular ethic of modern capitalism. His answer is Protestantism. Weber maintains that the Reformation did not mean the elimination of the church's control over everyday life. Instead, it meant a new form of control in which a religiously based secular ethic and a worldly asceticism replaced the otherworldly asceticism of Catholicism and the indifference it had toward the rewards of this life.[37] Protestantism gave positive spiritual and moral meaning to worldly activities and imparted an ethos of planning and self-control to economic activity. The Protestant sects joined the idea that the gods bless with riches those who please them with a kind of religious conduct embodying the notion that honesty is the best policy. It thus delivered to capitalism its special ethos: the ethos of the modern bourgeois middle classes.[38]

The relationship between the Protestant ethic and the spirit of capitalism is most clearly illustrated in the doctrines of Calvinism and its emphasis on predestination. The doctrine of predestination holds that only a small proportion of men are chosen for eternal grace and that the meaning of individual destiny is hidden in impenetrable mystery. Furthermore, the elect do not differ visibly from the damned. Thus one cannot know his destiny. He must simply consider himself to be chosen and combat all doubts as temptations of the devil. The Calvinist creates his own salvation, or at least the conviction of his salvation, by the performance of deeds and in the service of a "calling." This requires systematic and continuous self-control in the performance of each deed rather than an accumulation of deeds as the Catholic church had asserted.[39] In its emphasis on deeds, Calvinism rejected pure feelings and emotions and eliminated the idea that salvation could be granted by the church. Weber contends that whereas Catholics saw magic as the means to salvation with the priest as the magician, Calvinists demanded a life of good works with no place for the Catholic cycle of sin, repentance, atonement, and release, followed by new sin. Calvinism sought to subject man to the dictates of a supreme will and to bring man's actions under constant self-control guided by ethical standards.[40]

Calvinism also sought to destroy spontaneous, impulsive enjoyment by insisting on ordered individual conduct and by transforming monastic asceticism into a worldly asceticism while adding the positive idea of proving oneself in worldly activity.[41] Protestant asceticism holds that it is morally objectionable to relax in the enjoyment of one's possessions. The individual needs hard, continuous bodily or mental labor. The acquisition of wealth in the performance of one's calling is encouraged, but consumption should be limited. The combined effect of limiting consumption and freeing acquisitive activity is a compulsion to save and accumulate capital.

Weber concludes that the religious roots of modern capitalism soon gave way to the tenets of worldly utilitarianism, which has resulted in an orgy of materialism. But the religious epoch gave to its utilitarian successor an amazingly good conscience about the acquisition of wealth and comforting assurance about the unequal distribution of worldly goods.[42] It also legitimated the exploitation of labor since the employer's activity is also a "calling." But whereas the Puritan wanted to work because it was his "calling," modern man is forced to work in the "iron cage" of the new economic order, and the pursuit of material goods controls his life.[43]

Domination Based on Authority

Weber's second major type of domination is domination based on authority. Obedience in systems of domination based on authority, as was the case with domination based on constellations of interests, is dependent on the perception of legitimacy. The sources of legitimacy differ, however. Weber asserts that there are three sources of legitimacy for domination based on authority: charisma, tradition, and legality/rationality. These are pure, or "ideal," types, and the bases of legitimacy usually occur in mixtures in their historical manifestations.

Charismatic Authority

Charismatic authority derives its legitimacy from the personal qualities of the leader. Weber defines charisma as the "quality of an individual personality by virtue of which he is set apart from ordinary men and treated as endowed with supernatural, superhuman, or at least specifically exceptional powers or qualities."[44] Accordingly, charismatic authority is a form of rule over people to which they submit because of their belief in the magical powers, revelations, or heroism of the leader.[45] Weber states that the pure type of charismatic authority appears only briefly in contrast to the relatively more enduring structures of traditional and legal-rational authority. Charismatic authority is a force for revolutionary change and is irrational in the sense that it is not bound by any intellectually analyzable rule.

The leader in charismatic authority is constrained only by his personal judgment, and he is not governed by any formal method of adjudication.[46] Disputes are settled by prophetic revelation or Solomonic arbitration. The relationship between the leader and the led under charismatic authority is typically unstable. Although the authority of the leader is not derived directly from the will of his followers (obedience, instead, is a duty or obligation), the charismatic leader still must constantly prove himself through victories and successes, since charisma disappears if proof is lacking. In sum, the charismatic leader knows only inner determination and inner restraint. He "seizes the task that is adequate for him and demands obedience ... by virtue of his mission."[47]

Administration under charismatic authority, according to Weber, is loose and unstable. The leader's disciples do not have regular occupations, and they reject the methodical and rational pursuit of monetary rewards as undignified. Whatever organization exists is composed of an aristocracy chosen on the basis of charismatic qualities. There is no procedure for appointment, promotion, or dismissal, and there are no career tracks. There is no continuing hierarchical assignment of tasks, since the leader can intervene at will in the performance of any task. Perhaps most important, there are no defined spheres of authority or competence to protect against arbitrary exercises of power and no system of formal rules to ensure equal treatment and due process.[48]

Traditional Authority

Like charismatic authority, traditional authority involves personal rule, but unlike charismatic authority, it is not the product of crisis and enthusiasm. Rulers enjoy personal authority and followers are subjects, but the routine governs conduct. Traditional authority is based on respect for the eternal past, in the rightness and appropriateness of the traditional or customary way of doing things. It rests on piety for what actually, allegedly, or presumably has always existed.[49]

Weber argues that administration under traditional authority tends to be irrational because the development of rational regulations is impeded; there is likely to be no staff with formal, technical training; and there is wide scope for the indulgence of personal whims. A person, not an order, is obeyed as the leader claims the performance of unspecified obligations and services as his personal right. Traditional authority is a regime of favorites with a shifting series of tasks and powers commissioned and granted by a leader through arbitrary decisions.[50] Justice under traditional authority is a mixture of constraints and personal discretion. There is a system of traditional norms that are considered inviolable, but there is also a realm of arbitrariness and dependence on the favor of the ruler, who judges on the basis of personal relationships.[51]

Legal-Rational Authority

In legal-rational authority, legitimacy is based on a belief in reason, and laws are obeyed because they have been enacted by proper procedures. Thus, it is believed that persons exercising authority are acting in accordance with their duties as established by a code of rules and regulations.

In administration, the legitimacy of legal-rational authority rests on rules that are rationally established. Submission to authority is based on an impersonal bond to a generally defined "duty of office," and official duty is fixed by rationally established norms.[52] Obedience constitutes deference to an impersonal order, not an individual, and even giving a command represents obedience to an organizational norm rather than the arbitrary act of the person giving the order. Thus, the official does not exercise power in his own right; he is only a "trustee" of an impersonal, compulsory institution. The organization of the administrative staff under legal-rational authority is bureaucratic in form. The system of justice under legal-rational authority is a balance between formal or procedural justice and substantive justice, but with relative emphasis on the formal aspects of justice.

In outlining the bases of legitimacy, Weber purposely eschews the notion of an evolutionary, linear progress from one form to another. Instead, Weber sees a general trend toward rationalization, which is punctuated by spontaneous and creative bursts of charisma. The victory of charisma over the rational and the routine is never complete, however, and in the end charisma itself is routinized.[53]

The basic problem of charismatic leadership is one of succession: What occurs when something happens to the charismatic leader? In coping with the problem of succession, the charismatic situation starts to yield to a "routinization of charisma."[54] Weber states that when the personal authority of the charismatic leader is displaced by mechanisms or rules for formally ascertaining the "divine will," a routinization of charisma has taken place.[55] In regard to succession, as established procedures used to select a successor come to govern the process, the forces of tradition and rationalization begin to take effect, and charisma is disassociated from a person and embedded in an objective institutional structure. In the process, an unstable structure of authority is transformed into the more permanent traditional or legal-rational structures of authority. With routinization, discipline in the form of consistently rationalized, trained, and exact execution of received orders replaces individual action. With the development of legal-rational authority, either through the routinization of charisma or the breakdown of the privileges of traditional authority, there is a certain "leveling" influence with the recognition of authority treated as a *source* of legitimacy rather than as a *consequence* of authority. Thus, legitimacy in legal-rational authority takes on some democratic overtones.[56]

Law. The two major forms of domination based on authority discussed by Weber are the legal structure and bureaucratic administration. Weber asserts that law grows out of the "usages" and "conventions" found in all societies.[57] Law is distinguished from mere usage and convention, however, by the presence of a staff, which may use coercive power for its enforcement. Weber notes that not all legal orders are considered authoritative. Legal authority exists only when the legal order is implemented and obeyed in the belief that it is legitimate.

Weber says that there are two kinds of rationality associated with the creation of legal norms: substantive and formal. An act is substantively rational if it is guided by principles such as those embodied in religious or ethical thought. An act is formally rational when it is based on general rules. Conversely, an act is formally irrational if guided by means beyond the control of reason (e.g., prophetic revelation or ordeal) and substantively irrational if based on emotional evaluations of single cases.[58] Weber traces a developmental sequence in the rationalization of the law that begins with primitive procedures relying on a combination of magically conditioned formalism and revelation. Next comes a theocratic or patrimonial form of legal system. From this there emerges an increasingly specialized and logically systematized body of law.[59] Although economic interests play a limited role in the systematization and rationalization of law, there is at least a parallel between economic systems and legal structures. Modern capitalism is the prototype of purposively rational behavior, and the formal rationality of legal thought is the counterpart of purposive rationality in economic conduct.

Legal Domination and the State. The concepts of *legal domination* and *state* are not coextensive for Weber. Law, according to Weber, is not exclusively a political phenomenon. It exists wherever coercive means are available. Conversely, the state has at its disposal means of greater effectiveness than coercive ones. Nonetheless, Weber defines the state in terms of the specific means peculiar to it, that is, the use of violent force. The state is a relationship of people dominating people supported by means of the legitimate use of violence. It is a compulsory organization that structures domination and, in the modern state, concentrates the means of administration in the hands of the leaders.[60]

According to Weber, the state was originally created to protect interests, particularly economic interests, and arose from the struggle between the estates and the prince—between the holders of privilege and the holders of power. This resulted in an alliance between the monarchy and bourgeois interests that wanted to be free of administrative arbitrariness and the irrational disturbances of the privileged and that wanted to affirm the legally binding character of contracts. This process eventuated in a legitimate legal order in the form of the modern state.[61] The modern state is characterized by a body of law, bureaucracy, compulsory jurisdiction over territory, and a monopoly over the legitimate use of force. Government administration in the modern state is bound by rules of law and is conducted in accord with generally formulated principles. The people who occupy positions of power are not rulers, they are superiors, and they hold office temporarily and not rulers, they are superiors, and they hold office temporarily and possess limited authority. The people, on their part, are citizens, not subjects.[62]

The rise of the modern state, based on systematized and rationalized law and administration, has produced a conflict between the formal justice embodied in that state and substantive justice. The difference is that whereas formal justice derives its premises from formal concepts, substantive justice derives its premises from the experience of life.[63] In traditional society, Weber says, judicial administration aims at substantive justice and sweeps away formal rules of evidence. This may be rational in the sense of adherence to some general, fixed principles, but, Weber argues, not in the sense of logical rationality. Decisions in such a system may be based on considerations of equity, but they may equally well be made on the basis of expediency or politics.[64]

Bureaucracy. The second major form of domination based on authority is bureaucracy. In addressing the topic of bureaucracy and its role in society, Weber makes one of his most influential contributions. Weber did not invent the term *bureaucracy* nor was he the first to examine its role in society. Nevertheless, Weber has given us one of the most famous statements on the characteristics of bureaucratic organizations and surely one of the most penetrating and controversial analyses of the bureaucratic phenomenon.

Weber's analysis of bureaucracy is logically tied to his interest in legal-rational domination in the modern state. In fact, Weber considered bureaucracy to be a major element in the rationalization of the modern world and the most important of all social processes.[65] Weber asserts that domination both expresses itself and functions through administration. Organized domination calls for continuous administration and the control of a personal executive staff and the material implements of administration. Legal domination calls for an increasingly bureaucratic administration in which domination is based on systematic knowledge.

Weber defines an organization as an ordering of social relationships, the maintenance of which certain individuals take as their special task. The organization consists of members accustomed to obedience; an administrative staff that holds itself at the disposal of the masters; and the masters themselves, who hold a power to command not derived from a grant of power by others.[66] The orientation of human behavior to a set of rules is central to Weber's concept of the organization. Organizational rules regulate the possession and scope of authority in the organization.[67]

Weber identifies bureaucracy as the dominant organizational form in a legal-rational society. The development of bureaucracy is a product of the intensive and qualitative (as opposed to extensive and quantitative) enlargement of administrative tasks. In other words, complexity breeds bureaucracy. Uncharacteristically, Weber never defines "bureaucracy." He does indicate that "bureaucracy" refers to the exercise of control by means of a particular kind of administrative staff, and he specifies the features of the most rational form of bureaucracy, which he calls the "ideal type" bureaucracy. Those characteristics are as follows:

1. Administration is carried out on a continuous basis, not simply at the pleasure of the leader.
2. Tasks in the bureaucratic organization are divided into functionally distinct areas each with the requisite authority and sanctions.
3. Offices are arranged in the form of a hierarchy.
4. The resources of the bureaucratic organization are distinct from those of the members as private individuals (i.e., administrators do not own the means of administration). This characteristic derives from Weber's concept of office in which the official role entails specific duties to be performed, but the resources to fulfill those duties are provided by someone other than the official.
5. The officeholder cannot appropriate the office (i.e., the office cannot be sold by the official or passed on by heredity).
6. Administration is based on written documents.
7. Control in the bureaucratic organization is based on impersonally applied rational rules. Thus it is not simply the existence of rules but the quality and mode of application of those rules that distinguishes the bureaucratic organization.[68]

Weber also outlines the terms of employment in the bureaucratic organization:

1. Officials are personally free and are appointed on the basis of a contract.
2. Officials are appointed, not elected. Weber argues that election modifies the strictness of hierarchical subordination.
3. Officials are appointed on the basis of professional qualifications.
4. Officials have a fixed money salary and pension rights.
5. The official's post is his sole or major occupation.
6. A career structure exists with promotion based on merit (though pressure to recognize seniority may also exist).
7. The official is subject to a unified control and disciplinary system in which the means of compulsion and its exercise are clearly defined.[69]

Weber states that the bureaucratic mechanisms described above exist only in the modern state and the most advanced institutions of capitalism. The ideal-type bureaucracy possesses rationally discussable grounds for every administrative act, it centralizes and concentrates the means of administration, it has a "leveling" effect in that it does away with plutocratic privilege and rests on equality in the eyes of the law and equal eligibility for office, and it creates permanent authority relationships.

Weber clearly believes bureaucracy to be the most rational and efficient organizational form devised by man. Bureaucracy is rational in that it involves control based on knowledge, it has clearly defined spheres of competence, it operates according to intellectually analyzable rules, and it has calculability in its operations.[70] Bureaucracy is efficient because of its precision, speed, consistency, availability of records, continuity, possibility of secrecy, unity, rigorous coordination, and minimization of interpersonal friction, personnel costs, and material costs.[71] In Weber's words,

> Experience tends universally to show that the purely bureaucratic type of administrative organization—that is, the monocratic variety of bureaucracy—is, from a purely technical point of view, capable of attaining the highest degree of efficiency and is in this sense formally the most rational known means of carrying out imperative control over human beings. It is superior to any other form in precision, in stability, in the stringency of its discipline, and in its reliability. . . . It is finally superior both in intensive efficiency and in the scope of its operations, and is formally capable of application to all kinds of administrative tasks.[72]

Note that Weber does not argue that bureaucracy is the most efficient of all conceivable forms of organization, merely more efficient than the known alternative forms of administration. The alternatives, according to Weber, are collegial and avocational administration. He contends that these alternatives are inadequate beyond a certain size limit or where functions require technical training or continuity of policy.[73] Weber is particularly determined in his opposition to democratic administration, a form of collegial administration. Weber contends that even simple forms of democratic administration are unstable and likely to fall into the hands of the wealthy, since those who work do not have time to govern. Moreover, as soon as mass administration is involved, democratic administration falls prey to the technical superiority of those with training and experience and thus to domination by technical experts.[74] Weber also has substantial reservation about the broader form of collegial administration. Collegiality, he argues, almost inevitably involves obstacles to precise, clear, rapid decisions and divides personal responsibility. Collegial administration impairs promptness of decision, consistency of policy, the responsibility of the individual, the requisite ruthlessness toward outsiders, and the maintenance of discipline within the group. Weber asserts that it is impossible for either the internal or the foreign policy of great states to be carried out on a collegial basis. And, as is the case with democratic administration, collegial administration will eventually give way to the technical superiority of the hierarchical organization.[75]

Weber considers bureaucracy and capitalism to be mutually supportive social structures. The capitalist market demands what bureaucracy provides—official business discharged precisely, unambiguously, continuously, with as much speed as possible, and according to calculable rules that make bureaucratic behavior predictable.[76] Moreover, capitalism and bureaucracy share an emphasis on formalistic impersonality in their relationships. In the market, acts of exchange are oriented toward the commodity, and those acts, Weber asserts, are the most impersonal relationship into which humans can enter. Market ethics require only that partners to a transaction behave legally and honor the inviolability of a promise once given. The private enterprise system transforms even personal relationships in the organization into objects of the labor market and drains them of all normal sentiment.[77] The bureaucratic organization, on its part, also offers the elements of calculability and depersonalization. Bureaucratic organizations operate *sine ira ac studio* (without bias or favor) and thereby exclude irrational feelings and sentiments in favor of the detached, professional expert.[78] By eliminating incalculable emotional elements, bureaucracy offers the attitudes demanded by the apparatus of modern culture in general and modern capitalism in particular. The demand for legal equality and guarantees against arbitrariness requires formal, rational objectivity in administration, not the personal choice of traditional authority nor the emotional demands for substantive justice in a democracy.[79]

Although Weber admires the rationality and efficiency of bureaucratic organizations, and respects the concept of justice embodied therein, he also associates bureaucracy with an oppressive routine adverse to personal freedom.[80] Weber observes that bureaucracy has penetrated all social institutions, public and private, and that bureaucracy limits individual freedom, renders the individual incapable of understanding his own activities in relation to the organization as a whole, and favors the "crippled personality" of the specialist.[81] Thus, though bureaucracy extends human capacities, it also increases the forces to which man is subject and may not even be just, since the propertyless masses may not be well served by a doctrine of formal equality before the law.[82] Unfortunately, Weber sees only reversion to small-scale organizations as a means of avoiding the dysfunctional consequences of bureaucratic organizations, and that would deprive society of bureaucracy's benefits.[83]

Weber's Political Perspectives

When one moves from Weber's sociological analysis to his political writings, some shifts in emphasis, if not changes in direction, are encountered. Weber's political writings place more emphasis on class conflict, less on ideal interests, and capitalism is treated as an independent phenomenon, not just part of the processes of rationalization. Also, whereas Weber's sociology focuses on the achievements of bureaucracy, his political writings stress the limitations of bureaucracy and the likely future struggle between political leadership and bureaucracy.

Democracy and the Nation-State

The "state," according to Weber, represents the monopoly of the legitimate use of force over a given territory and is an "ultimate" in that it cannot be integrated into a more comprehensive whole.[84] The "nation," however, is more than coercive control over a territory; it is also a community of sentiment. A nation exists where there is some common factor among people, where this common factor is regarded as a source of value and produces a feeling of solidarity, and where the feeling of solidarity finds expression in autonomous political institutions or at least creates a demand for such institutions.[85]

Culture is a complex of characteristics or values that constitutes the individuality of a particular national community. Weber asserts that there are reciprocally interdependent relationships between the state and its culture. The state can survive only if it can harness the solidary feelings of national community and culture in support of its power. Conversely, the national community preserves its distinctive identity by the protection it receives from the state. Weber adheres to the position that nations and the cultures they incorporate should be preserved. Weber contends that the state should serve national and cultural values and that politics is the appropriate sphere for the pursuit of these nonmaterial values.[86] The ultimate value, Weber contends, is the power position of the nation in the world, with struggle and conflict being permanent features of social life. Even more, Weber believes that conflict should be encouraged because the highest qualities of life (i.e., qualities of independence engendered by struggles with the difficulties of life) can be developed only through conflict.[87] This extends even to the ultimate conflict, war, which, Weber contends, creates a sentiment of community and gives a consecrated meaning to death. Only in war can the individual believe that he is dying *for* something.

Weber supports democracy as a means of providing leadership for national ends, but it is a "democracy" of a special type, and even then his support is at best reluctant. Weber warns against viewing democracy as a panacea for society's ills. He argues that democracy is inevitably governed by the "law of the small number" (i.e., that politics is controlled from the top by a small number of people). Democracy changes the rules for the selection of a leader, but leaders are still selected.[88] Instead, Weber defends democracy as a postulate of practical reason. It is to be preferred simply because it is the only reasonable alternative to authoritarianism. Democracy permits mass involvement, but on an orderly and regular basis, and it is consistent with the requirements of modern institutions and their demands for equality of status.[89]

Nevertheless, Weber believes democracy to be distinguished not by direct mass involvement but by the use of demagogy, the regular use of the vote in choosing leaders, and organization by mass political parties. The influence of a democratic elite is viewed by Weber as not only inevitable but desirable. Weber warns against the evils of "leaderless" democracy in which professional politicians who have no "calling" rule. Weber argues that democracy requires leadership. In his words,

> In a democracy the people choose a leader in whom they trust. Then the chosen leader says, "Now shut up and obey me." People and party are no longer free to interfere in his business. . . . Later the people can sit in judgment. If the leader has made a mistake—to the gallows with him![90]

Political leadership is required to ensure the supremacy of the political over the bureaucratic. It is also required to ensure the supremacy of the political over the economic by focusing on social unity in the face of the divisiveness of class and material interests.[91] Although Weber warned against leaderless democracy, he was also aware that democracy could lead to "Plebiscitary Caesarism" in the form of an individual carried to absolute power by the emotionalized masses.[92] What is needed is not just leadership but charismatic leadership. This requires more than popularity and it is different from caesaristic rule. The charismatic leader is one who is truly destined to rule and is suited for his tasks by supernatural gifts.[93]

The importance of leadership to Weber is reflected in his discussion of the role and functions of the politician. The objective of politics, Weber tells us, is to share power or to influence the distribution of power, and politics itself is any kind of independent leadership in political associations.[94] Consequently, the politician must have a capacity for independent action, he should not sacrifice his personal judgment for official duties (i.e., he should be willing to resign if that is necessary for him to live up to the responsibilities of leadership), and he must have skill in the struggle for power.[95] The politician should combine passion and a feeling of responsibility with a sense of proportion —passion in devotion to a cause and a sense of proportion developed by establishing some distance between himself and others.[96] He must fight vanity and avoid seeking power for power's sake. These attributes, Weber suggests, are most likely to be found among those whose economic position is sufficiently secure that they can "live for" politics, not have to "live off" it.[97] According to Weber, the prototypical modern politician is the lawyer who is both available for service and has the skills required for effective participation in the struggle for power.[98]

The functions of the politician are to give direction to policy in a continuing struggle with bureaucratic and party officials and to counter the influence of class conflict and material interests by giving expression to a common interest underlying superficial perceptions of class interests. In regard to the latter function, Weber differs from Marx in believing that divisions of class can be overcome within the capitalist system and that workers and entrepreneurs have a common interest in the rationalization of industry. Nevertheless, he also recognizes that capitalism has led to the pursuit of material interests (a "dance around the golden calf"), it has replaced personal relationships with impersonality, and it has led to conflict between those with property and the propertyless.[99] This has resulted in a degeneration of the national political outlook and the subordination of the true function of politics to sectional and class interests. Weber argues that politics should be neither merely the pursuit of power nor simply an extension of economic activity in the form of class or interest-group activity. Instead, political leadership should draw people to an awareness of common interests, including a common interest in the perpetuation of capitalism.

Weber further contends that the honor of the political leader lies in his exclusive personal responsibility for what he does. Unfortunately, the ethical bases for the assumption of personal responsibility are ambiguous. Weber distinguishes between two kinds of ethics: the ethic of ultimate ends and the ethic of responsibility. Under the ethic of ultimate ends, one feels responsible only for seeing that the "flame of pure intention" is not quenched and action is taken regardless of the consequences. Under the ethic of responsibility, one is held accountable for the foreseeable results of his actions.[100] The ambiguity stems from two sources. First, Weber argues, no ethic can tell us to what extent an ethically good purpose justifies an ethically dubious means. Second, one must face the reality that some of the tasks of politics can be performed only by use of violence, an ethically dubious means. The ambiguity poses a paradox. On the one hand, everything that is striven for through political action employing violent means and following an ethic of responsibility endangers the salvation of the soul. On the other hand, if one pursues a goal following a pure ethic of ultimate ends, then the goals themselves may be discredited because responsibility for consequences is lacking. Weber admits that he cannot prescribe whether one should follow an ethic of ultimate ends or an ethic of responsibility, or when one should be followed and when the other. He does assert that only when the two supplement each other does one have a "calling" for politics.[101]

Weber's emphasis on political leadership was prompted, in large part, by his aversion to bureaucratic domination. Weber considered the ideologies of his day (primarily capitalism and socialism) to be of small consequence compared to what he perceived to be the nearly inexorable process of bureaucratization. Weber argues that bureaucrats will develop interests of their own and start to shape policy with the attendant danger that the rule of law will be undermined in the absence of effective political leadership.[102] Weber asserts that the official, according to his proper vocation, should not engage in politics. He should engage only in the impartial administration of his office.[103] The honor of the civil servant, Weber says, is vested in his ability to execute conscientiously the orders of superior authorities, "exactly as if the order agreed with his own convictions."[104] If the administrator receives orders with which he disagrees, he should make his views known to his superior; but if the superior insists, the administrator must comply to the best of his ability. In short, a sense of duty should be placed above personal opinion. This should be part of the administrator's ethic and is required for the rule of law.

The problem arises when the bureaucracy attempts to overstep its rightful functions and capabilities. Weber believes bureaucrats to be, along with feudal lords, the primary exponents of power and prestige for their own political structure.[105] The aggrandizement of bureaucracy can subvert the rule of law, since the bureaucracy, which cannot be inspected and controlled, becomes a law unto itself. Moreover, Weber contends that the permanent official is more likely to get his way than is his nominal superior, who is not likely to be a specialist and thus be at the mercy of his expert subordinate. Knowledge becomes an instrument of political power, and secrecy protects the bureaucrat's monopoly on information.

Weber considers the bureaucratic machine to be one of the hardest of social structures to destroy. Bureaucracy is *the* means for achieving rationally ordered societal action. Nevertheless, the bureaucrat is also part of a community of functionaries who have an interest in seeing that the bureaucratic mechanism continues to function. These officials may develop into a status group whose cohesion stems, not from economic interests, but from the prestige of a style of life that fosters the values of status, security, and order.[106] Even more, bureaucrats may become a privileged class and use their positions for personal advantage. As a power group, bureaucrats may develop a code of honor that includes not only a sense of duty but also a belief in the superiority of their own qualifications.[107] Once in power, the bureaucracy is difficult to dislodge because few among the governed can master the tasks performed by the bureaucracy. Democracy requires the prevention of a closed status group of officials from taking power and the minimization of the authority of officialdom. But the "leveling" consequences of democracy may occur only in regard to the governed rather than their bureaucratic masters, in a process to which Weber refers as "passive democratization."[108]

The central political question for Weber is how to prevent bureaucracy from exceeding its functions or, stated conversely, how to maintain the supremacy of the politician. That is no simple matter. Collegial administration is slow and obscures responsibility; a structural separation of powers is inherently unstable, and one power is likely to become dominant; amateur administration does not provide the requisite expertise; direct democracy is possible only in small groups and also does not provide expertise; representative democracy must rely on political parties, which themselves are bureaucratized. Bureaucracy, Weber maintains, can be controlled only from the top. Charismatic leadership may be the solution, if there is one. It is, at least, the best hope. Politicians are the indispensable counterweight to bureaucracy, and both parliamentary and plebiscitary bases of leadership are necessary to prevent rule by a clique of political notables and governmental officials who will control the rule of law rather than be subject to it.[109]

Nor is the economic sphere immune from possible bureaucratic domination. This, Weber argues, is as likely to be the result of the quest for the bureaucratic values of order and security as it is the result of a power drive by bureaucratic officials.[110] Weber sees the bureaucratic threat in the economic sphere as emanating from two sources: from socialism, which seeks to replace capitalism with a bureaucratic order; and from the possibility that the bourgeoisie itself will go "soft" and precipitate a decline in capitalist values. Weber argues that socialism will make autonomous economic action subject to the bureaucratic management of the state. Economic transactions accomplished by political manipulation will replace the rationality and individualism of a capitalist economy. Weber believes that a system of bureaucratic rule is inevitable, but socialism will accelerate the process of bureaucratization and thus lead to serfdom.[111] Capitalism also faces dangers from within. Ironically, capitalism is itself a prime reason for the bureaucratization that threatens to stifle individualism. In addition, capitalism has encouraged the pursuit of material goods and the desire for a secure subsistence. This, Weber contends, will result in a "vast army of state pensioners and an array of monopolistic privileges," and the demise of the entrepreneurial spirit of capitalism.[112]

Despite an undeniably pessimistic strain, Weber avoids schemes involving inevitable social development or unavoidable historical cycles. There is the notion of a recurrent struggle between routinization and charisma. When the world becomes overly bureaucratized, the prophets and the Caesars return. The future is thus a field of strategy, not a repetition of, or unfolding of, the past. Social life is "polytheism of values" among which choices are possible, and charisma, says Weber, is the metaphysical vehicle of human freedom.[113]

Conclusion

The main points of Weber's substantive sociology may be summarized as follows:

1. A fundamental dynamic of civilization has been the process of rationalization.

2. The process of rationalization is reflected in various forms of domination or exercises of power perceived to be legitimate.

3. The two basic types of domination are domination based on constellations of interests and domination based on authority.

4. Domination based on constellations of interests is manifested in religious and economic associations.

5. Domination based on authority is manifested in the operations of the state and bureaucratic organizations.

6. The legitimacy of domination based on authority is derived from three sources: charisma, tradition, and legality/rationality.

7. There has been a general historical trend toward increasing rationality in social relationships, but that trend has not been unilinear. Instead, the advance of rationalization has been punctuated by outbursts of charisma and reversions to tradition.

8. Bureaucracy is the dominant organizational form in a legal-rational society and it derives its characteristics—predictability, calculability, and impersonality—as well as its sense of justice from the society in which it resides.

9. Whereas the past has been marked by a struggle between charisma and the forces of depersonalization, the future will see a struggle

over who will enact the rules in a legal-rational society, a struggle that will pit the political leader against the professional bureaucrat.

Although Weber is held in an esteem that approaches reverence, he has not been without his critics. Indeed, scarcely a facet of Weber's work has not been the subject of careful scrutiny and, often, intense controversy. There is widespread agreement on one criticism. Weber's writing style is, at best, difficult, and the striking difference between the clarity of Weber's spoken word and the opaqueness of his written word is often noted.[114] Weber both defended and explained his sometimes tortured constructions by stating, "Personally I am of the opinion that nothing is too pedantic if it is useful in avoiding confusions."[115] It is not clear that Weber avoided confusion, but his writing certainly qualifies as oftentimes pedantic. Another general criticism of Weber's work is his tendency to rely more on assertion than demonstration or proof. This is probably inevitable given the compass of Weber's interests and the sweep of his ideas. Nonetheless, his dismissal of important ideas is, at times, almost casual. For instance, Weber simply rules out some forms of democracy as being "impractical," and popular sovereignty is peremptorily reduced to the status of "popular fiction."[116]

But the bulk of the criticisms have focused on Weber's methodology, his historical analysis, and his analysis of bureaucracy. The critique of Weber's methodology centers on his use of the "ideal type" construct. The ideal type is intended to combine attributes in a logically consistent manner. It is to be based on, but not confined to, historical manifestations that approximate the ideal type. There are several problems with Weber's use of the ideal-type construct. One is that the construct can be used in a self-serving manner. Consider, for instance, Weber's treatment of the concept of capitalism.[117] He defines a particular form of capitalism (an ideal type, if you will) that has as its essence a "spirit" that emphasizes honest accumulation as a "calling." Moreover, he traces the causal roots of this brand of capitalism to ascetic Protestantism. Note that this form of capitalism need never have actually appeared in its "pure" condition in history, which means that an empirical test of the causal relationship is at least inappropriate and perhaps impossible. Note too that Weber is dealing with a narrowly defined economic phenomenon whose relationship to ascetic Protestantism may be more definitional than causal and which excludes other forms of economic activity generally considered to be "capitalistic." Mouzelis takes the critique of Weber's ideal type a step further in arguing that Weber's use of the construct does not always conform to Weber's self-imposed requirement of internal logical consistency. In particular, Mouzelis contends that Weber's ideal-type bureaucracy is not necessarily rational and efficient, and, consequently, Weber's posited combination of bureaucratic characteristics may not be "objectively possible."[118] Finally, it is argued that the use of ideal types alone does not accomplish Weber's theory-building objectives. To constitute a theory, it is held, the types should be "arranged and classified in a definite order of relationship."[119] This Weber failed to do.

Weber has also been criticized in regard to his historical analysis. Most of this criticism has been directed at Weber's analysis of the causes of capitalism. Although Weber acknowledges the likelihood of causal pluralism, his own analysis is largely confined to the influence of religious ideas on economic activity. Moreover, while Weber sought to demonstrate that ideas preceded interests in the development of capitalism, he does not demonstrate that *both* Calvinism and capitalism were not the product of prior material interests.[120] Finally, it is argued that Weber failed to deal with the processes by which the religious ideas of a dominant status group actually became an everyday standard of behavior for the common man.[121] This omission leaves open the possibility that forces other than religious ideas may have been instrumental in giving rise to capitalism, and even its particular "spirit."

Yet all of these criticisms pale in comparison to the reaction to Weber's formulation of the concept of bureaucracy.[122] It has been argued that bureaucracy is not necessarily rational, it may not be efficient, that other forms of organization may well be more efficient, and that bureaucracy, by virtue of its structural and procedural complexity, may permit, if not encourage, evasions of individual responsibility. A particularly penetrating analysis is that of Robert Merton.[123] Merton accepts Weber's construction of the bureaucratic phenomenon, abides by Weber's ground rules on the intent and use of the ideal type (i.e., it must stand only the test of internal logical consistency or objective possibility), and goes to the heart of the Weberian bureaucracy (i.e., the impersonal application of the rules) in formulating his critique.

For Merton, the problem of bureaucracy comes in the form of a paradox. The paradox is that the very organizational features Weber thought to be associated with rationality and efficiency may instead be associated with irrationality and inefficiency. Merton cites as a case in point the consequences of the impersonal application of the rules in a bureaucratic organization. The impersonal application of the rules is intended to enhance organizational rationality and efficiency by encouraging a high degree of reliability and conformity in behavior in the organization. Problems arise, however, when these traits (reliability and conformity) become exaggerated. And, Merton argues, this is likely to be the case in bureaucratic organizations given a number of specified formal and informal dynamics. As rule enforcement assumes increasing significance, the organization develops what Merton refers to as a "punctilious adherence to formalized procedures," more commonly known as "red tape." Eventually, the enforcement of rules becomes an end in itself, and this results in a "displacement of goals" as an instrumental value (the enforcement of rules) is substituted for a terminal value (the accomplishment of organizational goals) as the purpose of organizational activity. Organizational rules become "sanctified" or imbued with a moral legitimacy of their own, and the organization develops rigor mortis and becomes unable to adapt to changing circumstances. In sum, Merton argues that bureaucracy contains "the seeds of its own destruction" in its emphasis on rules and the bureaucratic environment itself produces a mentality that encourages the enforcement of rules regardless of their consequences for the accomplishment of organizational objectives.

Weber is likely to remain a subject of both respect and controversy. On matters administrative, his particular genius was to place administration in a broad historical context and to associate the processes of bureaucratization with the processes of rationalization in the Western world. Moreover, Weber associated the mechanisms of bureaucracy with familiar concepts of justice, such as due process and equal application of the law, thus lending bureaucratic organization a significance that transcends even considerations of rationality and efficiency.

Notes

1. H. Gerth and C. Wright Mills, *From Max Weber: Essays in Sociology* (New York: Oxford University Press, 1946), 6.

2. Ibid., 8.

3. Reinhard Bendix, *Max Weber: An Intellectual Portrait* (Berkeley: University of California Press, 1960), 3.

4. Karl Loewenstein, *Max Weber's Political Ideas in the Perspective of Our Time* (Amherst: University of Massachusetts Press, 1966), 94 and 98.

5. Gerth and Mills, *From Max Weber*, 26.

6. David Beetham, *Max Weber and the Theory of Modern Politics* (London: Allen & Unwin, 1974), 19.

7. Bendix, *Max Weber*, 8.

8. Gerth and Mills, *From Max Weber*, 39.

9. Donald G. MacRae, *Weber* (London: Fontana/Collins, 1974), 26.

10. Ibid., 39.

11. Max Rheinstein, *Max Weber on Law in Economy and Society* (New York: Simon and Schuster, 1954), xviii; and Gerth and Mills, *From Max Weber*, 49.

12. MacRae, *Weber*, 20.

13. Max Weber, *The Theory of Social and Economic Organization*, trans. A. M. Henderson and Talcott Parsons (New York: Free Press of Glencoe, 1947), 92 and 96.

14. Gerth and Mills, *From Max Weber*, 157.

15. Max Weber, *The Protestant Ethic and the Spirit of Capitalism* (New York: Scribner's, 1958), xiv.

16. Gerth and Mills, *From Max Weber*, 186–87.

17. Bendix, *Max Weber*, 259.

18. Max Weber, *The Methodology of the Social Sciences*, trans. Edward A. Shils and Henry A. Finch (New York: Free Press, 1949), 94.

19. Rheinstein, *Max Weber on Law*, xxx.

20. Weber, *Methodology of the Social Sciences*, 98–99.

21. MacRae, *Weber*, 66.

22. Weber, *Methodology of the Social Sciences*, 82.

23. Ibid., 20–21.

24. Ibid., 1.

25. Gerth and Mills, *From Max Weber*, 143–44.

26. Weber, *Methodology of the Social Sciences*, 4.

27. Gerth and Mills, *From Max Weber*, 149.

28. Beetham, *Max Weber and the Theory of Modern Politics*, 29.

29. Gerth and Mills, *From Max Weber*, 180.

30. Nicos P. Mouzelis, *Organisation and Bureaucracy* (Chicago: Aldine, 1967), 15–16.

31. Rheinstein, *Max Weber on Law*, 324. Weber defines authority as a command of a definite content finding obedience on the part of specific individuals. See Martin Albrow, *Bureaucracy* (New York: Praeger, 1970), 39.

32. Gerth and Mills, *From Max Weber*, 288.

33. Weber, *Theory of Social and Economic Organization*, 42–50.

34. Weber, *Protestant Ethic*, 18–19.

35. Ibid., 1(e). Weber, for instance, considers capitalism to be more rational than centralized planning. Central planning, according to Weber, does not have the advantage of a price system, which reduces the scope of required decisions; it is limited by inadequate knowledge; planning authorities may serve only their own interests; planning decisions may be unenforceable; and it is likely to encounter difficulty in maintaining property rights and labor discipline. See Weber, *Theory of Social and Economic Organization*, 37–39.

36. Weber, *Theory of Social and Economic Organization*, 184–86.

37. Weber, *Protestant Ethic*, 40.

38. Gerth and Mills, *From Max Weber*, 313 and 321.

39. Weber, *Protestant Ethic*, 103–15.

40. Ibid., 119.

41. Weber ascribes the following characteristics to Protestant asceticism: (1) There are inhibitions against immersion in the world; (2) there is a drive for mastery over worldly things so as to make the world over in a transcendental image; (3) there is an emphasis on rationality through the systematization of conduct according to practical norms; accordingly, the goal is not mere mastery, but *rational* mastery; (4) there is an ethical universalism in that all are treated by the same impersonal standards; (5) there is high functional differentiation in which each serves God's will in his own particular "calling." See Weber, *Theory of Social and Economic Organization*, 80–81.

42. Weber, *Protestant Ethic*, 177.

43. Ibid., 181.

44. Weber, *Theory of Social and Economic Organization*, 358.
45. Weber offers the concept of charisma as one from which value judgments about particular individuals perceived as having charisma have been excluded. Ibid., 359.
46. Bendix, *Max Weber*, 295–96.
47. Gerth and Mills, *From Max Weber*, 246.
48. Bendix, *Max Weber*, 302; and Weber, *Theory of Social and Economic Organization*, 360.
49. Gerth and Mills, *From Max Weber*, 296.
50. Weber, *Theory of Social and Economic Organization*, 343.
51. Gerth and Mills, *From Max Weber*, 296.
52. Ibid., 299.
53. Mouzelis, *Organisation and Bureaucracy*, 19–20.
54. Gerth and Mills, *From Max Weber*, 54.
55. Ibid., 250.
56. Weber, *Theory of Social and Economic Organization*, 73 and 386.
57. A usage is a collective way of doing things that individuals perpetuate without being required by anyone to do so. A convention is a collective way of doing things that is perpetuated because failure to do so would provoke disapproval by persons in the environment. Convention is distinguished from mere usage in that it carries with it a sense of obligation or duty. Bendix, *Max Weber*, 389.
58. Rheinstein, *Max Weber on Law*, xl and xli.
59. Weber attributes the rationalization of legal systems in the West to several factors including the rise of an economic system and other interests that were served by the systematization of the law, the concept of a higher or natural law, which led to the notion that general law should prevail over special law, and the influence of Roman law. Ibid., 304.
60. Gerth and Mills, *From Max Weber*, 78–83.
61. Rheinstein, *Max Weber on Law*, 345–48.
62. Bendix, *Max Weber*, 418–22.
63. Rheinstein, *Max Weber on Law*, xli and xlii.
64. Ibid., 264. Weber holds much the same opinion of the "popular justice" of the jury system. The jury system, he says, appeals only to the layman who feels annoyed whenever he encounters formalism and satisfies only the emotional demands of the underprivileged classes. Ibid., 318.
65. Albrow, *Bureaucracy*, 43.
66. Weber, *Theory of Social and Economic Organization*, 56; and Rheinstein, *Max Weber on Law*, 335.
67. Albrow, *Bureaucracy*, 38–39.
68. Weber, *Theory of Social and Economic Organization*, 330–32; Albrow, *Bureaucracy*, 43–44; Gerth and Mills, *From Max Weber*, 196–98.
69. Weber, *Theory of Social and Economic Organization*, 333–34; Albrow, *Bureaucracy*, 44–45; Gerth and Mills, *From Max Weber*, 198–204.
70. Beetham, *Max Weber and the Theory of Modern Politics*, 69.
71. Rheinstein, *Max Weber on Law*, 349.
72. Weber, *Theory of Social and Economic Organization*, 337.

73. Ibid., 415.

74. Rheinstein, *Max Weber on Law*, 331–34.

75. Weber, *Theory of Social and Economic Organization*, 397–402. On more specific devices, Weber does not like functional representation because it leads to mere compromise rather than general agreement, and he does not like workers' councils because disagreements are settled on the basis of economic power, not spontaneous agreement.

76. Gerth and Mills, *From Max Weber*, 215.

77. Rheinstein, *Max Weber on Law*, 190–92.

78. Ibid., 351.

79. Ibid., 355.

80. Gerth and Mills, *From Max Weber*, 50.

81. Mouzelis, *Organisation and Bureaucracy*, 19.

82. Gerth and Mills, *From Max Weber*, 221.

83. Weber, *Theory of Social and Economic Organization*, 338.

84. Gerth and Mills, *From Max Weber*, 48.

85. Beetham, *Max Weber and the Theory of Modern Politics*, 122.

86. Ibid., 44.

87. Ibid., 39–42.

88. Ibid., 103.

89. Ibid., 104–5. Democracy, in Weber's view, should incorporate features such as universal suffrage, popular representation, the initiative and the referendum, and the popular election of the head of state. See Loewenstein, *Weber's Political Ideas*, 25–26.

90. Gerth and Mills, *From Max Weber*, 42.

91. Beetham, *Max Weber and the Theory of Modern Politics*, 217.

92. Loewenstein, *Weber's Political Ideas*, 8 and 26.

93. Ibid., 74–76.

94. Gerth and Mills, *From Max Weber*, 77.

95. Bendix, *Max Weber*, 441.

96. Gerth and Mills, *From Max Weber*, 115.

97. Beetham, *Max Weber and the Theory of Modern Politics*, 228.

98. Bendix, *Max Weber*, 442–43.

99. Beetham, *Max Weber and the Theory of Modern Politics*, 218–20.

100. Gerth and Mills, *From Max Weber*, 120–21.

101. Ibid., 127.

102. Bendix, *Max Weber*, 485.

103. Gerth and Mills, *From Max Weber*, 95.

104. Ibid.

105. Ibid., 160.

106. Beetham, *Max Weber and the Theory of Modern Politics*, 81.

107. Ibid., 73.

108. Gerth and Mills, *From Max Weber*, 226.

109. Bendix, *Max Weber*, 457.

110. Ibid., 463.

111. Gerth and Mills, *From Max Weber*, 49–50.

112. Bendix, *Max Weber*, 461–62.

113. Gerth and Mills, *From Max Weber*, 72.

114. See, for instance, Albrow, *Bureaucracy*, 54; and Rheinstein, *Max Weber on Law*, vii.

115. Weber, *Methodology of the Social Sciences*, 20.

116. Beetham, *Max Weber and the Theory of Modern Politics*, 266.

117. Weber, *Protestant Ethic*, 7.

118. Mouzelis, *Organisation and Bureaucracy*, 47–48.

119. Weber, *Theory of Social and Economic Organization*, 28.

120. Weber, *Protestant Ethic*, 7.

121. Bendix, *Max Weber*, 275.

122. See Albrow, *Bureaucracy*, 54–61, for a summary of these critiques.

123. Robert K. Merton, "Bureaucratic Structure and Personality," *Reader in Bureaucracy*, ed. Robert K. Merton et al. (New York: Free Press, 1952), 361–71.

CHAPTER 2

Frederick W. Taylor:
The Man, the Method, the Movement

As was the case with the writings of Max Weber, a question likely to occur to the reader on first encountering the works of Frederick Taylor is why they should be included in a text on public administration. It would seem to be anomalous, at least on the surface, that an author who was almost exclusively concerned with private-sector management should be included in a volume dealing with the public sector.

The reason for doing so is that the definition of the field of public administration widely accepted in Taylor's day encouraged, indeed demanded, such an inclusion. That definition was founded on the premise that administration should be separated from political and policy concerns and that administrators should be limited to, in Woodrow Wilson's words, "the detailed and systematic execution of public law." It was argued that by taking politics out of administration, a generic administrative function—namely, the appropriate ordering of means to given ends—had been identified. Accordingly, it was permissible to search for general administrative techniques in the private sector, and even in other constitutional systems, that could be used to enhance efficiency in the operation of American government. With this charge, attention naturally turned to the techniques of Scientific Management, which were directly concerned with the question of efficiency and had achieved a large measure of public notoriety, if not always acclaim. Scientific Management attracted the enthusiastic support of many in government who believed that those techniques could be applied in the public sector. Taylor himself thought the techniques of Scientific Management to be applicable to the public sector, since, in his judgment, the average public employee did little more than one-third to one-half of a good day's work.

Thus the reason for the inclusion of a review of Taylor's works in this volume is that Scientific Management was perceived as a way to achieve greater efficiency in the management of the public business. But this simply transforms an apparent anomaly into an irony. The irony is that a movement seen by most as a series of expedients to improve efficiency was seen by its originator as primarily a mechanism for social reform. Taylor saw Scientific Management as a "mental revolution" in which a "scientific" approach could be brought to bear not only on the performance of physical tasks but on all social problems. Only in the larger frame of social reform can one comprehend the evangelical zeal of the adherents of Scientific Management and the passion of the opposition.

In this chapter, Taylor as a man and Scientific Management as both a method and a movement are discussed. I pay more attention to Taylor's life than is the case for most authors in this volume because of the intimate relationships among the man, his methods, and the movement as Taylor's virtues, and his vices, are reflected in Scientific Management. On methods, I consider time-and-motion studies, wage-incentive schemes, and functional organization as three of the primary emphases in the techniques of Scientific Management. On Scientific Management as a movement, I look at efforts to spread the gospel of Scientific Management and some of the controversy that surrounded those efforts.

Life

Frederick W. Taylor was born in Philadelphia on 22 March 1856 into a family with deep roots in American culture and a strong religious heritage. His father, Franklin, was a fourth-generation English Quaker and his mother, Emily, a sixth-generation English Puritan. Franklin earned an undergraduate and a master's degree from Princeton University and was an attorney in Philadelphia. He was something of a gentleman of leisure, however, and did not actively practice his profession, pursuing, instead, his interests in literature and history. He has been described as "devoid of aggressiveness and combativeness," and little of the father was to be found in the son.[1] But Taylor's mother apparently exerted a powerful influence on her son. Emily Winslow Taylor's character reflected her Puritan background, which "fostered a bold sense of inquiry, dissatisfaction, revolt, a new vision, discipline, and a passion for making the new vision prevail."[2] All these attributes were to be found in Emily Taylor and later, even more decidedly, in her son Frederick. Emily was an expert linguist, an abolitionist, and a feminist whose home in Germantown became a salon for innovators and reformers. Whereas Franklin appears to have played a relatively minor role in the rearing of Frederick and his brother and sister, Emily was a major force, presiding over her children's education and running a household described as "a thing ruled regular."[3]

As a child, Frederick Taylor demonstrated little interest in his parents' social and philosophical concerns. The family lived abroad for

48

several years, but the only apparent effects on Frederick were that he developed a lasting aversion to travel and a similarly lasting dislike for Germans.[4] Although Taylor was rather austere in his personal life, he had a love of games; this combination of control and playfulness were carried, in somewhat changing measure, throughout his lifetime. Taylor was active in sports as a child and later participated in crew, baseball, skating, and gymnastics while at Exeter Academy. Taylor was also a member of the Young America Cricket Club and an avid tennis player, playing on the winning team in the U.S. Lawn Tennis Doubles Championship in 1881. In the late 1890s Taylor developed an interest in golf and played daily. Sports were not Taylor's only extracurricular activity. He also sang tenor in the choral society and developed a reputation for his female impersonations on the stage.[5] Nonetheless, there was usually a sense of purposefulness to Taylor's play. Taylor's interest in mechanical inventions, for instance, was manifested in his sports activities. Among his inventions were a spoon-shaped handle for a tennis racket, a two-handled putter (later outlawed), and a method of tightening tennis nets with an iron socket.

As a student, Taylor proved to be more diligent than brilliant, but with generally good results. At age sixteen, Taylor entered Phillips Exeter Academy to prepare for the study of law. Despite demonstrating a rebellious spirit evidenced by being caught reading a book during chapel and cheating on an exam, Taylor worked hard and earned good marks.[6] Near the end of his time at Exeter, however, Taylor suffered from a vision problem that his parents attributed to studying too much by kerosene lamp. The result was that, though Taylor planned to study law and passed the entrance examination to Harvard University with honors, he decided not to enter Harvard. Instead, in an abrupt and curious change of direction, Taylor chose to become an apprentice machinist at the Enterprise Hydraulic Works, a small firm in Philadelphia where he spent four years. Thus, from a budding lawyer, a prospective engineer was born.

After serving his apprenticeship at Enterprise Hydraulic, Taylor assumed a position as an ordinary laborer at the Midvale Steel Works. The choice proved to be fortuitous. Midvale, at that time, was owned by a friend of the Taylor family and run by William Sellers, an innovative engineer who took a personal interest in Taylor's development. At Midvale, Taylor progressed through the stages of an ordinary laborer, but at a pace seldom achieved by the ordinary laborer. Taylor worked originally as a time clerk and machinist, became a gang boss after two months, and was chief engineer after only six years at Midvale.

It was at Midvale that the rudimentary concepts of Scientific Management began to form in Taylor's mind. As a laborer, Taylor had identified with the workman and his mores, including sympathy for a practice Taylor would later resoundingly condemn, "systematic soldiering," or informal output restrictions imposed by the work group. When Taylor became a part of management, his outlook and identifications changed markedly. Taylor took his primary loyalty to be to management, and he launched a concerted attack on systematic soldiering. Taylor's supervisory style was authoritarian in nature, and he became known as something of a "holy terror" in his relationships with his men.[7] Those relationships were at one point so tattered that Taylor exchanged physical threats with some members of his work group. Taylor's attempts to combat systematic soldiering led him to institute two important components of what was later to be known as Scientific Management: time-and-motion studies and a piecework incentive plan. Taylor reorganized the tool room, standardized the tools, and created five positions that were the precursors of "functional foremen": an instruction card clerk, a time clerk, an inspector, a gang boss, and a shop disciplinarian. In addition, Taylor began his study of metal cutting, which would eventually consume twenty-five years of experimentation.

While at Midvale, Taylor also found time to take up the study of engineering. He negotiated a rather unusual arrangement with Stevens Institute in which he actually appeared at Stevens only to take examinations.[8] Taylor received a degree in mechanical engineering from Stevens in 1883. Ironically, in the light of his career interests, Taylor received little training in mathematics or accounting. He later remedied these deficiencies by hiring competent mathematicians to assist him and taught himself the basics of accounting. In 1886 Taylor joined the American Society for Mechanical Engineering and began a long and fruitful relationship that would see the association serve as a public forum for the presentation of most of Taylor's ideas on Scientific Management. Taylor would later serve as president of the society.

In 1890 Taylor left a successful career at Midvale and entered into what were probably the most difficult years of his life. While at Midvale, Taylor had made some contacts with the navy, which led to an association with a group called the Manufacturing Investment Company, a wood pulp and paper manufacturing firm with a patent on a process for manufacturing wood pulp from lumber-mill by-products. Taylor's venture into management was not entirely successful. Taylor, as was his wont, was apparently more concerned with improving productivity than the financial position of the firm. What Taylor did develop while he was with Manufacturing Investment was a deep distrust of big business, which was to have a lasting impact and shape his later programs of social reform.[9]

Taylor left Manufacturing Investment in 1893 to become a consulting engineer, introducing various elements of Scientific Management in a number of firms. This period was marked less by his success in consulting than a coming together of most of the major elements of Scientific Management. In 1895 Taylor presented his first report to the American Society of Mechanical Engineers in a paper entitled "A Piece Rate System."[10] Although, as the title suggests, Taylor proposed a new wage-incentive scheme, he was more concerned with the system of management than the scheme embedded in it. It was also during this period that Taylor made a series of investments that formed the basis of his personal wealth and subsequently enabled him to devote most of his time to promoting Scientific Management.

In 1898 Taylor took a position with Bethlehem Steel Company in what was to be a most productive association. While at Bethlehem, Taylor installed a system of production management and functional supervision that incorporated many of the basic ideas of Scientific Management. Taylor also collaborated on the invention of a high-speed tool steel, touted as the most important machine-tool invention of Taylor's lifetime.[11] The money received from the patent on this process was the largest single increment to Taylor's personal fortune. After Taylor left Bethlehem in 1901, he spent the rest of his life basically as a publicist, educator, and social reformer in advancing the cause of Scientific Management, and his attentions shifted, accordingly, from the technical aspects of Scientific Management to its social implications.

Over his lifetime, Taylor developed a philosophy of life, work, and society that shaped his approach to the development of a science of management. Although Taylor scorned formal religion, his view of life reflected his Quaker and Puritan background. Taylor's grand aim was control. He believed that hard work yields morality and that weaknesses must be curbed by doing what is right.[12] Character is developed and reinforced by doing things that are tiresome, monotonous, and unpleasant.[13] This set of beliefs plus Taylor's distrust of anything not based on provable facts determined both the focus of Taylor's science of management and the methods he employed in elaborating it. This basic philosophy was also reflected in Taylor's disciplined life style. Taylor dressed only for utility; he did not drink alcohol, coffee, or tea; and even his approach to pastimes, as we have seen, was highly structured.[14] It has been said that the aesthetic was not in Taylor's blood. If he had a concept of the aesthetic, it was probably the elimination of the superfluous.[15]

Taylor's attitude toward life was also reflected in his attitude toward work. Though Taylor reportedly had a strong personal distaste for manual labor, he described his years as an apprentice and the winter of 1895, which was spent cutting metal, as the happiest of his life.[16] Taylor was both celebrated and condemned for his often tactless and cold-blooded references to workingmen, but he had a respect for, and identification with, the workman. Indeed, Taylor purposely adopted the life style and habits of the worker including a penchant for swearing, which sometimes caused him difficulty in more formal circles.[17]

Taylor's approach to Scientific Management constituted a harsher critique of management than of the workers. Taylor felt that management was the basic cause of inefficiency, since it had not assumed its fair share of responsibility for the design and performance of work. Thus workers "soldiered" because management had not performed its functions properly. Taylor's attitude toward the workman can perhaps be more appropriately characterized as one of noblesse oblige than castigation. Comparing college professors to workingmen, Taylor claimed, "We are all made of the same clay, and essentially of the same mental as well as physical fibre."[18] Taylor thought education as a gentleman demanded actual experience as well as respect both for a day's work and the men who do it. Taylor ranked character, common sense, and education, in that order, as the elements of a good man.[19]

As a social reformer, Taylor is probably best described as a "conservative radical." Taylor was surely inclined to the radical side of things, as is evidenced by his distrust of big business, his scathing criticism of management practices, and his opposition to capitalism devoid of human consideration and characterized by financial privilege.[20] Yet Taylor rejected socialism, felt that labor unions had outlived their usefulness, and had little sympathy for what he called the "semi-philanthropic" gestures of the labor reformers of his day.[21] Though Taylor would later be identified with the Progressive movement, his direct concerns never extended much beyond the shop level, and his interest in the "labor problem" developed rather late in his career.

In assessing Frederick Taylor as a man, the lasting impression is one of basic dualities and conflict. His passion for games versus his dedication to hard work and discipline, his tactless reference to workmen versus his deliberate adoption of their life style, his passion for orders versus a personal habit of leaving things laying about, his plague of nightmares versus his preoccupation with control, his distaste for manual labor versus his reported pleasure in doing it, his dislike of clerical routines versus his praise of the monotonous grind, the incidents of reading a book in chapel and cheating on an exam at Exeter versus his concern for character and integrity illustrate the dualities and suggest the conflicts. In sum, Taylor's personal life was characterized by tension and inner turmoil. Taylor has been described as a man marked by an excess of his virtues, but he was also a man apparently engaged in a struggle against a perceived inner weakness in which a frenzy for order was a counterpart of the disorder within him.[22] And Taylor the man has an integral impact on Scientific Management as a method and as a movement.

The Method

Taylor identifies the basic social problem of his day as one of inefficiency. His objective is to increase efficiency by capitalizing on the
difference between what can be done by a "first-class" man and an
ordinary worker and, in the process, produce both high wages and lower
labor costs.

Taylor blames both management and the worker for inefficiency,
but reserves his sternest criticism for management, which he contends
is responsible for nine-tenths of the problem.[23] Management, Taylor
charges, is deficient both in terms of its lack of knowledge as to what
constitutes a proper day's work and in its indifference about proper
managerial practices. The worker contributes to the problem of inefficiency through "systematic soldiering" or the purposeful and organized
restriction of output. But even here Taylor lays the ultimate blame at
management's doorstep, since management's ignorance and indifference encourage systematic soldiering on the part of the workmen.

Taylor argues that traditional styles of management, which employ
a driving method of supervision (a combination of authoritarian rule
and physical compulsion), and an incentive system (piecework) that
discourages efficiency by lowering rates of compensation as productivity increased, combine to foster systematic soldiering. Even under the
best of previous managerial practices— initiative and incentive management—Taylor contends that too much responsibility is placed on
the worker and too little on management. Under initiative and incentive management, a worker is simply hired and sent out to perform specified tasks with little in the way of instruction or guidance from management. The result is all too often inefficiency, since the worker is not
likely to know how best to perform his assigned tasks. Taylor characterizes initiative and incentive management as a "lazy manager's
philosophy" in which management has shirked its primary responsibilities in regard to job design.[24]

To correct these deficiencies, Taylor proposes an approach to management embodying a radically altered division of responsibilities between management and the workers. Management is to assume a much
larger portion of the burden and is to take primary responsibility for a
scientific search for the best way of performing organizational tasks.

Taylor argues that there are two kinds of workmen: first-class and
second-class. A first-class workman is both able and willing to do a task
efficiently, and Taylor maintains that every man is a first-class workman at some kind of work. A second-class worker, in contrast, is physically able to perform a task, but will not do so because he is lazy. Taylor has little patience with, or sympathy for, a second-class workman.
As he puts it, Scientific Management has no place for a bird who can

sing, but won't.[25] It is management's responsibility to locate and/or develop first-class workmen, place them in positions suitable to their talents, provide them with good working conditions and appropriate implements, and give them detailed instructions on the best method of performing their tasks.

All of this is to be based on the development of a science of management that is to replace rules-of-thumb passed on from workman to workman. Taylor's objective is to seek, coordinate, and systematize knowledge, and by processes of observation, comparison, and abstraction, to deduce general laws of management.[26] This scientific endeavor is to concentrate on two kinds of experiments—the control and operation of machines and the standardization of human actions—with the intent of making man as predictable and efficient as the machines he tends.

Although Taylor believes it advisable, and necessary, to utilize the knowledge of the workers in regard to the performance of their tasks, he does not think they are capable of developing a science of management themselves. Instead, Taylor charges management with the basic responsibility for developing the required science and planning the work. In other words, management is first to make itself efficient before expecting efficiency from the workers. Once the proper method has been discovered, workers are simply responsible for executing the plan. Authority is to be exercised through an unveiling of scientific laws, not as an expression of arbitrary rule, but Scientific Management is to be implemented through the enforced standardization of methods, the enforced adoption of the best implements, and enforced cooperation between and among management and the workers.[27]

Taylor summarizes this approach in his famous statement of the principles of Scientific Management. Those principles are as follows:

1. The development of a science of management
2. The selection and training of the workman
3. Bringing science and the workman together
4. An equal division of work and responsibility between management and worker[28]

Thus, under Scientific Management, science would replace rule-of-thumb, harmony would replace discord, cooperation would replace individualism, maximum output would replace restricted output, and each man would be developed to his greatest efficiency and prosperity.[29]

In pursuit of these objectives, Taylor devoted most of his productive lifetime to the quest for a science of management. In the course of this quest, Taylor discovered and/or implemented a series of innovations pertaining to the machinery of production, the organizational environment, and the people who used the machines and populated the organizations. Some of these developments, such as the invention of mechanical devices, the development of cost accounting techniques, machine-room layout and design, purchase and store methods, tool standardization and tool-room reorganization, and mnemonic classification systems, while important, fall beyond the purview of the present discussion. I concentrate instead on three central components of Taylor's Scientific Management: time-and-motion studies, wage-incentive systems, and functional organization.

Time-and-Motion Studies

As stated earlier, Taylor believes that the basic causes of inefficiency are the ignorance on the part of management as to the proper time required to perform a task and the systematic soldiering on the part of workmen that such ignorance encourages. Accordingly, a primary task for Scientific Management is to establish appropriate standards for task performance. These standards are to be based on scientific investigations of tasks performed using optimal methods rather than simple observations of actual performance in the workplace. The intent is thus not to measure the actual performance of the average workman but to determine what a first-class workman could do employing scientifically determined techniques.[30]

The primary tool of analysis in these investigations is time-and-motion studies. The general procedure employed in time-and-motion studies is to break down physical activities into their component parts, specify the optimal routine for the performance of each component part, and discover the most efficient method for recombining the parts into the more complex task. More specifically, time-and-motion studies involve the following steps:

1. The worker is provided with the best implements, appropriately placed.
2. The task is analyzed and divided into elementary units.
3. Useless movements are discovered and discarded.
4. The analyst studies a skilled workman performing the task with the aid of a stopwatch. The objective here is to discover the quickest and best method for making each elementary movement. Such investigation is to be guided by a series of "principles" of physical activity; for example, the two hands should begin and complete their motions at the same time, the two hands should not be idle at the same time except during periods of rest, and the motions of the arms should be made in opposite and symmetrical directions and should be made simultaneously.

5. The elementary movements of the task are grouped in an appropriate sequence to maximize overall efficient task performance.

6. The proper method of task performance is described and recorded and the time required to perform the task is determined.

7. An allowance is made for unavoidable delays. Based on his investigations, Taylor asserts that 20 to 27 percent should be added to the actual working time to allow for unavoidable delays.

8. Allowances should be made for the time it takes a new employee to learn the job.

9. Allowance should be made for rests and the intervals of rest required for a worker to recover from physical fatigue.[31]

The product of time-and-motion studies is thus a specification of the nature of a task, how the task is to be done, and the time required for the performance of a task accounting for the capacity, speed, and durability of the worker. Since no two workmen work at exactly the same speed, performance standards should be set somewhere between the performance of a first-class man and the performance of an average man with the standards being gradually increased as the worker becomes more familiar with the system.

Once the basic time-and-motion study was performed, instruction cards containing the procedures derived were used in the training of other workers. The instructions contained on these cards were often formed in exquisite detail. For instance, the instructions for the operation of a lathe consisted of 183 steps, all of which were to be accomplished in the manner specified and in the order listed.[32] Taylor's suggested procedure is to choose *one* man and allow him to work under the new system with a higher rate of pay. Other workers are expected to come voluntarily into the program as its attractions became apparent.

Although Taylor sought the "one best way" of performing various physical tasks, he never asserted that time-and-motion studies were an exact science. Instead, he felt that "laws" relating to humans were subject to greater variability than those relating to physical things, and he reportedly could be content with "good enough" while still searching for the "best."[33] Thus standards established through time-and-motion studies are to be accepted only conditionally. Those standards are not to be altered, however, unless a new method of performing the task is discovered. This is required to prevent arbitrary changes in standards as productivity increases. Taylor felt that such changes had served as a disincentive under previous managerial practices with workers being penalized by lower marginal rates of compensation when productivity increased to unexpected levels.[34] The trick, of course, is to establish correct standards in the first place and then stick to them.

Wage-Incentive System

The distinguishing feature of Taylor's incentive system is the prior establishment of standards of work performance through time-and-motion studies. Consequently, Taylor felt that the actual method of reward—be it day work, piecework, task work with a bonus, or differential piecework—was a relatively unimportant part of the system. In Taylor's opinion, factors such as special incentives, higher wages, shorter working hours, better working conditions, and individual rewards for the worker based on performance all overshadow the importance of the specific method of payment.

Taylor's basic approach to incentives is, first, to give each worker a definite task with detailed instructions and an exact time standard for the performance of each element of the task. When this has been accomplished, the worker is to be paid extraordinary wages for performing the task in the allotted time and ordinary wages if the time allotment is exceeded. As noted, Taylor felt that the primary failing of previous incentive systems had been that they did not start with a sure knowledge of the time required to perform a task. Consequently, workers were encouraged to soldier either if standards were based on actual performance or, as was the case in some incentive schemes, if standards were increased as the workers produced more. Taylor also objected to gain-sharing plans, such as those proposed by Towne and Halsey.[35] These plans provided that, when work is done in a shorter time and at a reduced cost, the gain in profits was to be shared in a prescribed ratio between management and the workers. Taylor argued that such plans shared a common failure in not establishing objective performance standards. In addition, he felt that these plans were deficient in that they did not recognize the personal contribution of each worker. Moreover, the delay between performance and reward reduces the plan's ability to motivate the worker to produce more. Thus Taylor would have incentives based on prior standards of work performance with each worker rewarded on an individual basis and performance linked immediately (daily) to reward.

Although Taylor thinks the particular system of payment to be relatively unimportant, he generally supports the differential rate system he had devised while at Midvale. Under the differential rate system, the worker is assigned a clearly defined task with a specified time allowed to perform the task. The task assignment, according to Taylor, should be made so difficult that it can be accomplished only by a first-class worker in the time specified. If the worker fails to perform the task in the required time, or if there are imperfections in the work performed, the pay rate is set at a level that is scarcely an ordinary day's pay. This base rate is to be determined by an analysis of payment for similar work in the relevant labor market.

If the worker accomplishes the task in the specified time without imperfections, a bonus of 30 to 100 percent of the base pay is earned with the specific amount of the bonus dependent on the work involved. For routine shop work, the bonus is to be 30 percent of base pay. For labor requiring severe bodily exertion and fatigue, the bonus is to be 50 to 60 percent. For jobs requiring special skill, the bonus is to be 70 to 80 percent. For work involving both skill and physical exertion, the bonus is to be 80 to 100 percent.[36] Taylor also advises against paying the worker too much, since this only results in demoralizing the worker, discouraging thrift, and encouraging the worker to look for the opportunity to work less.

Thus, under Taylor's incentive system, like other pay schemes, success is rewarded by higher pay and failure is penalized by financial loss. Nevertheless, Taylor's system is distinguished from others because it is based on prior knowledge of what constitutes a good day's work. Given this knowledge, management is protected, since it is not likely to encounter unexpectedly high labor costs resulting from unanticipated increases in productivity, and the worker is protected, and thus not encouraged to soldier, since the work standards will not be changed in the absence of the discovery of a new way of doing the work.

Functional Organization

Taylor's prescriptions for organizational structure are a radical departure from previous practices. Previously the military model of organization had prevailed, stressing unity of command at each level of the organization and culminating in a single executive body at the apex of an organizational pyramid. Under this arrangement, the foreman was responsible for a wide range of functions including hiring, training, supervising, and firing his subordinates. Foremen were often hired on a contract basis and simply charged with getting the work done, with little direction from management.[37]

Taylor believed this arrangement to be deficient in two regards. First, it demands an undue amount of technical expertise from top management. Second, it expects too much from the foreman and, as a result, effectively precludes direct control by management over the workers. Consequently, Taylor proposes both a decentralization of authority from general management and a centralization of authority from the foreman. The new locus of authority and responsibility is to be the planning department. In the process, Taylor divides the tasks previously performed by the foreman and allocates them to a number of "functional foremen."

The decentralizing aspect of Taylor's functional organization is the establishment of a cadre of technical experts in positions of power in the organization. This power is not to be fixed at the top level of the organization but in a planning department, and authority is to be exercised on the basis of knowledge, not mere position. The experts in the planning department are to be relatively free from bureaucratic controls exercised from above. Organizational executives are to limit themselves to handling problems that cannot be handled in the planning department. Top executives are to have a general knowledge of all the steps necessary in the accomplishment of organizational tasks, and they are to stay apprised of the character and fitness of important men working under them. But operational control for top executives is to be based on the "exception principle."[38] That is, the executive is to receive condensed reports of organizational activities and concern himself only with exceptions from normal performance.

Functionalization also means centralization to the extent that some activities previously performed by the foreman are to be elevated to the planning department in order to establish management's central responsibilities in the areas of job design and planning and to institute direct managerial control over the workers. The planning department, consistent with its importance in Taylor's scheme of things, is assigned a wide range of functions including performing time-and-motion studies, maintaining proper inventory levels, providing for the maintenance of equipment, analyzing orders for machines or work, and establishing a system of classification for materials and equipment. Although Taylor is not very precise on the point, the department is to be composed of a number of offices, such as a time-study office, a pay department, an information bureau, an employment bureau, and a rush-order department.[39]

Four of Taylor's functional foremen are to be assigned to the planning department: the route clerk, the instruction card man, the time clerk, and the disciplinarian.[40] The route clerk is to oversee the work flow, study specific jobs and decide the best method of doing them (both the required operations and the sequence of operations), indicate the tools to be used, make a chart showing the course of work through the shop, and determine the order in which various jobs are to be done. The instruction card man is to study the drawings and worksheet prepared by the route clerk, prepare detailed instructions for the performance of each operation, and indicate the length of time required for each operation. The time clerk is to be responsible for preparing pay and written reports, reviewing time cards to determine eligibility for bonuses, and allocating work costs to the proper accounts. The disciplinarian is to review trouble between workers and their bosses, hire and fire, and attend to other personnel matters.

The remaining four functional foremen are assigned to the shop and made responsible for the proper execution of the plan.[41] These foremen are called the gang boss, the speed boss, the inspection foreman, and the repair boss. The gang boss is to set up the job, organize and situate the required machinery, give instruction cards to the workers, and route the work through the shop. The speed boss is to see to it that machines are run at the proper speed and that the appropriate tools are used. In addition, the speed boss is to ensure that the job is performed in the prescribed fashion, and he is to instruct the worker on the use of machines. In case of failure, the speed boss is responsible for ascertaining the causes and demonstrating that the work could be done in the required time. The inspection foreman is to examine the products and ensure that they conform to standards. The repair boss is to be responsible for the adjustment, cleanliness, and general care of the machines, and he is to keep a record of repairs and maintenance.

Taylor's preferred style of supervision for these functional foremen is to hold a plum for the worker to climb after, crack the whip with an occasional touch of the lash, and work shoulder to shoulder with the worker, pushing, teaching, guiding, and helping.[42] Though force is to remain available, it is to serve only as a supplement to appeals to self-interest. The worker is expected to do what he is told and, in effect, become one in a complex train of "gear wheels" constituting the overall organization.

It should be noted that in abandoning the military style of organization with its emphasis on unity of command, Taylor is making the worker directly responsible to eight foremen. To avoid conflict, Taylor requires that the duties of the various foremen be precisely defined so that none interferes with others. More important, Taylor argues that an effective unity of command is retained in the organization, since knowledge is to be enshrined as the single master.[43] The organizational hierarchy is to be based on abilities with each individual encouraged to rise to his highest level of competence. This is to include the movement from worker to managerial status; and Taylor countenances, indeed encourages, a higher ratio of what he calls "brain workers" to "hand workers."

These three components—time-and-motion studies, wage-incentive systems, and functional organization—constitute the core of Taylor's Scientific Management. But Taylor would object to the notion that these, or any other listing, of procedures and techniques capture the essence of Scientific Management. For Taylor, Scientific Management is more than a "series of expedients to increase efficiency." Instead, Scientific Management requires a "mental revolution" on the part of both management and workers as science replaces rule-of-thumb and mutual confidence between management and workers replaces "suspicious watchfulness."[44] It was in pursuit of this mental revolution that

Frederick W. Taylor

Taylor embarked on a campaign to promote the spread of Scientific Management in the early 1900s.

The Movement

In his early efforts, Taylor's interests were largely technical and his objective that of efficiency. Not until 1899, in a speech to Bethlehem managers, did Taylor even suggest that Scientific Management could be reduced to a body of principles.[45] In 1901 Taylor abruptly changed course, and the inventor and engineer became an educator and social reformer. In so doing, Taylor turned his attention from the technical aspects of Scientific Management to its social consequences, with particular emphasis on the "labor problem."

At the turn of the century, the labor force was in a virtually permanent state of turmoil and unrest with a high level of antagonism between management and the workers. Taylor believed that the application of the techniques of Scientific Management could address the causes of the conflict between labor and management by defining a proper day's work, by providing just compensation for the worker, and by giving management a good rate of return on its investment. In this way, attention could be diverted from contention over division of what Taylor calls "the surplus" to increasing that surplus and, in the process, serving the interests of both management and the workers.[46] That is, management could get what it wants (lower labor costs) and the workers could get what they want (higher wages) by increasing efficiency.

Taylor's concept of the organization under Scientific Management is thus one in which harmony would replace discord and cooperation would replace conflict, with an underlying compatibility of interests between management and the workers exposed through the application of Scientific Management techniques. As Taylor puts it,

> The majority of men believe that the fundamental interests of employees and employers are necessarily antagonistic. Scientific Management, on the contrary, has for its very foundation the firm conviction that the interests of the two are one and the same; that prosperity for the employer cannot exist through a long period of years unless it is accompanied by prosperity for the employee and vice versa.[47]

Indeed, Taylor identifies "close and intimate cooperation" between management and the worker as integral to the mental revolution embodied in the doctrines of Scientific Management.

Although Taylor stresses cooperation in the workplace, authority is not to be shared equally by management and the workers. Taylor's approach can probably be better described as a form of benevolent paternalism in which hierarchy is to remain the primary mechanism of control and coordination in the organization. Nevertheless, Taylor contends that management is to be as severely disciplined as the workers under Scientific Management. The exercise of authority is to be based on the mandate of right reason resting on scientific laws, and those laws are to be as binding on management as hierarchical authority is to be on the worker. Management is thus to be a senior partner in a scientific enterprise in which knowledge is to be enshrined as the ultimate master with management deriving its authority from superior competence. Taylor simply believes the worker to be less competent and thus unable to construct the required science of management. In Taylor's words:

> in almost all of the mechanic arts the science which underlies each act of each workman is so great and amounts to so much that the workman who is best suited to actually doing the work is incapable of fully understanding this science without the guidance and help of those who are working with him or over him, either through lack of education or through insufficient mental capacity.[48]

Indeed, Taylor contended that an "intelligent gorilla" would be at least as useful as the Eastern European immigrants he found working at Bethlehem.[49]

Taylor sees the organization under Scientific Management as constituting a mutually beneficial exchange with significant rewards accruing to both management and the workers. The benefits to management are an increase in output with lower labor costs. Taylor estimated that the application of the principles of Scientific Management would result in a doubling of output per man and per machine and reported that those companies already employing the techniques of Scientific Management were more prosperous than ever before.[50]

Benefits to the workers come in a variety of forms. Most obviously, the worker would receive higher compensation under Scientific Management. Though the worker would generally not recover the full benefits of increased productivity (because of the cost of developing new techniques and implements), he would receive significantly higher wages. Moreover, Taylor claimed that the 30 to 100 percent higher wages received under Scientific Management had proven to be satisfactory with no contention raised about the distribution of the surplus.[51] More indirectly, the worker would benefit from lower consumer prices made possible by lower labor costs. But Taylor feels that the primary benefit to the worker was more intangible in nature: the development of a better character. Taylor contends that training under Scientific Management aids the worker in general intellectual and moral development. Under Scientific Management, workers would be given more interesting work that would more fully develop their talents. Moreover, Scientific Management would produce not only a better worker but also a person who would be able to live better, save money, and become more sober.[52]

In terms of the social reform movements of the day, Scientific Management would fall among those Haber calls "systemizers."[53] This movement, comprised basically of engineers, looked to technological expertise, hierarchy, and discipline for a solution to the labor problem. Taylor's particular interests took him from mechanical efficiency to the interface between man and the machine. Taylor believed that far from ignoring the human factor, as his critics charged, he alone was meaningfully addressing the labor problem, and he had little brief for the other reform movements of his day.

The Industrial Betterment movement was dismissed by Taylor as a collection of "semi-philanthropic aids," which were of "distinctly secondary importance." Industrial Betterment, a forerunner of the later Human Relations movement, argued that human happiness was a business asset, that well-being for the worker would yield hard work and greater productivity, and that the natural goodness of man would flourish if nurtured in a benevolent environment.[54] In order to achieve a higher level of human happiness, the Industrial Betterment movement supported a variety of reforms, such as comfortable lavatories, lunchrooms, kindergartens, athletic grounds, night schools, safety training, and free lectures. Although not entirely discounting such reforms, Taylor's approach to the labor problem was based on a contrasting set of premises. Whereas Industrial Betterment assumed that morality and well-being would yield hard work, Taylor argued that hard work would yield morality and well-being. Whereas Industrial Betterment thought better working conditions would bring out man's "natural goodness," Taylor asserted that the natural weaknesses in man must be curbed by insisting that he do what is right through hierarchical controls.

Taylor was similarly disdainful of the union movement. Though Taylor believes that unions play a useful role in relieving the worker of the worst excesses of previous managerial practices, he feels that they have outlived their usefulness. Unions, Taylor argues, foster the restriction of output by making the work of the least efficient the standard of performance. In addition, Taylor accuses unions of employing abhorrent tactics. In Taylor's words, "The boycott, the use of force or intimidation, and oppression of nonunion workmen by labor unions are damnable; these acts of tyranny are thoroughly un-American and will not be tolerated by the American people."[55] Taylor hopes to avoid the tendency toward unionization through "systematic individualization" in which individuals rather than positions are rewarded, and rewards are based on scientific assessments of productivity. Taylor tempered his position, however, by stating that Scientific Management should not be implemented unless it was agreeable to both management and the workers and even suggested that there was no reason why a joint commission of employers and workers could not be established to set daily tasks.[56]

Scientific Management's intended reach transcended even this concern with the labor problem. Harlow Person, a president of the Taylor Society, expressed this broader intent in stating the hope that "we may discover that the philosophy, principles, and techniques [of Scientific Management] are applicable to conservation problems of entire nations, and perhaps of an entire world."[57] Even further, Person asserted: "The very survival of democratic institutions may depend on a lifting of productivity to new degrees of adequacy which will rapidly eliminate starvation, establish a feeling of greater economic security, and destroy impulses to follow false leaders along paths of violence toward a totalitarian world."[58] For Taylor, the diffusion of character is the essence of democracy, and that character was to be instilled by adopting both the mentality and the techniques of Scientific Management.

After leaving Bethlehem in 1901, Taylor largely withdrew from direct contact with the technical work of Scientific Management and became increasingly concerned with promoting the cause. Taylor's primary vehicle for promoting Scientific Management was a series of publications; his platform, at least initially, was the American Society of Mechanical Engineers (ASME), which he had joined in the 1880s while he was still at Midvale. During 1902 and 1903, Taylor worked on the manuscript for *Shop Management*, a report on the progress of Scientific Management.[59] In this manuscript Taylor's emphasis began to shift from efficiency to the social implications of Scientific Management. *Shop Management* was presented as a paper to the ASME in 1903 and subsequently published in book form by the society. In 1906 Taylor presented "On the Art of Cutting Metals" to the ASME as his presidential address.[60] Although largely technical in nature, the paper signaled Taylor's most significant mechanical invention—high-speed tool steel —which represented the culmination of some twenty-five years of research. In 1909 Taylor completed his best-known and most controversial work, *The Principles of Scientific Management*.[61] In *Principles*, Taylor completed a transition in which the social implications of Scientific Management were emphasized almost to the exclusion of technical matters. Taylor submitted this manuscript, as he had all his manuscripts, to the ASME for consideration for publication. The ASME balked at its publication, however, given the publicity then attendant to Scientific Management and Taylor's stress on nontechnical material.[62] The paper was held by the ASME for nearly a year without action. As a result, Taylor withdrew the manuscript and had it published at his own expense for distribution to ASME members. *Principles* was subsequently serialized by *American Magazine* and published by Harper and Brothers in 1911. Thus Taylor's most famous work did not bear the imprimatur of the ASME, and a rift was evidenced within the society between those who believed an engineer to be simply a technician and those who supported a broader role of social responsibility. This rift was to grow in the years following and eventuate in the formation of separate organizations by Taylor and his associates to promote Scientific Management.

Taylor's publications gained him some notoriety, but the Scientific Management movement acquired widespread public attention through hearings conducted by the Interstate Commerce Commission (ICC) on railway rates in 1910. The hearings became a forum for a confrontation between the railroads seeking higher rates and the Progressives, represented by Louis Brandeis, who argued that a rate increase would not be necessary if the railroads were simply operated more efficiently.[63] Brandeis's concern for efficiency brought him into contact with exponents of Scientific Management, from whom he solicited testimony. Interestingly, in view of the fact that the hearings served as a springboard to public fame for the Scientific Management movement, Taylor did not testify. Instead, testimony was received from three prominent Taylor associates: H. L. Gantt, Frank Gilbreth, and Harrington Emerson. Once Taylor realized the significance of the hearings, however, he worked closely with Brandeis.

The ICC hearings precipitated a period of intense public scrutiny of the techniques and philosophy of Scientific Management. In 1912 Congress launched an investigation into whether or not Scientific Management should be forbidden in government agencies. Taylor did testify at these hearings and was subjected to extensive, and often hostile, questioning by members of the House Investigating Committee.[64] The hearings were the beginning of a five-year congressional examination and debate over the desirability of employing the techniques of Scientific Management in the federal government and ended in legislation prohibiting it.[65]

Although limited by his wife's ill health, Taylor participated in a number of other activities designed to promote the cause of Scientific Management. Between 1901 and 1914, Taylor lectured annually at the Harvard Graduate School of Business Administration; he participated, on a limited basis, in the application of Scientific Management techniques at federal arsenals; and at his home in Philadelphia he entertained a steady stream of visitors who came to learn about Scientific Management from the master.

Meanwhile, the practice of Scientific Management was spreading through business and government. Although by 1910 Taylor conceded that no single firm had adopted Scientific Management in its entirety, he estimated that 50,000 workmen were working under some form of Scientific Management.[66] In government, there was a great deal of enthusiasm for, and some limited attempts to apply, the principles of Scientific Management. Probably the most extensive efforts were at federal shipyards and arsenals. Between 1906 and 1908, the Mare Island Shipyards near San Francisco became the first "scientifically managed" government plant.[67] By 1908, the Watertown Arsenal in Massachusetts had become a model plant with a 50 percent decrease in material cost and a doubling of output per man.[68] At the local level, the bastion of progressive reform at the turn of the century, Scientific Management evinced a great deal of interest. The most thorough applications were in New York and Chicago.[69] Members of New York City's Bureau of Municipal Research, a leader in the reform movement, occasionally entertained Taylor in their offices and became enthusiastic advocates of Scientific Management. In Philadelphia, Taylor's home city, a director of Public Works was appointed to institute Scientific Management procedures.

Interest in Scientific Management also spread abroad. *The Principles of Scientific Management* was translated into nine languages: French, German, Dutch, Swedish, Russian, Lettish, Italian, Spanish, and Japanese.[70] Interest in Scientific Management boomed in England, and in France Georges Clemenceau ordered that Scientific Management principles be applied in all military plants.[71] Later, Scientific Management was endorsed, albeit on a qualified basis, even in the Soviet Union, where Lenin had once characterized Scientific Management as a form of cruel bourgeois exploitation. Beguiled by its scientific attainments, Lenin urged its adoption as part of a policy to centralize authority and as a necessary step on the road to socialism.[72]

Taylor was personally rather conservative in his approach to social reform, but Scientific Management quickly became identified with broader social movements: the Progressive movement and a larger campaign against waste and inefficiency. The Progressive movement preached the gospel of efficiency in the name of a democracy that was to be led by an elite cadre of experts. Efficiency became the watchword of the day as the Taft Committee on Economy and Efficiency was established at the federal level and a host of efficiency commissions sprung up at state and local levels of government. Scientific Management was even embraced by the women workers' movement, despite

Taylor's assertion that women were less efficient than men, less regular in their attendance, and should look forward to getting married.[73]

Within the Scientific Management Movement itself, the Society to Promote Scientific Management (later to be called the Taylor Society) was formed in 1911. In addition, a group of Taylor associates struck out in a number of directions, not all of which were to Taylor's tastes. Among the most prominent of them were H. L. Gantt and Frank Gilbreth. Gantt's technical concern was production-control techniques. He also adhered to a technocratic social philosophy in which an expert elite was to put down the rule of the mob. Gantt advocated an economic system that was to transform industries into public-service corporations run by committees of producers, distributors, and consumers. In 1916 Gantt formed the New Machine, an organization designed to acquire political and economic power.[74] Taylor would castigate Gantt for straying too far from his technical concerns.

Frank Gilbreth was most closely identified with time-and-motion studies, and he developed a photography method of conducting those studies. Gilbreth's life was later popularized in the book and the subsequent movie *Cheaper by the Dozen*. Gilbreth has been described as a "talented technician, a flamboyant personality, and an aggressive and occasionally unscrupulous promoter."[75] Gilbreth formed the Taylor Society, but he later broke with Taylor, who considered him to be overly preoccupied with time-and-motion studies to the exclusion of other elements of Scientific Management.

As Scientific Management received greater public attention, it also attracted significant opposition. The opposition was led by labor unions, particularly the metal trades unions, which protested the application of Scientific Management at the Watertown Arsenal.[76] Union protests against Scientific Management led to the aforementioned congressional inquiry that ended in legislation prohibiting the use of the techniques of Scientific Management in federal agencies. Socialists, following Lenin's line, denounced Scientific Management as a form of capitalist exploitation.[77] Even in the ASME, long a forum for Taylor's ideas, opposition developed. In 1912 the ASME appointed a committee to investigate Scientific Management.[78] Although the results of the investigation were inconclusive, Taylor and his associates chose to work largely outside the ASME thereafter.

Following Taylor's death in 1915, the Scientific Management movement continued, but in altered form. Splits among Taylor's disciples diluted the impact of their efforts and eventually compromises with the forces of the opposition and changing social, political, and economic conditions altered the course of reform. By the 1920s, unions had reached a compromise with advocates of Scientific Management in which unions accepted time-and-motion studies in return for Scientific

Management's acceptance of collective bargaining.[79] The exponents of Scientific Management even incorporated elements of industrial democracy in their doctrines, and unions became supporters of "humanized" Scientific Management. The result of the compromises was less controversy, but also a substantial loss of distinctiveness and fervor in pursuit of the cause. By the 1920s, the Scientific Management movement had largely retreated from comprehensive strategies of social reform and returned to its initial concentration on technical matters.

Conclusion

Taylor, in developing Scientific Management, made undoubted contributions to the understanding of, and prescriptions for, the management of organizations. Yet he is probably better characterized as a synthesizer than an innovator. That is, Taylor's contribution was less the introduction of new ideas than the integration of existing ideas into a coherent system. In this synthesis, Taylor extended the perspectives of both the engineers and industrial reformers. The engineering perspective was extended from machines to men. The labor-reform perspective was extended from men to machines. And it was the man-machine interface that was the primary focus of Taylor's efforts. In addition, Taylor advanced the cause of systematic investigation by the precision of his measurements, which replaced the prior reliance on rules-of-thumb. Scientific Management was clearly a movement right for its time, and its impact is still evident, particularly in industrial engineering.

Although limited in its perspective, Scientific Management also suggested the importance of cooperation in the workplace and called for an end to the arbitrary exercise of managerial authority. Taylor was hardly a humanist, but he did recognize the interests of the workers, at least to the extent that they shared with management a stake in higher productivity. Thus suspicion and mutual distrust were to be replaced by a joint pursuit of shared objectives.

Despite these contributions, Scientific Management is limited both in regard to its scope and its scientific accomplishments. In its scope, Scientific Management neglects the impact of factors external to the organization and considers only some factors internal to the organization. Taylor never extended his technical studies much beyond the shop level. The broader financial aspects of the firm were of little concern to him. Taylor's sole venture into the broader areas of management at Manufacturing Investment Corporation was something less than a stunning success, and he developed a reputation among those who employed him as having a talent for "making money fly."[80] Taylor gave the impression that he would pursue efficiency regardless of the cost, and his techniques, like the man, tended to suffer from an excess of their virtues.

Taylor has been most roundly, and perhaps unfairly, condemned for an alleged neglect of the human factor in the organization. It is probably fairer to state that Taylor operated on the basis of a limited set of assumptions about the nature of man and his relationship to the organization. Taylor assumed, at least implicitly, that the ordinary worker was only segmentally involved in the organization (i.e., he had interests other than work) and that he was seeking instrumental rewards from his organizational involvement (i.e., rewards that would allow him to acquire his primary gratifications elsewhere). In addition, Taylor assumed that the worker would rationally pursue his self-interest relatively uncontaminated by his feelings, attitudes, and private goals. Given this image of man and his relationship to the organization, Taylor assumed that behavior could be rendered predictable by the proper manipulation of monetary incentives. This view is not so much wrong as it is partial. Subsequent research has indicated that individual behavior in the organization is influenced by a considerably broader range of variables, including a host of social and psychological factors that Taylor adjudged irrelevant to productivity.

Finally, Taylor was not entirely successful in achieving his scientific objectives. Although Taylor claimed that Scientific Management is "a true science resting upon clearly defined laws, rules, and principles," the claim is of dubious validity.[81] The claim to be a science is subject to interpretation. Taylor defined science simply as "classified or organized knowledge," and Scientific Management would seem to qualify by the definition (though other, more stringent, definitions are possible). [82] The claim of having arrived at clearly defined laws, rules, and principles is more difficult to support. Taylor admitted that laws relating to human behavior are subject to greater variability than are those relating to physical phenomena, and he believed that time-and-motion studies, a central component of Scientific Management, could not be reduced to an exact science.[83] Indeed, as we have seen, the latter point led to a falling out between Taylor and Frank Gilbreth, one of Taylor's leading disciples.

Perhaps even more critically, Taylor never arrived at scientifically determined standards of work performance or rates of compensation. Performance standards did not reflect the "one best way" of performing a job. Instead, the prescribed methods were "state-of-the-art" solutions subject to change on the discovery of a better method. The choice of a "first-class workman" to perform the task and establish the standards was largely arbitrary and dependent on self-selection through a volunteer process. The choice of an actual standard by which to evaluate work performance was similarly arbitrary. Since no two men work at exactly the same pace, work standards were to be set at some unspecified point between the performance of the observed first-class workman and the average workman. Rates of basic compensation and the size of the bonus that was to be a function of that basic wage were to be established by two criteria, neither of which was entirely objective in nature. First, the base wage was to be barely sufficient to allow the worker to sustain himself. Second, the base wage was to be comparable to wages received by workers performing similar tasks in a relevant labor market. Thus the matter of an appropriate division of rewards was left unsettled and remained a major point of contention between Taylor and his critics, particularly the labor unions.

Scientific Management was truly a creature of its inventor and, as such, shared both his virtues and his shortcomings. It embodied a work ethic and social morality that transcended a scientific and technical enterprise. If Taylor failed in his scientific ambitions, he succeeded far beyond his original intentions in capturing the public's imagination and altering some traditional concepts of management.

Notes

1. Frank Barkley Copley, *Frederick W. Taylor: Father of Scientific Management*, vol. 1 (New York: American Society of Mechanical Engineers, 1923), 45.

2. Quotation from Stuart P. Sherman, "What Is a Puritan?" in ibid., 28.

3. Ibid., 53.

4. Ibid., 66.

5. This penchant was later carried to a curious extreme when Taylor would try out his wife's horses by donning her skirts and riding sidesaddle through town. Ibid., 374.

6. Daniel Nelson, *Frederick W. Taylor and the Rise of Scientific Management* (Madison: University of Wisconsin Press, 1980), 25.

7. Copley, *Frederick W. Taylor*, 153.

8. Ibid., 127.

9. Nelson, *Frederick W. Taylor*, 53–54.

10. Frederick W. Taylor, "A Piece Rate System," in *Scientific Management*, ed. Clarence Bertrand Thompson (Easton, Pa.: Hive Publishing, 1972), 636–83.

11. Nelson, *Frederick W. Taylor*, 86.

12. Samuel Haber, *Efficiency and Uplift: Scientific Management in the Progressive Era 1890–1920* (Chicago: University of Chicago Press, 1964), 20.

13. Ibid., 7.

14. Copley, *Frederick W. Taylor*, 83.

15. Ibid., 110.

16. Taylor's "testimony" before the special house committee, in Frederick W. Taylor, *Scientific Management* (New York: Harper & Brothers, 1911), 125.

17. Copley, *Frederick W. Taylor*, 89.

18. Ibid., 188.
19. Ibid., 126.
20. Ibid., 387.
21. F. W. Taylor, *Shop Management* (New York: Harper & Brothers, 1947), 200.
22. Haber, *Efficiency and Uplift*, 5.
23. Copley, *Frederick W. Taylor*, 292.
24. Ibid., 241.
25. Taylor, "Testimony," in Frederick W. Taylor, *Scientific Management* (New York: Harper & Brothers, 1911), 175.
26. Copley, *Frederick W. Taylor*, xxiv.
27. Frederick W. Taylor, *The Principles of Scientific Management* (New York: Harper & Brothers, 1919), 83.
28. Ibid., 36–37.
29. Ibid., 140.
30. Taylor, *Scientific Management*, 25.
31. Copley, *Frederick W. Taylor*, 227.
32. James March and Herbert Simon, *Organizations* (New York: Wiley, 1958), 14.
33. Copley, *Frederick W. Taylor*, 265.
34. Ibid., 211.
35. Nelson, *Frederick W. Taylor*, 14–16.
36. Frederick Taylor, "Shop Management" in Taylor, *Shop Management*, 26.
37. Nelson, *Frederick W. Taylor*, 7.
38. Copley, *Frederick W. Taylor*, 302.
39. Taylor, "Shop Management," 111.
40. Copley, *Frederick W. Taylor*, 324–25.
41. Ibid.
42. Ibid., 321–22.
43. Ibid., 290.
44. Ibid., 10.
45. Nelson, *Frederick W. Taylor*, 90.
46. Taylor, "Testimony," 30.
47. Taylor, *Principles*, 10.
48. Ibid., 41.
49. Nelson, *Frederick W. Taylor*, 91.
50. Taylor, *Principles*, 28.
51. Taylor, "Testimony," 147.
52. Taylor, *Principles*, 74. Taylor's favorite example was "Schmidt" (actually Henry Noll), who was taught to load pig iron under the techniques of Scientific Management. Noll, unfortunately, later lost his job and home because of excessive drinking. See Nelson, *Frederick W. Taylor*, 98.
53. Haber, *Efficiency and Uplift*, 19.
54. Ibid., 20.
55. Taylor, "Shop Management," 191.
56. Taylor, "Testimony," 145.
57. Harlow Person, "Foreword," in Taylor, *Scientific Management*, xvi.

58. Ibid.

59. Taylor, "Shop Management."

60. Taylor, "On the Art of Cutting Metals," in Thompson, *Scientific Management*, 242–67.

61. Taylor, *Principles.*

62. Nelson, *Frederick W. Taylor,* 174.

63. Ibid.

64. Taylor, "Testimony."

65. Haber, *Efficiency and Uplift,* 69.

66. Taylor, *Principles,* 28.

67. Nelson, *Frederick W. Taylor,* 155.

68. Ibid., 166.

69. Haber, *Efficiency and Uplift,* 110–11.

70. Copley, *Frederick W. Taylor,* xx.

71. Haber, *Efficiency and Uplift,* 120.

72. Ibid., 129.

73. Copley, *Frederick W. Taylor,* 464.

74. Haber, *Efficiency and Uplift,* 44.

75. Nelson, *Frederick W. Taylor,* 131.

76. Haber, *Efficiency and Uplift,* 68.

77. Ibid., 65. However, the socialists were also beguiled, as was Lenin, with the potential benefits of the application of Scientific Management.

78. Nelson, *Frederick W. Taylor,* 182.

79. Ibid., 202.

80. Haber, *Efficiency and Uplift,* 16.

81. Taylor, *Principles,* 7.

82. Taylor, "Testimony," 41.

83. Copley, *Frederick W. Taylor,* 234.

CHAPTER 3

Luther H. Gulick:
The Integrated Executive

Whereas the works of both Max Weber and Frederick Taylor would appear, at first blush, to be related only tangentially to the study and practice of public administration, Luther Gulick and his writings are directly and obviously central to those concerns. If there is a single person who personifies public administration in the United States, it is Luther Gulick. Indeed, his status in the field is such that he is sometimes referred to as the "Dean of Public Administration." That title is well earned. Gulick's life spans most of the period of the conscious study of public administration; his ideas, as they have evolved over time, mirror both many of the changes in the field and some enduring themes that underlie those changes; and his record of public service is perhaps unparalleled in the field, and at least achieved by only a very few.

The enduring themes are the most germane to our interests here, and I use the works of Luther Gulick as indicative of a line of thought that has had, and continues to have, substantial impact on the conduct of public administration in the United States. Gulick's work reflects many of the emphases of the reform movement of the early twentieth century as it applied to public-sector organization and management. He adopts Wilson's theme that a science of administration should be constructed, founded on basic principles applicable in both the public and private sectors. The common objective is to achieve greater efficiency in public-sector operations. These themes are elaborated with Gulick's particular stress on structural reform in the name of consolidation and integration, centralization to enhance executive power, professionalization to improve the quality of personnel in the public sector, and the rationalization of decision-making and management processes to assure greater effectiveness and efficiency in service delivery.

Perhaps the strongest of Gulick's emphases is the enhancement of executive power both within organizations and among the organizations of the executive branch. A strong executive is required to coordinate properly the fragmented activities performed in individual public organizations and in the public sector as a whole. Unified and concentrated leadership is necessary to rationalize operations and to locate responsibility at the apex of the organizational pyramid. In the relationship between branches of government, the executive should plan, propose, and implement public policies and programs, while the legislature should be restricted to review and approval.

There is a regard in which Gulick differs significantly from many of his contemporaries. That difference is Gulick's stance on the politics/policy-administration dichotomy. Gulick rejects the common contention of the time that the two domains can be, or should be, separate and distinct. Gulick argues that such a separation is impractical, impossible, and undesirable. Instead, we should develop a system that allows the fullest use of the expertise of the public administrator, including expertise on matters of public policy.

One gets from Gulick the overall sense that government has an important and useful role in society and that the administrator plays a vital part in the performance of necessary governmental functions. In this way, too, Gulick reflects both the temperament of the time and the sense of mission so characteristic of the reform movement. Gulick had a passion for his mission that is clearly evidenced in his writings and even more powerfully in his administrative career.

Life

Luther Halsey Gulick was born in Osaka, Japan, on 17 January 1892.[1] The middle of three children of missionary parents, he was the third Gulick to bear the name Luther Halsey and shared it with an uncle who was the co-inventor (along with James Naismith) of basketball. The Gulick family was of Dutch descent, tracing its American roots to 1653, and numbered among its members a long line of scholars, doctors, teachers, scientists, authors, missionaries, and pastors. Gulick's father, Sidney Lewis Gulick, was an astronomer and mathematician as well as a theologian. His mother, Cara May (Fisher), the daughter of a California banker and ranch owner, was a professionally trained nurse.

Gulick lived in Japan during much of his youth. He describes himself as being full of mischievous adventure (he almost burned down his house while trying to make gunpowder), hot-tempered, active, and spoiled—characteristics that prompted a mission elder to comment on his father's departure from Japan, "Yes, we were sorry to have Dr. Gulick leave us; but after all he did take Luther with him." The Gulick family returned to the United States in 1904, spending a winter in Germany where Gulick studied at a local technical high school and learned to speak German.[2] In 1906 Gulick moved to Oakland, California, to stay with his maternal grandmother and attend high school. An apparently industrious youth, Gulick worked for a bookstore and delivered newspapers, finding his most dependable customers to be saloon-keepers and the madams of two brothels. His schoolwork went well in Oakland, but he reports that he made few friends.

The following year, Gulick was awarded a scholarship by Hotchkiss, a boarding school in Lakeville, Connecticut, where he spent his next three years. Gulick's studies at Hotchkiss focused on Greek, Latin, and mathematics; he participated in debate, joined the literary society, and was on the school track team until he broke an ankle, which ended his athletic endeavors. After a shaky start, and despite some problems with spelling, Gulick performed well at Hotchkiss, achieving honor-roll status and the top rank in his class. He developed what he describes as an "overly competitive nature," however, which was manifested, for instance, in a tenacity in debate that was considered ungentlemanly and would soon cause him difficulty.

During the summer of 1910, Gulick traveled to England as a deck-hand on a cattle boat and bicycled across the British Isles. On his return to the United States, he learned that his scholarship at Hotchkiss had been terminated because he was a "disturbing factor." Since he had placed well on national examinations, Gulick decided not to return to Hotchkiss, applying instead for admission to Oberlin College in Ohio where he was accepted on a provisional basis. He soon gained full admission by achieving Dean's List status in his first semester. Gulick earned his keep while at Oberlin by washing dishes, scrubbing floors, and beating rugs at a boarding house for missionary children; cutting lawns; selling magazines; and promoting lectures and concerts. During the summers, he worked as a section hand for a railroad, sold aluminum pots and pans, worked on a farm, poured cement for a mausoleum, and was a swimming instructor at a girl's camp in New Hampshire. He also made his first entry into politics in 1912 by managing a local campaign for Theodore Roosevelt's Bull Moosers.

Gulick received a B.A. degree in political science from Oberlin with honors and membership in Phi Beta Kappa in 1914.[3] On graduation, Gulick entered Oberlin's Theological Seminary with the intent of following his father in missionary work. Though he received an M.A. degree in philosophy in 1915, Gulick was beset by what he calls "agnostic uncertainties," which resulted in a major change in direction in his career plans. Gulick came to believe that the essence of spiritual life is not in the formal elements of religion but in the basic values of "fundamental honesty, individual human dignity, justice and human rights, the opportunity for creative fulfillment, social responsibility, 'charity' as defined by St. Paul, selfless devotion to noble causes, and deep emotional participation in the Universe." He maintained his parents' commitment to the advancement of humankind, but decided that his best contribution could be made through social work and government rather than as a missionary.

Consequently, Gulick applied to Columbia University, which he entered in the fall of 1915 as a Ph.D. student with a fellowship in political science and public law. Even more important, Gulick came into contact with the New York Bureau of Municipal Research where he attended courses at the bureau's Training School for Public Service and commenced what was to be a lifelong association. Gulick specialized in administration and budgeting and, in 1917, secured a position as secretary of the Joint Special Committee on Finance and Budget Procedure of the Massachusetts General Court (legislature). This experience produced the material for his Ph.D. dissertation and was later published as *Evolution of the Budget in Massachusetts.*[4] After a year's stint in the army, where Gulick served as a captain and staff member of the Statistics Branch of the General Staff, he was appointed director of the Training School for Public Service and secretary of the Board of the Bureau and embarked on what was to be a singularly distinctive career in the public service.

During the 1920s, Gulick received his Ph.D. from Columbia University and was appointed director of the Bureau of Municipal Research which was reconstituted as the National Institute of Public Administration.[5] Under Gulick's leadership, and with an expanded mandate, the institute undertook administrative studies in several states over the following twenty years.[6] Gulick himself served as chairman of the Governmental Research Association, director of research for the New York Taxation and Retrenchment Commission, and a member of the National Tax Association's Committee on a Model Tax Law in addition to performing his duties as director of the institute.

In the 1930s Gulick added a national dimension to his interests. In 1931 he was promoted to Eaton Professor of Municipal Science and Administration at Columbia University, a position he held until 1942. In 1933 Gulick was appointed secretary and director of the Social Science Research Council's Commission of Inquiry on Public Service Personnel. From 1933 through 1936, he was director of the Regent's Inquiry into the Character and Cost of Public Education in the State of New York. Between 1935 and 1937, Gulick served as a member of the President's Committee on Administrative Management and coedited the famous *Papers on the Science of Administration*, to which he contributed two papers.[7]

With the coming of the 1940s and the onset of World War II, Gulick went to Washington, serving in a wide array of capacities. Gulick acted as a consultant to both the Treasury Department and the secretary of war. In addition, Gulick worked with the Bureau of the Budget, was in charge of the technical aspects of the reorganization of the

Smaller Plants Corporation, organized and acted as chairman of the Advisory Committee on Education in the office of the Coordinator for Inter-American Affairs, and served as a member of the Census Advisory Committee of the Department of Commerce.

A central concern for Gulick during the war years was postwar plans and operations. He served as coordinator of postwar programs in the National Resources Planning Board, a member of the staff of the Office of Foreign Relief and Rehabilitations Operations, and acting chief of the Secretariat of the United Nations' Relief and Rehabilitation Administration. While working for a year on the White House staff as an aide for administrative matters, Gulick became involved in war-reparation matters and, in that capacity, traveled to Europe, Russia, Japan, and the Philippines.[8]

Returning to New York after the war, Gulick resumed his activities with the Institute of Public Administration. Between 1950 and 1953, Gulick was executive director of a review of New York government and, in 1954, was appointed the first city administrator of New York, a position he filled until 1956. In 1959 Gulick was appointed to the New York City Commission on Government Operations.

In the 1960s and 1970s, and as Gulick moved into his seventies and eighties, his level of activity continued almost unabated. In 1962 Gulick was made chairman of the board of the Institute of Public Administration. He also served as a member of the New York City Charter Revision Commission, co-chairman of a New York City zoning committee, member of the Mayor's Committee on Professional, Technical, and Managerial Manpower, chairman of a commission on a model-city charter, member of the Mayor's Committee on the Transition (1965–66), member of the Board of Trustees of the National Recreation and Park Association, and consultant to various foreign countries and international organizations. In 1982, at the age of ninety, Gulick was appointed chairman emeritus of the Institute of Public Administration.

Gulick has received a host of awards in recognition of his distinguished record of public service. Among the most prominent of these are the Distinguished Citizen Award of the National Municipal League, the Twenty-Fifth Anniversary Citation and the Dwight Waldo Award of the American Society for Public Administration, the Distinguished Service Award of the National Academy of Public Administration, the National Planning Award of the Regional Planning Association, and the Gruenberg Award of the Governmental Research Association.

The Role of Government in Society

Gulick had few pretensions about his abilities as a theorist. In his words, "I shall leave to the political historians and philosophers the comprehensive and systematic interpretation of the world, as I am neither historian nor philosopher. My interests and experience are rather in getting things done through administrative and civic action."[9] Nonetheless, one can derive from his writings at least a general orientation concerning the role and functions of government in society. Gulick asserts that man is a social animal with facile hands, a restless curiosity, and an inventive and retentive mind. Man's nature calls for social contact and his limitations for a specialization of "knowledge, skill, taste, art, and emotion."[10]

Government, according to Gulick, is the means by which willful, strong, and selfish men can live together cooperatively. The necessity of governmental activity arises when private actions based on self-interest and guided by the "unseen hand" of the market prove to be inadequate. Government functions to control conduct in the name of maximum freedom and to provide cooperative community services, that is, activities that can be performed better, more economically, or more satisfactorily on a cooperative basis. In all of this, government should manifest a "decent human sympathy for the weak."[11]

Although government must act, Gulick does not believe that it should act unilaterally. He maintains that "in a pluralistic society, there is no place for an exclusive pursuit by the central government of national goals and programs embracing public and private activities."[12] Instead, the public and private sectors should become partners in a cooperative enterprise serving the common good with planning a vital ingredient in this cooperative venture. Gulick argues that planning should be multidisciplinary in character and will inevitably be based on value judgments. Thus, planning must involve all relevant disciplines and should solicit the views of special-interest groups as well as the opinions of the "ordinary public."[13] Since limits on knowledge limit the precision of planning, Gulick asserts that planning should deal with the marginal value of incremental change rather than fix absolute priorities and should function as a general guide, not an immutable blueprint, for change.[14]

Gulick identifies market failure as a primary justification for governmental action, but he does not consider it to be the sole cause of the growth of government. Enlargement of the role of the public sector, he argues, may also be attributed to pressure from "enthusiasts, bureaucrats, and politicians for enlarged budgets," and he maintains that there is no evidence of "survival of the fittest" among governmental agencies.[15] Survival, according to Gulick, may well be as much a tribute to inertia as to adaptability. Therefore, extensions of governmental activity should be preceded by a careful examination of the consequences of such action for society, and attempts to make the state omnipotent should be resisted.[16] The role of the state should be limited because of uncertainty about the future; lack of wisdom, experience, knowledge, and character among leaders; lack of administrative skill and technique; the vast number of variables involved in comprehensive action; and the absence of orderly methods of developing new ideas and programs in a totalitarian state.[17] Democratic government in a pluralistic society, according to Gulick, is superior to totalitarian government in its ability to generate new ideas, the presence of the corrective effect of free criticism, and the requirement of the common man's appraisal of the end product. Although Gulick acknowledges that totalitarian governments have little difficulty in regimenting attitudes and thus securing the consent of the governed, he feels them to be prone to a "hardening of the arteries" without sufficient channels of communication for proposing or assessing change.[18] Gulick concedes that there are no fixed limits on the role of government. Nevertheless, he argues that the state should not, and is not likely to, encompass all human activity.

In order to perform properly its required duties, a substantial reordering of functions is required. Gulick asserts that neither the public nor the legislature is capable of the planning needed by an effective government. The public, according to Gulick, cannot deal with the intricacies of planning. Thus the responsibility for planning must be delegated by the public and discharged by the governmental system.[19] The legislature, on its part, has no central focus of responsibility and cannot act in an expeditious and coherent fashion. Gulick maintains that we should be less concerned with checks and balances in executive-legislative relationships than with the distinction between policy planning and execution on the one side and policy adoption or veto on the other.[20] Gulick's ideal government is one in which the chief executive, supported by a special staff, draws the plans; the legislature accepts or rejects proposed policies; the executive carries out the adopted plan; and the public exercises general control through participation in political parties and pressure groups. This allocation of functions, Gulick believes, would produce a unified management necessary not only for efficiency and effectiveness but also for meaningful democratic control as responsibilities are more clearly defined and assigned.

Gulick also calls for a redefinition of responsibilities in the federal system. Gulick contends that national legislators too often enact policies that ignore the necessities of state and local governments, while state and local governments sometimes take action as though there were no federal government or national problems.[21] In contrast to his recommendation for a functional allocation of duties between the executive and legislative branches, Gulick argues that it is not possible to achieve a clear separation of functions in the federal system. Instead, he supports "pragmatic solutions" in which functions are divided into their local, state, and federal "aspects" with responsibilities assigned accordingly. These assignments would be flexible and subject to change based on continuing planning and cooperation among authorities at each level of government.[22]

Gulick's own notions about the proper responsibilities of the several levels of government have changed over time, although he generally advocates a major role for the federal government. During the Great Depression, Gulick argued for the assumption of substantial new powers by the federal government, including control over the entire field of business, transportation, banking, and taxation and "basic control" in the areas of wages, hours, working conditions, prices, distribution, profits and finance, and general trade practices.[23] He later tempered this sweeping pronouncement in maintaining that where divergence and local adaptation are required, responsibilities should be decentralized with the smallest unit capable of embracing the geographical extent of a problem and able to command the appropriate professional service assuming responsibility.[24] Even where national policies are required, grass-roots administration is still desirable if clear standards of delegation are established to ensure uniform enforcement of policy and adequate protection of individual rights.

The Role of Administration in Government

The dominant theme during much of the time in which Gulick wrote was that politics and policy considerations should be separated from administrative matters. Gulick's own position is that it is impractical, impossible, and undesirable strictly to separate politics and policy from administration. For Gulick, administration involves the determination of major policy; the development and adoption of specific programs; the creation of the organization; provision of personnel; authorization of finances; administrative supervision, coordination, and control of activities; and the audit and review of results.[25] Under his broad definition, Gulick maintains that administration is necessarily involved in both politics and the policy process.

Gulick attributes two meanings to the word *politics.* In its vulgar sense, politics means seeking selfish advantage or advancement through the control of rulers. In its true sense, politics means actions by which rulers control.[26] The problem is that there is no objective way of distinguishing between vulgar and true politics, since the distinction lies in the motivation of the actor rather than in the action itself. Therefore, attempts to control the vulgar aspects of politics in administration run the danger of denying the true political function of administration. Furthermore, efforts to keep politics in its vulgar sense out of administration have proven to be impractical. Prohibition of political activity in a system of checks and balances, Gulick contends, results in a virtually powerless government that "can't go wrong because it can't go at all." Efforts to eliminate politics from administration by setting up independent public agencies only frustrate efforts to establish an integrated government capable of planning.[27] In sum, Gulick maintains that the old dichotomy between politics and administration has broken down, and he argues that a new doctrine should be developed that permits "the fullest possible use of the expert in an appropriate framework of political and professional responsibility."[28]

Gulick's own formulation is a rather tenuous accommodation of politics, policy, and administration. Gulick distinguishes among the roles of politicians, political appointees, administrators, and technicians in determining degrees of political and policy involvement. The role of the politician is to maintain equilibrium in the overall system by monitoring and adjusting the relationships among the experts, bureaucrats, and interest groups. Political appointees are to act as intermediaries, explaining the experts to the public and the public to the experts.[29] The administrator's role is to understand and coordinate public policy and interpret policy directives to the operating services, but with unquestioned loyalty to the decisions of elected officials. The administrator differs from the political executive in that the administrator does not make final decisions on policy, does not advocate policies before the public, and does not succeed or fail on policy positions. Finally, the technician generally should be limited to the consideration of "technical matters."[30]

Though the roles ascribed to these several actors indicate, in rough fashion, the relative degree of involvement in policy and political activity, Gulick concedes that the acts of all public officials are a "seamless web of discretion and action" and that discretion is likely to involve the official in policy considerations.[31] The amount of discretion decreases as one moves from the elected official to the technician. Nevertheless, not all policy matters are referred to the top, and, consequently, much discretion inevitably resides at the bottom where "public servants touch the public."[32] Moreover, any particular decision is political, not technical, if the public deems it to be such.[33] Therefore, the differences among the roles in regard to policy and political involvement are differences in degree rather than differences in kind; the successful administrator must understand, and be able to deal with, the strategic dimensions of the politico-administrative system in which he must operate.[34] Effective administration rests on singleness of purpose, clarity of policy, and public support. Gulick's charge to administrators is to fuse knowledge and skills with public desires, political forces, and common sense; evolve a course of remedial, structured action; and take steps to secure the authority to act.[35] This entails "political" activity in its true sense and injects the administrator into the policy process.

Science and Administration

The policy/politics-administration dichotomy had been the basis on which early authors in the field had hoped to construct a science of administration. By separating administration from policy and politics, it was argued, administration could be defined as a value-free endeavor and thus the legitimate subject of scientific analysis.

Although he rejects the policy/politics-administration dichotomy, Gulick also aspires to the application of scientific methods to administrative matters. According to Gulick, "Through science and the scientific spirit man has freed himself, at least in his material existence, from the complete domination of habit."[36] He believes that the same methods and spirit can be applied to investigations of human behavior and, indeed, thinks it "inevitable that there should be in every field of human endeavor an effort to reduce experience and phenomena to measurable terms."[37] In regard to public administration, Gulick sees the scientific method as a way to "substitute for ignorance, competence; for the amateur, the professional; for the jack-of-all-trades, the expert; for superficial facility, increasing differentiation and specialization; and for the untutored novitiate, the trained executive."[38]

Gulick argues that we must move beyond the mere collection of easily accessible facts, law, and practices and problem-oriented applied research to a scientific pursuit of solutions to the problems of modern government. These problems range from the details of management to the philosophy of society. A science of administration would embody "a system of knowledge whereby men may understand relationships, predict results, and influence outcomes in any situation where men are organized at work together for a common purpose."[39] The scientific pursuit entails intellectual examination and classification of phenomena, testing hypotheses by experiment and exploration, and the application of discovered truths to the world of nature with continuous questioning of results.[40] The objective is the discovery of "principles" or "immutable laws of administration," which can be distilled and simplified for practical application to administrative matters.[41]

Having rejected the politics/policy-administration dichotomy, Gulick is faced with the problem of the role of values in administration and a redefinition of an appropriate domain for scientific analysis. Gulick states that values are concerned with the assessment of the desirability of ends; he acknowledges that values, so defined, are inevitably involved in administration and are not amenable to scientific investigation. Consequently, science cannot embrace the entirety of administrative activity. He contends, however, that values are not involved in statements of "variations and interrelationships"; scientific analysis can reveal what, under certain conditions, is likely to occur. Thus the appropriate domain for a science of administration is the investigation of relationships between actions and outcomes. Gulick contends that the only value endemic to the scientific endeavor itself is efficiency, although in application, efficiency must be accommodated to other social and political values.[42]

Gulick is aware of the problems in developing a science of administration. The social sciences have an elusive subject matter, since human beings are dynamic and, to some unknown extent, unpredictable.[43] Furthermore, the study of human behavior raises the problem of establishing appropriate controls for scientific experimentation. Nonetheless, Gulick considers scientific research to be a necessity and "a powerful ally, if not an indispensable adjunct of efficient democracy."[44]

Gulick is also aware of the potential dangers of scientific "expertise." He notes that we are confronted by specialists who know more and more about less and less, that experts may assume that they know better than the people what they need, and that experts may assert knowledge and authority in fields in which they have no competence. These dangers are significant because Gulick observes, "a government program which relies upon a professional group of experts will, within a generation, come under the leadership and direction of that profession."[45]

The answer to the dangers of technocracy, according to Gulick, is a sense of professionalism that imposes responsible self-discipline and recognizes that final action cannot be taken by experts. In a democracy the common man must be the ultimate judge of what is good for him. This does not mean that the expert is unnecessary. Rather, the requirements of democracy impose on the expert and the administrator an obligation to communicate better with both political leaders and the common man and to educate them about the conditions conducive to effective administration. As Gulick puts it, "To move democracy, you must not only develop the facts through research but you must develop also the vocabulary of the leaders and the support of the masses."[46]

Administrative Organization

Gulick agrees with the objectives of the early reform movement in the United States, but he differs on the appropriate strategy for reform. The original "good government" movement concentrated on specific abuses and sought reform through the electoral process. What is needed, Gulick contends, is reform of the basic structure and underlying processes of administration. Functions must be defined, work divided, structures and relationships formalized, staffs professionalized, and activities rationalized.[47] This entails reforms such as a short ballot, a strong executive branch, consolidation of agencies, and the adoption of more "businesslike" practices in government. On the last point, Gulick suggests that public administration and private administration are part of a single broad science despite differences in objectives and emphases. Both deal with groups of men working toward specified goals with a division of labor; both arrive at policy decisions through planning; both coordinate, direct, and hold accountable; both seek to maximize results through incentives and the best use of men, materials, and time; both must be sensitive to public opinion and to the continuity of the enterprise in a changing environment.[48]

Gulick asserts that administrative reform should be guided by a new set of "principles." American government had originally been based on principles derived from an aversion to executive power and a desire for representativeness. These principles were as follows: Many governmental officials should be elected (the long ballot); elections should be held frequently; a system of checks and balances should be constructed to contain executive power; many heads are better than one (i.e., a preference for committee leadership); and anyone is competent to hold any governmental position.[49] Experience, says Gulick, has demonstrated the defects of these principles. The election of many officials and frequent elections have produced neither good government nor democratic government; the system of checks and balances has resulted in "more brakes than driving power"; multiheaded agencies have deprived the system of responsible and energetic leadership; and inexperienced men have proven to be incapable of handling important executive and technical work.[50]

What is needed, Gulick maintains, is an administrative branch capable of planning and implementing democratic policies. He advises that administrative reform be guided by the following principles:

1. Related work should be administered as a unit.
2. All agencies should be consolidated into a few departments.
3. Each unit of administrative work should be placed under a single, responsible official selected on the basis of proven ability, technical knowledge, and experience.
4. The power of the department head should be commensurate with his responsibility.
5. Each head of a large department should have a staff for performance evaluation.

6. Responsibility for each function should be vested in a specific official.

7. The number of elected officials should be reduced.

8. Boards or commissions should not be used for administrative work. They should be limited to quasi-legislative and quasi-judicial functions.

9. All administrative work should be headed up under a single chief executive, who should be directly elected by, and responsible to, the voters or their representatives.

10. The chief executive should have the power to appoint and discharge department heads and to direct their work.

11. The chief executive should have a research staff to report on the work of the departments and search for improved methods of operation.[51]

In short, the administrative branch should be integrated and placed under the leadership of strong and competent executives with a powerful chief executive overseeing the entire process.

Reform also requires both a rational division of work and subsequent integration *within* each organization as part of an integrated executive branch. According to Gulick, the division of work and the integrated organization are "the bootstraps by which mankind lifts itself in the process of civilization."[52] Division of work is necessary because men differ in nature, capacity, and skill; because one man cannot be in two places at the same time; because one man cannot do two things at the same time; and because man is limited in his range of knowledge. Integration is required to provide central coordination among the "unit tasks" defined by the division of work in the organization. Accordingly, the theory of organizations is concerned with the structure of coordination imposed on the divided work of the organization.

One ingredient of integration is the grouping of similar tasks in the organization. Gulick identifies four bases on which the unit tasks of an organization may be grouped: purpose (tasks grouped by the service rendered), process (tasks grouped by the skill or technology employed), clientele or materiel, and place. Although Gulick emphasizes the importance of purpose in coordinating efforts in the organization, he notes that the selection of any particular base will depend on the stage of organizational development, technological changes, the size of the organization, and the specific advantages and disadvantages attached to the use of a particular base in a given organization.[53]

The concentration on division of work and grouping of unit tasks in the organization is what Gulick calls a "bottom-up" perspective on the organization. This perspective properly emphasizes the "principle of homogeneity" or the grouping of similar tasks. Nevertheless, the bottom-up view, if taken alone, ignores the necessities of control and coordination in the organization. Therefore, Gulick also advises a "top-down" view, noting that if subdivision and specialization in the organization are inevitable, coordination is a necessity.[54] He identifies two primary mechanisms of control and coordination in the organization: the structure of authority, and ideas or singleness of purpose.[55]

Coordination through the structure of authority is, of course, a central mechanism of control. It requires a single overall directing executive authority, the provision of a supervisor for each job, and the determination of the unit tasks into which the overall job will have to be divided.[56] In establishing the structure of authority, Gulick warns that the effective span of control at each level of the organization is limited by the knowledge, time, and energy of the supervisor. The span of control can be extended, however, where work is routine, repetitive, measurable, and homogeneous in character.[57]

Leadership is also a vital element of coordination through authority. Gulick asserts that the principle of unitary, concentrated leadership is almost universal, and he advises that leaders be given both power and, with particular reference to the public sector, the time to use it. Gulick assigns a wide range of functions to the executive summed up in the acronym POSDCORB. The letters of the acronym stand for the functions of the executive, which are Planning, Organizing, Staffing, Directing, Coordinating, Reporting, and Budgeting. The executive organization should be structured around these functions, and, according to Gulick, none of the functions should be performed outside the executive office.[58] Gulick attaches special importance to the planning function. Planning is the means by which purpose is translated into programs and involves the identification of key controllable items that are to be manipulated to achieve organizational objectives.[59] Gulick asserts that planning should be performed by specialists, but he advises that those in charge of planning should also be in charge of operations to ensure both a proper correlation between plans and operations and the effective implementation of the plans.

Although Gulick stresses the structure of authority and the role of leadership as coordinating mechanisms in the organization, he acknowledges that reliance on hierarchy alone is not sufficient to produce an integrated organization. The organization must also employ coordination by ideas, thereby developing the desire and will to work together with a singleness of purpose. This means that the tasks of the administrator must be accomplished more by persuasion than by coercion and discipline. Gulick states that "the way to solve problems is by personal negotiation, with all of the cards on the table, not by inconsiderate, independent, and precipitate action."[60] Coordination through ideas, according to Gulick, can render the absurdities of hierarchy "sweet and reasonable," and he considers a clear statement of purpose to be the best guarantee of effective administration.[61]

An integrated executive structure in government, according to Gulick, provides not only coordination but also a single focus of leadership and political responsibility more amenable to democratic control than a series of autonomous units.[62] He cautions that we should also be cognizant of the limits of integration imposed by constraints on effective knowledge, decision-making capability, and management technique.[63] Thus a balance must be struck between the desire for integration and the limits of its applicability.

From Principles to Particulars

As noted previously, Gulick considers himself to be a man of action, and much of his career has been devoted to the application of the ideas and principles just reviewed. In discussing these applications, it is useful to start with a brief look at the Institute of Public Administration, which was both a source of many of Gulick's beliefs and an instrument for their implementation.

The institute, originally called the New York Bureau of Municipal Reasearch, was founded in 1906 and was an integral part of the efficiency movement in America.[64] Although they were concerned with economy and efficiency, however, the leaders of the bureau were also driven by a "profound devotion to democracy," manifested in their call for responsible and responsive government and the education of the citizenry.[65] The founders of the bureau sought the expansion of governmental functions in order to make democracy "a living, vital thing."[66] Thus the work of the bureau was not simply to achieve efficiency but to encourage a more positive role for government, as well as to create the enlightened citizenry considered necessary for true democracy.

The bureau, described by Gulick as "a power house and idea factory" for the efficiency movement, was centrally involved in the pursuit of administrative principles and their practical application.[67] The aims were to promote efficient and economical government; to promote the adoption of scientific methods of accounting and the reporting of municipal business; to secure constructive publicity; and to collect, classify, analyze, correlate, interpret, and publish the facts.[68] Basic emphasis was placed on the concentration of executive responsibility and the development of appropriate planning, coordinating, budgeting, and personnel practices.[69]

The bureau, and later the Institute of Public Administration, pursued its objectives through two major mechanisms: the governmental survey and the Training School for the Public Service. The governmental survey, the bureau's primary instrument of analysis, entailed the grouping of administrative activities into major functions, the assignment of an investigator to each function, the analysis of statutory and constitutional provisions regarding each function, and an investigation of the actual organization and operation of the agencies involved.[70] Recommendations were then developed with the objective of better unifying, standardizing, clarifying, coordinating, and controlling governmental activities. These recommendations were discussed with agency executives for possible implementation, and reports were issued to the public in accord with the bureau's mission of civic education.

The second major mechanism was the bureau's Training School for Public Service, established in 1911. The school's purpose was to "train men and women for administrative responsibility, for unofficial public service, and for governmental research."[71] The program encompassed one year of study plus a three-month internship. The staff of the bureau served as instructors and the city as a laboratory as students were assigned to bureau studies to develop their skills.[72]

Gulick's personal interests, which were bred of his experience with the bureau and shaped his leadership of that organization, have been largely in the fields of public finance, personnel, and metropolitan government. While still a student at the Training School for Public Service, Gulick was appointed secretary of the Joint Special Committee on Finance and Budget Procedure in Massachusetts. The experience produced a lasting interest in public finance and shaped many of his ideas about budgetary reform. Gulick generally has supported increased executive responsibility in financial matters with a correspondingly reduced role for the legislature, both of which are intended to free the purposeful executive from legislative indecision.[73] Gulick also advocated "functionalized," or program, budgeting employing performance indicators for review and evaluation. Finally, Gulick prescribed a substantial measure of centralization of financial responsibility within the states. He urged that the state have jurisdiction over the administration of all taxes except the property tax, local taxes levied for purposes other than regulation, and a few other taxes that can "naturally be administered by local units."[74]

Gulick's second major area of interest has been personnel. Here, Gulick supported a "positive career service" in the public sector. This, he argued, will place politics on a higher plane of issues and men, not jobs and special privileges, and will secure the effective personnel necessary for a democracy to carry out the decisions and desires of the people.[75] Gulick's proposed formula was "pick 'em young, tell 'em everything, and treat 'em rough, but fairly."[76] In other words, public employees should be recruited early, they should have an apprentice period to learn the job, and "weak sisters" should be left behind.

Gulick's proposed career system would extend to all nonpolitical top positions in government and would consist of five career classifications: unskilled services, skills and trades service, clerical service, professional and technical service, and the administrative service. There should be competitive examinations for all career classifications, based on the particular skills required for each classification. A probationary period should be served by all public employees, and strict controls should be placed on temporary appointments to avoid circumvention of the competitive examination requirement. Advancement in the career service should be based on merit, and good salaries and adequate retirement benefits should be offered to attract and retain qualified employees. Safeguards should be built into the system to protect employees from arbitrary dismissal.[77]

As one would expect, given his lifelong association with the Institute of Public Administration and New York City government, Gulick also has been centrally concerned with the problems of metropolitan government. Gulick's ideas on metropolitan government have been generally consistent with his concept of federalism discussed earlier, that is, assignment of responsibilities to the various levels of government according to "aspects" of functions and reliance on the smallest unit of government capable of dealing with a problem. There are some equivocations on the matters of executive versus legislative powers and the centralization of fiscal responsibilities.

As did the reform movement in general, Gulick attached great importance to the city. He has stated that the city "offers the masses democratically the opportunity for the highest culture and it schools men in freedom, self-control, and social adaptation to change."[78] Nevertheless, Gulick recognized that urban life poses problems as well as opportunities. Cities suffer from congestion, concentrations of minorities and the poor, the necessity of providing services to people who do not live there, and a lack of fiscal resources. The problems of the city, Gulick argued, are not due solely to size. The costs of scale are at least partially mitigated by the economies of scale, and Gulick contended that no "laws" limit the size of metropolitan government.[79] Instead, the metropolitan problem is one of bad political engineering and inadequate management devices. Gulick asserted that government has failed to act in many areas and suffers from fractionalization in those functions that have been undertaken. An inadequate revenue base coupled with an unbalanced population and a lack of political resources and clearheaded leadership, he argued, have rendered metropolitan governments unequal to the tasks they face.

Gulick identified several alternative approaches to the solution of metropolitan problems: the creation of limited-purpose agencies for the metropolitan area, transfer of fractionated activities to the next higher level of government, the creation of local multiple-purpose agencies, solving problems serially by intergovernmental contracts, establishing a department of local affairs at the state level, the reconstruction of the county, and the creation of a new layer of government for the metropolitan area. Whatever its particular form, the essential elements of metropolitan governance are flexibility and political viability in establishing boundaries; geographical, social, and economic comprehensiveness; joint action on interrelated activities; a representative body drawn from the area as a whole; the protection of local communities in their continuing responsibility for local functions; and an adequate fiscal structure.[80] Gulick's preferred solution, despite his general insistence on executive control and his suspicion of legislative bodies, was the creation of a Metropolitan Council that would rely on voluntary cooperation among the responsible political executives and community leaders of the existing jurisdictions.[81] The council would be a legislative body composed of the chief elected officials in the metropolitan area as well as directly elected members.

Although metropolitan governance is important, federal support is also required. According to Gulick, the ultimate solution to metropolitan problems requires action at all levels of government with the federal government centrally involved and leadership coming from the President.[82] Each level of government should deal with aspects of functions that fall within its domain in a fiscal system that combines intergovernmental payments and the delegation of independent taxing power to appropriate state and local units.[83]

Conclusion

The major components of Gulick's approach to government and administration may be summarized as follows:

1. Government should play a positive role in society by acting when private actions prove to be inadequate in serving the common good. Wherever possible, cooperative arrangements between the public and private sectors should be established with planning an essential element of all public endeavors.

2. The executive branch at all levels of government should propose and implement policies, while the legislative branch should be limited to the approval or rejection of executive proposals.

3. Within the executive branch, the chief executive should be

strengthened through more powerful hierarchical controls, improvement in staff support, consolidation of executive departments, and, at the state and local levels, reduction in the number of elected officials.

4. Collaborative relationships among federal, state, and local governments should be developed with "aspects" of functions allocated to the appropriate levels of government. In particular, the federal government should acknowledge the national aspects of problems at the state and local levels and assume a leadership role in addressing those problems.

5. Administrators are necessarily involved in political and policy matters, and administrative theory should be reformulated to accommodate the use of professional expertise in a full range of administrative functions.

6. Scientific methods should be employed to discover general principles of administration that can be applied to achieve greater efficiency and effectiveness in governmental operations.

7. Executive branch organizations should be internally integrated with top leadership coordinating activities through the structure of authority and by developing a unity of purpose within the organization.

In short, Gulick's recipe for administrative reform entails the assumption of new functions by government; more efficiency in the functions undertaken; centralization within executive agencies and for the executive branch as a whole; and governance by experts subject to direct control by an elected chief executive, veto by the legislature, and general oversight by the public.

Assessing Gulick's ideas is rather difficult because many of his ideas have changed, or at least moderated, over the course of his lengthy career. Moreover, he often seems to be led more by his passion for reform than the findings of systematic research. As a result, Gulick's thoughts are sometimes marked by unresolved tensions, and his pronouncements often lack empirical support.

At points, Gulick's ideas seem inconsistent. For instance, although Gulick is renowned for his advocacy of integrated structures, he is willing to tolerate a federal system in which there is no unity of command, no definition of functional responsibility, no clear chain of command, and in which authority is not commensurate with fiscal responsibility. More often, the tension is evidenced in opposing considerations. Thus Gulick suggests a large role for the state, but asserts that there are limits to the role the state can, and should, play; he supports planning, but says there are limits to the degree to which planning can be effectively performed; he argues for integration, but recognizes there are limits on the extent to which integration is possible; he supports a career civil service with protection from political interference, but he also wants to strengthen the political chief executive in relationships with executive agencies; he would enlarge the role of the expert, but acknowledges the problem of controlling the expert in a democratic society. The problem is not so much that there are opposing considerations on all these matters—that is probably inevitable. The problem is where the balances should be struck and/or under what conditions a particular course of action should be pursued. Gulick provides no clear solutions for these critical problems.

A similar problem arises in regard to some of the "principles" of administration that Gulick espouses. Consider, for instance, the principles of homogeneity and integration. The principle of homogeneity states that similar tasks should be grouped in the organization. The problem is that all activities cannot be grouped along a single dimension. Nor is there a dominant alternative. Instead, the combination of methods used in grouping tasks should be determined by examining the advantages and disadvantages of the various bases for grouping organizational tasks. Gulick fails to provide concrete criteria for choosing among the bases, however, and offers little more than informed speculation about the probable consequences of any particular selection. On the principle of integration, Gulick argues that an integrated organization will produce efficient and effective administration, automatic coordination through clearly specified channels of communication, and clear assignments of responsibility that make democratic control more effective. This is certainly plausible. But an equally plausible case can be made that "red tape" is more likely than effectiveness and efficiency in the integrated organization, that integration will discourage communication by virtue of elongated channels of communication and organizational formality, that responsibility will be obfuscated rather than clarified in the labyrinth of bureaucracy, and that an integrated executive branch headed by a powerful chief executive may result in tyrannical government.

Unresolved tension also characterizes Gulick's approach to organizational management. Gulick would rely primarily on the hierarchical structure of authority to achieve control and coordination in the organization. Even "coordination through ideas" is seen by Gulick as a method of hierarchical control and a way to make that control seem reasonable. The question is whether hierarchically integrated organizations are sufficiently attentive to the wide range of needs that have been found to motivate people in organizations. Gulick is sensitive to this issue. He asserts, for instance, that our primary task should be to "release the hidden energy in human nature" and that "nothing must take second place to our effort to understand the patterns of human awareness and how men who are working together in teams can find release for their full energies."[84] But Gulick fails to address the potential incompatibilities between hierarchically integrated organizations and the satisfaction of human needs in the organization. For instance, the hierarchically integrated organization would have a limited span of control to ensure close and direct supervision. Yet it has been argued that close supervision dampens morale and inhibits the assumption of individual responsibility on the part of subordinates. Hierarchical integration is commonly associated with an elaborate division of labor to capitalize on the economies of specialization, whereas job enlargement (i.e., less specialization), it is argued, promotes a greater sense of identification with the overall mission of the organization and a greater sense of individual achievement in task performance. The hierarchically integrated organization requires centralized decision-making procedures, but decentralized and participatory decision procedures have been supported as a way of giving the individual a greater sense of involvement in the organization and increasing the likelihood of individual acceptance of organizational decisions.

Finally, some of Gulick's positions appear to be more value commitments than "scientific" statements. His support for a strengthened and integrated executive branch is a case in point. Gulick contends that executive leadership will lead to more efficient and effective administration and will result in a higher degree of democratic control. He provides little evidence in support of this contention. Moreover, Gulick's acceptance of the value of executive leadership conflicts with other values, such as representativeness and neutral competence.[85] The conflict with representativeness is that a powerful executive branch may escape both meaningful electoral controls (witness to that point is the oft-heard charge of an "imperial Presidency") and the controls provided by the "checks and balances" of the legislative branch (a problem that would be exacerbated by Gulick's proposal to limit severely the powers of the legislature). The conflict with neutral competence is that executive leadership requires more control by political officials over appointed officials and thus puts the administrator in a position of potential conflict between professional standards and hierarchical directives.

These problems should not diminish an appreciation of the significance of Gulick's contributions to the study and practice of public administration. Ideas such as those expressed by Gulick are deeply engrained in both. The ideas that the study of public administration should be integrally related to the practice of public administration, that citizen enlightenment is required for effective democracy, that businesslike techniques should be adopted to improve the efficiency of governmental operations, that executive leadership is required for effective administration, that professionalism should be encouraged in the public service, and that government should be made more responsive and responsible both defined the focus of public administration for a generation of scholars and remain as central themes in the discipline. It should also be noted that the very normative emphasis that frustrates Gulick's search for a science of administration also accounts, in large measure, for the lasting impact of his ideas.

Moreover, Gulick's contributions to public administration should be assessed at least as much in terms of what he did as what he said. Gulick's long service with the Institute of Public Administration, his involvement with the President's Committee on Administrative Management, his administrative record during the war, his varied activities in the administration of New York City, as well as the awards and honors associated with his activities, stand as elegant testimony to his distinguished status in the discipline.

Notes

1. Information on Gulick's early life is taken from autobiographical notes provided by Professor Paul Van Riper of Texas A&M University. Other information is drawn from material provided directly by Dr. Gulick.

2. Gulick's early, largely informal schoolwork went badly until it was discovered that he had poor eyesight (he eventually lost sight in one eye). He remained a slow reader throughout his life and did not read for pleasure until after his retirement.

3. He became engaged to Helen McKelvey Swift, whom he later married, in the same year.

4. Luther Gulick, *Evolution of the Budget in Massachusetts* (New York: Macmillan, 1920).

5. Later to be called simply the Institute of Public Administration.

6. The states included Massachusetts, New York, Virginia, South Dakota, Delaware, Tennessee, New Jersey, Michigan, and Maine.

7. Luther Gulick, "Notes on the Theory of Organization," in *Papers on the Science of Administration*, eds. Luther Gulick and L. Urwick (New York: Institute of Public Administration, 1937), 3–45; and "Science, Values, and Public Administration," ibid., 191–95.

8. He also attended the Potsdam Conference in 1945 and the meeting of the foreign ministers in Paris in 1946.

9. Luther Gulick, *The Metropolitan Problem and American Ideas* (New York: Knopf, 1962), 4.

10. Luther Gulick, "What the City Does for and to Its Citizens," *Public Management Journal* 21, no. 12 (December 1939): 335.

11. Gulick, *Metropolitan Problem*, 14.

12. Gerhard Colm and Luther Gulick, *Program Planning for National Goals*, Planning Pamphlet no. 125 (Washington, D.C.: National Planning Association, 1968), 5.

13. Luther Gulick, "The Concept of Regional Planning," *Public Policy* 12 (1963): 108.

14. Ibid., 102.

15. Luther Gulick and Charles F. Aufderhar, "The Increasing Cost of City Government," *American City Magazine* 31, no. 1 (July 1924): 15; and Gulick, "Notes on the Theory of Organization," 43.

16. Luther Gulick, *American Foreign Policy* (New York: Institute of Public Administration, 1951), 229.

17. Gulick, "Notes on the Theory of Organization," 40.

18. Luther Gulick, *Administrative Reflections from World War II* (University, Ala.: University of Alabama Press, 1948), 127.

19. Luther Gulick, "Politics, Administration, and the 'New Deal,'" *Annals* 169 (September 1933): 58.

20. Ibid., 66.

21. Luther Gulick, "Planning and Cooperation," *State Government* 20, no. 3 (March 1947): 87.

22. Ibid., 86.

23. Gulick, "Politics, Administration, and the 'New Deal,'" 64.

24. Gulick, *American Foreign Policy*, 181–82.

25. Ibid., 57.

26. Luther Gulick, "Politics, Administration, and the 'New Deal,'" 59–60.

27. Ibid., 55–57.

28. Luther Gulick, "Next Steps in Public Administration," *Public Administration Review* 15, no. 2 (Spring 1955): 76.

29. Gulick, *American Foreign Policy*, 217–18.

30. Commission of Inquiry on Public Service Personnel, *Better Government Personnel* (New York: McGraw-Hill, 1935), 20–35.

31. Gulick, "Politics, Administration, and the 'New Deal,'" 61.

32. Ibid., 62.

33. Ibid.

34. Luther Gulick, "The Twenty-Fifth Anniversary of the American Society for Public Administration," *Public Administration Review* 25, no. 1 (March 1965): 4.

35. Ibid., 2.

36. Luther Gulick, *The National Institute of Public Administration* (New York: National Institute of Public Administration, 1928), 101.

37. Luther Gulick, "Wanted: A Measuring Stick for School Systems," *National Municipal Review* 18, no. 1 (January 1929): 3.

38. Gulick, *National Institute of Public Administration*, 52.

39. Gulick, "Science, Values, and Public Administration," 191.

40. Luther Gulick, "The Scientific Approach to the Problems of Society and Government," *University of Buffalo Studies* 15, no. 2 (March 1938): 29.

41. Luther Gulick, "Principles of Administration," *National Municipal Review* 14, no. 7 (July 1925): 400.

42. Gulick, "Science, Values, and Public Administration," 192–93.

43. Gulick, "Scientific Approach to the Problems of Society and Government," 31.

44. Gulick, *National Institute of Public Administration*, 45.

45. Gulick, *American Foreign Policy*, 216.

46. Luther Gulick, "The Recent Movement for Better Government Person-

nel," *American Political Science Review* 31, no. 2 (April 1937): 301.

47. Luther Gulick, "Metropolitan Organization," *Annals* 314 (November 1957): 57.

48. Gulick, "Twenty-Fifth Anniversary of the American Society for Public Administration," 1; and "Next Steps in Public Administration," 74.

49. *Proceedings of Sixteenth Annual Conference on Taxation under the Auspices of the National Tax Association* (New York: National Tax Association, 1924), 265.

50. Ibid., 266.

51. Ibid., 266–67; and Gulick, "Principles of Administration," 401.

52. Gulick, "Notes on the Theory of Organization," 4.

53. Ibid., 15, 21–30.

54. Ibid., 11, 6.

55. Ibid., 6. He also mentions habit or routine as a coordinating mechanism, but does not elaborate on the point.

56. Ibid., 7.

57. Ibid.

58. Ibid., 13–14.

59. Gulick, *Administrative Reflections from World War II*, 80.

60. Gulick, "Planning and Cooperation," 86.

61. Gulick, "Notes on the Theory of Organization," 39; and *Administrative Reflections from World War II*, 77.

62. Gulick, *Metropolitan Problem*, 81–82.

63. Ibid., 85–89.

64. See Gulick, *National Institute of Public Administration*, and Jane S. Dahlberg, *The New York Bureau of Municipal Research* (New York: New York University Press, 1966), for reviews of the history of the institute.

65. Dahlberg, *New York Bureau of Municipal Research*, v.

66. Ibid., 32.

67. Luther Gulick, "Perspectives in Public Administration: Past, Present, and Future" (paper delivered at C.W. Post Center, Long Island University, Greenvale, New York, 19 December 1979).

68. Dahlberg, *New York Bureau of Municipal Research*, 20–21.

69. Ibid., 174–227. This involved procedures such as executive budgeting, cost accounting, audit procedures independent of the executive branch, central control and standardization of governmental purchases, central control and compensation equalization in personnel, revenue control and improved methods of tax collection and property assessment, in-service training programs, and establishing standards for drawing organization charts.

70. Gulick, *National Institute of Public Administration*, 36–40.

71. Ibid., 55.

72. Ibid., 73. This apprentice system later gave way to more structured lecture and discussion courses in charters and municipal corporations, municipal organization, budgeting, public accounting and financial reporting, purchasing and storing of materials, civil service and personnel, taxation and revenues, public debt, engineering administration, police and fire administration, public welfare, education, governmental research, and the relationship between the administrators and the citizen. Frederick Taylor's *Scientific Management* was

required reading. See Dahlberg, *New York Bureau of Municipal Research*, 129. Initially, the school had an arrangement with Columbia University whereby its students could acquire general advanced training in government and administration. Later, under Gulick's leadership, the school moved away from basic graduate instruction and began accepting only advanced, experienced students for training.

73. For instance, Gulick cites, with tacit approval, Cleveland's budget reform proposal to the committee, consisting of the following procedures: (1) The governor should submit budget estimates to the legislature; (2) the governor should appear before the legislature to explain the estimates; (3) a legislative committee of the whole, meeting in joint session, should consider the governor's estimates; (4) the legislature should vote separately on the requests of each organizational unit; (5) members of the legislature should only be able to propose reductions in the governor's estimates; (6) the governor should submit a final budget to the legislature containing the actual and estimated revenues and expenditures for the two previous years and a statement of current assets, liabilities, and surplus or deficit; (7) if differences remain between the governor and the legislature, a public referendum should be held on the budget. See Gulick, *Evolution of the Budget in Massachusetts*, 131–33; and Dahlberg, *New York Bureau of Municipal Research*, 174.

74. *Proceedings of the Sixteenth Annual Conference on Taxation*, 267–68.

75. Commission of Inquiry on Public Service Personnel, *Better Government Personnel*, 81.

76. Luther Gulick, "Toward a Municipal Career Service," *Public Management Journal* 17, no. 11 (November 1935): 332.

77. Commission of Inquiry on Public Service Personnel, *Better Government Personnel*, 4–8.

78. Gulick, "What the City Does for and to Its Citizens," 356.

79. Gulick, "Metropolitan Organization," 58.

80. Gulick, *Metropolitan Problem and American Ideas*, 60.

81. Gulick, "Metropolitan Organization," 63–65.

82. Gulick, *Metropolitan Problem and American Ideas*, 129.

83. Gulick, "Planning and Cooperation," 87.

84. Gulick, "Next Steps in Public Administration," 75.

85. Herbert Kaufman, "Emerging Conflicts in the Doctrines of Administration," *American Political Science Review* 50, no. 4 (December 1956): 1057–73.

CHAPTER 4

Mary Parker Follett:
The Group Process

Mary Parker Follett was an innovative thinker who offered ideas that were not to gain major acceptance until some time after her death. Perhaps the distinguishing feature of Follett's work is her treatment of the role of social conflict. Follett argues that conflict itself is neither good nor bad, it is simply inevitable. Whether the consequences of conflict are good or bad depends on the uses to which conflict is put. If conflict is used to produce an interpenetration of ideas and integrative solutions, it is good. If it results in domination by one side or compromise in which both sides simply yield something, the results will be unsatisfactory. In other words, Follett argues that we can use conflict to produce harmony, not simply victory or accommodation.

This view of conflict is novel, particularly in the literature on organizations where the dominant paradigm has been one of the organization as a cooperative social system—even among authors, such as Taylor, who support hierarchical organizational structures. Follett also desires cooperation in the organization. But, for Follett, cooperation is a process and an outcome, not a precondition. Indeed, cooperation is likely to be the result of a merging of differences in the pursuit of the interest of the whole.

The preceding point is related to another of Follett's central themes: the importance of the group process. Follett contends that individuals achieve their true expression in group relationships. This happens as individual activities realize increased range and enhanced significance in the group setting. Follett considers the state to be both a logical extension of the group process and its highest expression. Both the group and the state serve a purpose greater than individual interests. Here, Follett offers a most provocative definition of the *general interest*. The general interest, according to Follett, is not simply the product of individual interests but the product of individual interests in social relationships, and the general interest is represented by the *social* interests defined in the group process. Interestingly, Follett has reservations about the ability of "ballot-box democracy" to produce the general interest so defined. Ballot-box democracy, to Follett, is likely to yield only the consent of the many to the rule by the few, when what is required is the creative interaction of all.

Follett's innovative thinking extends to questions of organizational management and is clearly related to her view of more general social processes. Swimming against the tide of ideas of her time, Follett urges horizontal flows of communication as opposed to the view that communication should follow the formal chain of command; she argues that control in the organization is pluralistic and cumulative (i.e., it arises from below) versus the conventional view that control should be concentrated in the apex of the organizational pyramid and cascade downward; she contends that authority should flow from the "law of the situation" (i.e., the objective demands of the work situation) rather than be based on personal imposition; and she maintains that leadership is the ability to create functional unity in the organization through the proper correlation of controls instead of personal power to command based on position.

These, then, are a few of Follett's seminal ideas, and her forte was the presentation of a few important ideas in a logically compelling fashion. Her writing has not just a logical flow, however, but was possessed of a certain rhythm. The aim of the following exposition is to capture both the flow and the rhythm of Follett's ideas and logic.

Life

Mary Parker Follett was born on 3 September 1868 in Quincy, Massachusetts.[1] Her family was English-Scottish-Welsh in extraction, and Mary was the older of the two children of Charles Allen and Elizabeth Curtis (Baxter) Follett. Follett's father was a machinist in a local shoe factory, and there were apparently strong bonds between father and daughter. Follett's mother, the daughter of a prosperous banker, suffered from ill health, which deprived her daughter of a childhood as she had the responsibility for taking care of an invalid mother and a younger brother.

Follett's early education was acquired at Thayer Academy in Braintree, Massachusetts. She graduated from Thayer in 1884 at the age of fifteen. In 1888 Follett entered what was to become Radcliffe College where she studied English, political economy, and history for two years. Follett traveled abroad in 1890 and 1891 to study at Cambridge University in England. She performed well at Cambridge, delivering a paper on the U.S. House of Representatives that was to form the basis for her first book, and she developed a lasting interest in English life. Her studies were cut short by her mother's illness, however, and she was forced to return home before she could sit for examinations. Returning to Radcliffe, Follett attended intermittently until 1898 when she received her A.B. degree, graduating summa cum laude at the age of twenty-nine. By this time, Follett's book *The Speaker of the House of Representatives* had already been published.[2]

On leaving Radcliffe, Follett embarked on a career in social work, supported by an inheritance from her mother's father. She was primarily involved with community centers in Boston where she pioneered in the development of evening programs in the public schools and vocational guidance programs. In 1918 Follett published her second book, *The New State*.[3] Originally intended as a report on her work with the community centers, the work blossomed into a major critique of American political theory and institutions in which Follett built on her knowledge of political science and added a new dimension—group dynamics—that was to be the central focus of the rest of her career. Follett's third book, *Creative Experience*, followed in 1924.[4] Probably her most important statement, *Creative Experience* elaborated on some of the themes introduced in *The New State* and focused even more centrally on the group experience. In 1925 Follett shifted direction, becoming a lecturer on industrial management, an area she believed to be among the most critical and promising in terms of human relations. She moved to England in 1929 where she continued her study of industrial conditions and lectured extensively.[5]

Mary Parker Follett was a woman of large frame, though not overly heavy, with dark brown hair and blue eyes. She was soft-spoken and unassuming in manner and reportedly had little taste for power or prestige. She did have a gift for making friends and a facility for winning confidence and esteem. Although she never managed a business, she developed a number of close relationships with leading industrialists on both sides of the Atlantic. Follett read Latin, Greek, French, and German and was interested in music, painting, nature, and travel. Never married, Follett lived with Isobel L. Briggs in Boston until 1926 and with Dame Katharine Furse in London from 1928 until shortly before her death in 1933.

Follett's early orientation was toward philosophical idealism, and evidence of that orientation crops up throughout her writings. Later, she became interested in the "new psychology" with its emphasis on group dynamics. Follett believed the study of institutions alone was not sufficient. What was needed, she argued, is the objective study of how people behave together. This requires empirical studies of human relations and social situations based on both participant observation and experimentation.[6] Of these two approaches, Follett chose participant observation, arguing that one cannot see experience without being a part of it.[7] According to Follett, life never stops long enough to be tested, and one cannot get outside life to view it.[8] Social life is in a constant state of flux and constitutes a complex unity built of mutual interrelationships and an interweaving of experience. One must be a part of life, either to observe it or to know it. Accordingly, Follett employed intimate knowledge based on personal observation to construct an approach to social life and industrial management that anticipated by half a generation the observations of others in the field.

The Group Process

Follett argues that the individual is a social being who finds both identity and a sense of fulfillment in a group experience. The group itself is more than a mob, a herd, or mere members.[9] Instead, the group is a cohesive and coherent entity whose processes can lead to changes in individual ideas and actions that produce mutual compatibility and harmony among its members. Thus the potential for social unity lies in the group process and involves an intermingling of differences and the emergence of a composite of ideas representing what is best for all.[10]

According to Follett, society can be understood only by a study of the flux of group relationships, which leads to unity.[11] In this setting, there are neither individuals independent of society nor a society independent of individuals. Rather, there is a reciprocal relationship between the individual and society in which the individual both shapes society and is shaped by it. Social unity is, in Follett's phrase, a "whole a-making" in the interweaving of individual activities as the individual and the society evolve together.[12]

For Follett, the core of the group process is creating, and her central concern is the processes by which groups can create something that individuals working separately could not have created. The group process is guided by the "law of interpenetration" and the "doctrine of the wholes." Under the law of interpenetration, members of a group are reciprocally conditioning forces as human interaction evokes new forms through the synthesis of differences.[13] The process of interpenetration and the emergence of synthesis results in a "whole," which, though not greater than the sum of its parts, is different from its parts.[14] Follett's "doctrine of the wholes" is that the whole cannot be understood by an analysis of its constituent parts. The whole is a dynamic entity produced by human interaction in which the interests of the whole are the interests of individuals *in social relationships*.[15] The interests of the whole emerge from a group process of the interpenetration and synthesis of ideas, actions, and feelings. The group purpose is not preexistent. Instead, purpose evolves from interaction and is embodied in the unification of differences as the group process gives rise to a feeling of "sympathy" in which the individual finds his or her own interests in the group's interest.[16]

Conflict and Its Resolution

The group process does not rest on the assumption of an a priori identity of interests. On the contrary, Follett asserts that differing interests, and conflict among them, are inevitable. Conflict as continuing unintegrated differences may be pathological, but the conflict itself is neither good nor bad. Furthermore, since conflict cannot be avoided, it should be used much as a violin uses friction to make music.[17] The task of society is to produce harmony and unity from dissonance and conflict as diversity is assimilated into the larger whole through the interpenetration and interweaving of ideas and actions.

Follett identifies three primary means for the resolution of social conflict: domination, compromise, and integration.[18] Domination, which encompasses coercion, persuasion, imitation, and voluntary submission, is inherently flawed because it ends in the victory of one side to a dispute. As a result, domination is not creative because it involves no interpenetration of ideas or interweaving of activities and is likely to produce antagonism in the defeated party.

Compromise is a similarly unsatisfactory method for the resolution of social conflict. Compromise, according to Follett, rests on the principle of "reciprocal abandonments" and the false assumption that, by some system of magic, subtraction (i.e., each party yielding something) may somehow become a process of addition.[19] In compromise, Follett argues, there is no qualitative change, only the vain hope that the truth lies somewhere between the competing sides. Compromise is "temporary and futile" and the partisanship on which it is based starves the cooperative nature of man.[20]

Integration. Follett's preferred method for the resolution of social conflict is integration. She argues that when conflicting interests meet, they need not oppose, only confront.[21] What should be sought in this confrontation of differing interests is an integration that gives all sides what they really want. Integration is thus the emergence of a creative synthesis produced by the interaction of differing interests that represents a harmonious marriage of those differences (like the nut and the screw).[22] Integration is neither solely cooperative nor solely competitive in nature. It is a synthesis of competition and cooperation that yields creative solutions.[23] Integration is not permanent, but a dynamic equilibrium in which succeeding disruptions are but moments in new integrations. Integration should be reflected not only on the intellectual level but also in concrete activities as conflicts are assimilated into the larger whole and actual control over behavior is established.[24]

Circular Response. The process by which integration is achieved is circular response. Follett maintains that social interactions are not characterized by simple cause-effect relationships in which a stimulus is the cause and a response the effect. Instead, social interactions are reciprocal, or circular, relationships in which the individual both affects, and is affected by, the social environment. Moreover, individual reactions are "always to a relating." As Follett puts it, "I never react to you, but ... it is I-plus-you reacting to you-plus-me."[25] To complicate things further, every situation is a relating of things which vary which means that the relating itself must vary. In sum, social situations are in a state of flux with each member of society in a condition of mutual interdependence with all others, as all of us create each other all the time.

Evocation. Circular response involves the interpenetration of ideas and activities and leads to integration by means of evocation in which each of us "calls out" something from others. Evocation, according to Follett, "releases something, frees something, opens the way for the expression of latent capacities and possibilities."[26] Thus evocation leads to creative adjustment of differing interests and the discovery of what Follett calls "plus-values" or values that represent creative responses to social conflict.[27]

Follett maintains that there is no result of the process of circular response, evocation, and integration, only moments in the process. Progress is an "infinite advance toward the infinitely receding goal of infinite perfection" and is determined by the capacity for cooperation.[28] Objectives are not preexistent but emerge from the evolving situation as experience generates will and purpose. Integration, represented by agreement, comes from the uniting of experience, and its significance is derived not from the fact that values are held in common but that they are created in common.[29] The collective will embodied in the integrative solution expresses agreements on ends larger than individual ends, but the collective will is based on the concrete claims of individuals, and the social interests defined are simply individual interests generalized.[30]

Conditions for Effective Integration

Follett concedes that not all disputes can be settled by integration.[31] Some differences may be irreconcilable. Moreover, integration may be discouraged by such factors as the relative ease of fighting, the enjoyment of domination, manipulation of the process by leaders, and lack of skill in the techniques of integration.[32] Nevertheless, Follett contends that the opportunities for integration are likely more numerous than might be expected and that we should be alert to those opportunities. Successful integration requires that opportunities be recognized, that differences be brought into the open, that significant rather than simply dramatic issues be the central focus, that broader issues be broken into parts that can be dealt with separately, and that interacting of different interests be encouraged.[33] The failure to integrate is likely to result in a loss of the expression of individual potentialities, a diminution of the power of the social unit, and a level of tension that is conducive to crowd manipulation.[34]

The Group and Individualism

Follett argues that her concept of the group does not deny the concept of individualism. On the contrary, she asserts that the group permits the truest expression of individuality. According to Follett, there is no separate ego. Instead, individuals are created by reciprocal activity, and "individuality" is the capacity for union or the ability to find one's place in the whole, not uniqueness.[35] The power of relating makes the individual of value, and the act of relating allows the individual to offer more to the group.

Furthermore, the group process does not result in the loss of individuality through either domination by others or domination by the whole.[36] The individual is not dominated by others because the group process involves the intermingling and the interpenetration of the ideas of all. The individual is not dominated by the whole because the individual is part of the whole. Thus the group process represents a synthesis of individualism and collective control in the form of collective self-control. There are not individual rights, only group rights; and the group does not protect rights, it creates them. The duty of the individual is neither to himself or herself nor to others, but to the group and the group serves the true and long-term interests of the individual.[37]

The Group and Freedom

Nor, Follett maintains, does the concept of the group deny the concept of freedom. For Follett, freedom is the "harmonious, unimpeded working of one's own nature," which is social in character, and "liberation from the tyranny of particularistic impulses."[38] Thus freedom is achieved through social relationships as the range and significance of individual activity is increased. From this perspective, the individual is not free simply when making "undetermined" decisions. Determinism is an inevitability as the individual is simultaneously determined and determining in social relationships. Instead, the individual is free when creating new opportunities, which is best done in a group setting governed by the law of interpenetration and the doctrine of the wholes. In Follett's words, they are free who "*win* their freedom through fellowship."[39] The group process seeks the freedom of all by means of

104

the authority of the whole and the function and contribution of each of its members.

Circular Response, Power, and Control

As the law of interpenetration and the doctrine of the wholes do not deny the concepts of individualism and freedom, the quest for integration through circular response, Follett contends, does not deny the reality of power and the existence of control. Follett asserts that the desire for power is a predominant feature of life and acknowledges that power will always be unequally distributed.[40] Rather than abolish power, integration through circular response both transforms power and increases it. Power is transformed from "power-over" to "power-with," and it is increased as greater power accrues to the whole, and thus to the individual, by virtue of the group's ability to satisfy a wider range of individual needs. Follett defines power as "the ability to make things happen, to be a causal agent."[41] She contends that the only genuine basis of power is the interweaving of experience produced by circular response. Consequently, power is jointly developed and it is coactive, not coercive.[42] Integration reduces the necessity of exercising power-over, and increases the possibility of exercising power-with, by reducing areas of irreconcilable difference in which the arbitrary exercise of power is required.

Whereas power is the capacity to make things happen, Follett defines control as "the application of power as a means toward a specific end."[43] Follett argues that control is impossible without unity and that the degree of control depends on how far the ideas and concrete activities of people can be united. Interaction in circular response *is* control, not simply a process by which it is established, and control is implemented as mutual interaction creates new situations.

The State and Social Life

According to Follett, the state is a logical extension of the group process and the highest expression of social life. Follett asserts that man joins groups to give expression to his multiple natures (the Law of Multiples) and that only the state can express the compounding and multiple compounding of natures involved in social life.[44] As the group will is an expression of the individual will at a higher level of purpose, so too is the state an expression of individual and group will at an even higher level of purpose. The true state gives rise to the great group unified by common ends with its sovereignty resting on the group process and the principle of integration.[45] As such, the state cannot leave us alone, it cannot regulate us, it can only express us.[46] The state is a fulfillment of the individual, and Follett states: "The home of my soul is in the state."[47]

The Role of Law

The supreme function of the state is the moral ordering of social relationships.[48] Nevertheless, laws that govern those relationships cannot be based entirely on fixed principles. Follett contends that there is no private conscience, only a socially conditioned conscience, and, as a result, we do not follow right, we create it.[49] Accordingly, law must be embedded in the social process and should not be a restraining force to protect interests but a positive force to broaden and deepen interests.

Follett maintains that the old idea of law was based on the concept of "contract" and particularistic interests and incorporated the notion that man could do what he wanted with his own.[50] This, she argues, has given way to the idea that law derives its authority from the fact that it was produced by the community and that the administration of justice should be a vital part of the social process. Nevertheless, Follett does not believe that the system of jurisprudence should be entirely pragmatic in character. Instead, law should be a blend of principle and precedent, both of which should be interpreted in the light of present experience.[51]

Planning

The prescribed positive role of the state is illustrated by Follett's support for national planning. She contends that large-scale planning is imperative and that such planning is the only alternative to chaos.[52] Planning, like law, should be an intrinsic part of the social process, however. Follett argues that coordination, not coercion, should be substituted for laissez-faire. That coordination should be in the form of the correlation of multiple controls at lower levels rather than superimposed state control. The state should act as a facilitator in the national planning process by providing for direct and voluntary contact among the heads of industry for the purpose of the self-coordination of their own activities.[53]

Ballot-Box Democracy

How can the "true state" be realized? Though Follett espouses democracy, she had little faith in existing democratic methods, which she referred to as "ballot-box" democracy, nor did she have much hope for the major reform proposals of her day. According to Follett, democracy was born of the pursuit of individualism and has been dominated by particularistic interests. First party domination and then a marriage of business and politics have inhibited individual participation in the political process and served parochial interests while seeking justification under the guise of majority rule.[54]

Ballot-box democracy, Follett argues, is not real democracy. Ballot-box democracy relies on brute numbers rather than a genuine union of interests and is based on the "law of the crowd," which employs suggestion or persuasion as its primary technique. Ballot-box democracy rests on the "doctrine of consent," which asserts that the few should decide while the many assent. This, according to Follett, is simply a rationalization for the arbitrary exercise of power. Mere acquiescence is not sufficient. Different kinds of information are required in the political process; fact situations change, which necessitates the continuing input of all interests; and the activities of the people are integral to that changing situation.[55] In short, consent does not capitalize on the potential contributions of the many. The tragedy of democracy, Follett alleges, is not that we have no public opinion but that we think we do.[56] In fact, there is no genuine confronting of real differences in ballot-box democracy and thus no creativity in producing a collective will. What is needed is not consent, but coaction.

Follett was similarly wary of the major reform proposals of her day as being adequate to the task of achieving the true state. Progressives, she argues, continue to emphasize the voter, not the man, by concentrating on the extension of suffrage.[57] Though Follett believed socialism to be the logical next step in industrial development, she charges that socialists seek a shortcut to the true state. Socialization of property must be preceded by socialization of the will.[58] The group theory of politics, or political pluralism, makes a contribution by recognizing the importance of group life. But pluralism fosters particularistic interests and relies on the balance of power theory. Pluralism thus frustrates attempts at integration because, by the time the balancing groups meet, it is likely to be too late to reach agreement. In their opposition to the monistic state, Follett argues, the pluralists have simply pitted the group against the state and run the danger of substituting group tyranny for state tyranny.[59]

Real Democracy

Follett asserts that we have not yet tried "real democracy" to achieve the true state. Perfection of the mechanisms of representation, reliance on majority rule, dependence on party organization, and submission to the law of the crowd are insufficient. Indeed, they are counterproductive. Democracy should not simply register opinions, it should attempt to create unity. This requires that new principles of interpersonal association be discovered and that minds be trained to work together constructively in the pursuit of the collective will. Follett's concept of real democracy rests on substantive participation by the many and a federalist political structure.

Participation

Follett maintains that the illusion of consent should be replaced by substantive participation to open the way for creative interpersonal relationships. An active and responsible citizenry will allow democracy to develop power from the interplay of daily concrete activities and inspire creativity through the interpenetration of ideas. Substantive participation and a mentality receptive to integrative solutions, in turn, will lead to the formulation of the collective will and its realization in the concrete activities of everyday life.

Although emphasizing participation, Follett disavows any "mystic faith in the native rightness of public opinion."[60] Instead, she places her faith in the ability of collective thought, evolved through the group process, to inspire creativity and integration, not simply degenerate into collective mediocrity.

Federalism

Follett asserts that substantive participation should take place in a federal political structure to produce effective representation. For Follett, the small group is the core of democracy, and the "democratic soul is born in the group" as individuals learn to be part of the social whole.[61] Small groups are thus a vital stage on the path toward a more complete whole.

Follett argues that the fundamental social group is the neighborhood group.[62] The neighborhood group facilitates understanding through acquaintance, provides regular and constant interaction, and involves more varied contact than do self-selected groups. The neighborhood group should assume responsibility for functions of its own to foster better citizenship, imbue its members with a creative attitude by encouraging constructive interpersonal relationships in "experience meetings," and act as a building-block for broader systems of representation.[63]

The process of representation should be cumulative with members of the smaller group selecting representatives for larger groups as one moves from neighborhood groups to district councils to city councils, to state governments, to the national government.[64] Representatives, on their part, should not merely be responsible for winning victories but for reaching agreement. This requires that representatives be allowed to exercise their own best judgment as to what is right rather than simply reflect the expressed interests of their particular constituencies. Yet the representative should not be an entirely free agent. The representative should maintain a reciprocal relationship with both the represented and the representative group and make the represented group aware of the activities of the representative group.[65]

Follett acknowledges that there may be problems with this system of representation. People from the same group may have different interests, and it may not be possible for one individual to act for another. Nevertheless, the general thrust of the federal structure should be to get ideas represented and to provide an appropriate forum for the integration of differences.

Follett maintains that there is an important role for leadership in the real democracy. Indeed, she contends that democracy is not opposed to aristocratic leadership and that the democratic process itself is a breeding ground for a new aristocracy as leaders emerge from neighborhood groups.[66] The function of leadership is transformed in real democracy, however. The leader is not to control the group but to express it by assisting the group in finding integrative solutions. The leader should also anticipate what public opinion will be and establish conditions for constructive change. In short, the leader is to release the energy of the group, unite energies to carry out purposes, and aid in creating new purposes.[67]

The Role of the Expert

As there is a role for leadership, so too is there a place for the expert in Follett's democracy of inequalities and complementary contributions. Democracy is not simply the people consenting to the rule of the expert, however, and Follett decries what she calls the "pernicious tendency" to make the opinions of the expert prevail by crowd methods.[68] Accurate information is required in the policy process, but there are limitations on the advice of the expert. In the first place, there is no *ante facto* will on which the expert can construct a policy. Instead, purpose and will emerge from a continuous process of mutual adjustment and integration. Moreover, the "facts" on which the expert is to base advice cannot be accepted at face value. Full and accurate information is often difficult to secure. Even if information is available, some things do not lend themselves readily to precise measurement. The facts themselves are not static and must be evaluated in the light of changing circumstances. The expert may choose which facts to present, and different facts may be elicited by different observers. Experts do not simply gather information, they condense and interpret it, raising the possibility that personal biases and preferences may contaminate the "facts."[69] Consequently, Follett argues that the findings of the expert must be balanced against the ideas of others as one form of experience is united with another. Democracy thus requires both expert advice and an active electorate with a government of popular control and centralized responsibility.[70] The expert should be more than on tap, but not on top.

Group Processes and the Industrial Organization

Although Follett was primarily interested in human relations and group processes in general, much of her later, and best-known, work focused on industrial organizations. Follett believed the basic principles of human behavior—interacting, evoking, integrating, and emerging—to be the same in business as in other group settings, and her analysis of business organizations is based on these fundamental concepts. Follett chose to concentrate specifically on industrial organizations for a number of reasons. First, she had access to business organizations, having established contact with several prominent businessmen during her career. Second, Follett thought the business setting offered original and interesting material for analysis, and she was attracted by the businessman's action-oriented approach to problems. Finally, and most important, Follett viewed the business organization as a social agency performing vital social functions. The greatest service business provides to society is work itself. Through work, business provides the opportunity for personal development and the occasion for the interweaving of activities from which "spiritual values" are created.[71] As such, business serves a broader social purpose than mere profit making and offers a place for pioneering in human relations. In business, technical knowledge could be combined with scientific investigations of cooperative human behavior to discover basic principles of organized activity. It is organized activity, Follett contends, that separates mediocre from high endeavor, and in the knowledge of organized activity lies the potential solutions to world problems.[72]

Coordination

From Follett's perspective, the primary task of the organization is the coordination of efforts, which transforms a collection of individuals into a working unit. Coordination is the reciprocal relating of all factors in the situation and results in the integrative unity of the organization. It is best accomplished by "cross-functioning," or the direct contact of persons and departments responsible for related activities.[73] Accordingly, communication and authority should flow horizontally, as well as vertically, in the organization. Furthermore, coordination should be a continuous process encompassing both planning and execution with each department basing its actions on what is good for the company as viewed from that department.

Control and Authority

Follett contends that control and authority flow from proper coordination, not, as is often assumed, coordination from control and authority. As noted previously, Follett defines power as the ability to make things happen. She defines control as "power exercised as a means toward a specific end." In other words, power is a capacity, while control is the exercise of power, or a process. Attaining control is a function of the ability to see the field of control as a complex whole and the ability to pass from one field of control to another, not simply predicting, but creating new situations.[74]

Follett notes two emergent aspects of control. First, control is coming to mean more the correlation of many controls (i.e., control is cumulative) rather than the superimposition of control by a central authority. Second, control is becoming more "fact control" than "man control."[75] That is, control is being exercised more on the basis of the demands of the situation as established by scientific investigation and less on the basis of personal and arbitrary mandate.

These characteristics of control are manifested in the exercise of authority (which Follett defines as "vested control") in the organization.[76] Follett describes the organization as an interweaving of functions with authority deriving from the unifying process of coordination. Accordingly, organizational authority is neither "supreme" nor is it delegated. Instead, authority is pluralistic and cumulative (i.e., it arises from below), and it is based on function rather than position. As such, authority is the outcome of interlocking activities and accrues to those with knowledge and experience and the skills to apply that knowledge and experience.[77]

Follett argues that we have been misled by "the illusion of final authority."[78] Authority is a process, not the final moment of decision. Authority is actually held by those with knowledge, not the person at the top, and involves a long series of interrelated activities prior to the act of decision. This does not mean that there is no final authority. Follett acknowledges that some questions have to be decided at the top of the organization.[79] Nevertheless, authority does not merely flow from the top of the organization. It is a reciprocally conditioning relationship based on circular response with functional knowledge and skill as the ultimate master.

As with control, Follett contends that the arbitrary exercise of organizational authority is diminishing. There are a number of drawbacks to the arbitrary exercise of authority. We lose what might be learned from the subordinate, friction is created, pride in work is destroyed, and the sense of individual responsibility is lessened.[80] Instead of exercising authority "over" subordinates, organizations have begun to develop "power-with" all members of the organization in response to what Follett refers to as "the law of the situation." The law of the situation requires sensitivity to "the interweaving, reciprocal responses and evolving changes that constitute the situation," and authority is determined by the objective demands of the work situation rather than personal imposition.[81] Thus, orders come from the work, not work from orders, and orders do not derive their validity from either the position of the superior or the consent of the subordinate but from the mutual contributions of the order-giver and the order-receiver.[82] In sum, authority resides in a function, is derived from the demands of the situation, and is the result of circular behavior.

The arbitrary exercise of authority can be avoided by assuring that all members know the purposes of the organization, giving reasons with an order whenever possible, not being disagreeable in giving orders, knowing the principles of work activity, mutually deciding which principles to apply, creating attitudes conducive to having orders carried out, and providing proper incentives in the organization.[83] Authority can be "depersonalized" by developing standard practices and habit patterns so that activity can be governed by technique rather than direct command. As the arbitrary and personal exercise of authority is reduced, a sense of functional unity is created, pride of craft is restored, and a sense of responsibility is engendered among all members of the organization.

Leadership

Follett's conceptions of authority and control do not eliminate the requirement of effective leadership in the organization. A different kind of leadership is required that follows the general pattern outlined by Follett for leadership in society. According to Follett, the old theory of leadership was based on the power of personality. A good leader was considered to be "one who has a compelling personality, who wields power, who constrains others to his will."[84] Actually, Follett contends, there are three kinds of leadership—leadership of position, leadership of personality, and leadership of function—and, of these, leadership of function is the most important.[85] Leadership of position is ineffective without functional capability. Position and function should coincide; but this is not always the case. Leadership of personality may only be an attempt to dominate by "masterful or persuasive" traits. Follett does not disregard personal qualities, but she does believe that they have been overemphasized. For Follett, organizing ability is more important than ascendancy traits, and learning the job is more important than the ability to exploit one's personality.[86]

In Follett's view, effective leadership is not based on position or personality but on the ability to create functional unity in the organization. The basic task of the leader is to organize and integrate experience. Somewhat more concretely, Follett identifies three leadership functions: coordination, definition of purpose, and anticipation.[87] Coordination involves educating and training individuals so that each can give what he or she is capable of giving, providing an opportunity for participation, and unifying the various contributions. In Follett's words, the executive is responsible for "making the organization chart a going affair."[88] Definition of purpose is required so that all may feel that they are working for a common end. Anticipation entails understanding the long-term good of the greater community and creating situations in which that good can be achieved. In order to perform these functions, the leader must have a thorough knowledge of the job, an ability to grasp the total situation, the capacity to create as well as direct power, the talent to see future directions, and a pioneer's sense of adventure.[89]

Although much of her discussion centers on the role and functions of the top executive, Follett believes the future will depend on more widely diffused leadership in the organization.[90] The need for leadership exists at many points in the organization, and each person should be prepared to answer the challenge of leadership of his or her own job. This diffusion of leadership does not mean that responsibility is likewise diffused. Centralization and decentralization can be accomplished simultaneously as the top executive retains responsibility for the whole, while each individual assumes responsibility for his or her own function in the whole.[91] In this way, the leader neither abandons responsibilities nor takes responsibility from others. Instead, the leader makes each feel his or her own responsibility. Contrary to the popular conception of the leader as a boss, Follett argues that the mark of a good leader is how little bossing he has to do.[92] The effective leader shows others what to do to meet their own responsibilities. The relationship between leaders and followers should be reciprocal, with leaders guiding and followers keeping their leaders in control by making suggestions, taking wrong orders back for correction, and keeping the faith in a common purpose.[93]

A relationship of particular concern to Follett is that between the executive and the expert. She notes that there is a trend toward specialization in the organization, and, as a result, most decisions are made by those with special expertise. Thus the exercise of authority more often represents the consent of the governors than the consent of the governed.[94] This creates an apparent dilemma. On the one hand, the executive cannot abdicate his decision-making responsibilities. On the other hand, he may not have the specific knowledge requisite to effective decision making. Follett's solution is to deny the dilemma. She counsels that the knowledge of the expert be joined with the knowledge of the executive. The opinion of the expert should not coerce, but enter into the decision process by means of circular response and integration.[95]

Worker Participation

Much of Follett's work emphasizes participation that fosters circular response and thus encourages integration of differences. Nonetheless, she gives only a qualified endorsement to full worker participation in the management of the organization. Follett believes that workers and management should share in joint control, but in a limited fashion. Participation, to Follett, means "everyone taking part, according to his capacity, in a unit composed of related activities."[96] The qualifying phrase suggests that worker participation does not necessarily mean industrial democracy. Follett does not believe, for instance, that workers should be allowed to elect their supervisors.[97] She feels that workers need not be consulted on all issues, only those on which they are competent to have some opinion.[98] More generally, Follett states that the worker should not be given a vote on something he does not know about, and, she contends, the worker cannot vote intelligently on how a business should be run.[99]

Instead of industrial democracy, employee participation should be an application of "functional power." This means that labor should expect only the degree of control that goes with its function.[100] The purpose of participation should be to join the capacities of workers and management so that labor can assist management, not by sharing existing power, but by developing joint power and thus creating new power.

The effectiveness of such participation requires that both management and labor learn the secret of the group process. Worker participation is not merely a procedure for collective bargaining. Follett views collective bargaining as a "temporary expedient" that neither gives labor a direct share in industrial control nor fosters the cooperative attitude required for circular response, evocation, and integration. Worker participation is not simply a means for forestalling trouble. Indeed, participation is likely to make things harder on management, not easier. Worker participation is not merely a medium for the exchange of information. Information should be united, not exchanged, by a cooperative study to get at the facts. Worker participation is not simply a means to gain consent. What is needed is cooperation, not consent. Worker participation is not merely a recognition of the "rights" of labor. Jobs, not rights, should be the focus of participation. Worker participation is not simply a way for management to avoid responsibility. That only passes the problem on.[101]

Worker participation, according to Follett, is a way to increase collective responsibility through the recognition of an identity of interests, an awareness of interdependence, an interpenetration of activity, and an integration of differing perspectives. The recognition of a reciprocal responsibility between management and the workers establishes the interweaving of experience as the only legitimate "boss" in the organization.[102]

Conclusion

Follett's work is distinguished more by the originality of her ideas than their number. The central thread of her analysis may be summarized as follows:

1. The group is the core of the social process and the means by which the individual achieves fulfillment.

2. The state is an extension of the group process at a higher level of objective and is the highest expression of social life. The true state is best achieved in a democracy with full participation and a federal structure based on neighborhood groups.

3. The organization is a group distinguished by the structured nature of its activities.

4. The primary task of the organization is the coordination of its activities to produce functional unity.

5. Functional unity in the organization, as in all groups, is best achieved through the interaction of related activities and the interpenetration of ideas in a pattern of circular response, evocation, and integration. This requires the participation of all members of the organization with each member contributing that which he or she is able to contribute.

6. In this context, organizational control and authority are derived from the process of functional relating and are based on knowledge and the law of the situation rather than position.

7. Organizational leadership performs the functions of providing the opportunity for participation and guiding individual endeavors in the pursuit of common purposes.

The main problem with Follett's work is that her idealism is showing. That idealism is perhaps most vividly reflected in her aversion to what she considers to be false contrasts. Thus Follett argues that we can have both collectivism and individualism and freedom, both circular response and power and control, both aristocracy and democracy, both executive control and the supremacy of expert knowledge, both centralization and decentralization. Even integration is defined as a solution to conflict in which everyone gets what he or she wants. In short, Follett has a tendency to say, in effect, that we can have everything at once. One need not question the possibility of combinations of these contrasting concepts to question the possibility of achieving all of them simultaneously.

Follett's idealism would not be a significant problem except that she claims to be dealing, not with what should be, but with "what perhaps may be."[103] Although it is not entirely clear what Follett means by this statement, it would seem to indicate that she intended to construct, not an ideal world, but a possible world. Accordingly, her construction must stand the test of achievability, not just desirability.

Follett's case rests on two fundamental assumptions: that attitudes can be changed and that interests are so structured as to permit integrative reconciliation. Attitudinal change is required for the integrative process to work properly. Individuals must develop a cooperative attitude that fosters a search for integrative solutions to conflict and aspire only to exercise "power-with" rather than grasp for "power-over." Follett was not blind to the baser side of human nature. She dealt with the subject of political power in her book on the Speakers of the House and acknowledges a human desire to exercise power-over.[104] Instead, Follett would appear to be engaging in "best-case" hypothesizing in assuming that those baser instincts can be overcome and human behavior can be what she would have it.[105] Whether such a change is possible is debatable. Follett offers little in support of her stand other than a hope that education can alter attitudes and an implicit belief in the malleability of human nature and the will to change.[106]

Follett's second assumption is that interests are so structured as to permit integrative reconciliation. This, of course, need not be the case. Consider the following possible configurations of interests:

1. A commonality of interests exists. In this case, there is no occasion for integration, since no differences exist. The appropriate mechanism of choice is not integration, but unanimity.

2. Interests are separate and unrelated. In this case, since there are no related differences, there is no occasion for integration. The mechanism of choice depends on the circumstance. Under a condition of unlimited resources, the likely mechanism of choice is mutual accommodation. Under a condition of limited resources, the likely mechanisms of choice are compromise or domination.

3. Interests are separate but related. This configuration of interests presents the possibility of integration, but only if the interests are compatible. If the interests are inherently in conflict, the likely mechanism of choice is, again, compromise or domination.

In short, the possibility of integration depends on a particular configuration of interests and the relative frequency of occurrence of that configuration is unknown. Furthermore, even if interests are in the appropriate configuration, disagreement over objectives and/or the means to achieve those objectives may remain as an impediment to integrative solutions.

One is driven to the conclusion that Follett's analysis of society and organization is only partial and remains largely untested. Nevertheless, she performs a substantial service by calling attention to the importance of integration and alerting us to the possibility of its use in resolving social conflict. Moreover, the ideas Follett presented and the dynamics she revealed anticipated later developments in the field of organizational behavior. Truly a person ahead of her time, Follett's actual contribution to the understanding of organizational life may not yet be fully recognized and her potential contribution not yet fully realized.

Notes

1. Material on Follett's life is taken from the *Dictionary of American Biography*, Supplement 1 (New York: Scribner's, 1944), 308–9; *Notable American Women, 1607–1950* (Cambridge, Mass.: Belknap Press of Harvard University Press, 1971), 639–41; and L. Urwick, ed., *The Golden Book of Management* (London: Newman Neame, 1956), 132–37.

2. Mary Parker Follett, *The Speaker of the House of Representatives* (New York: Longmans, Green, 1896).

3. Mary Parker Follett, *The New State: Group Organization, the Solution of Popular Government* (New York: Longmans, Green, 1918).

4. Mary Parker Follett, *Creative Experience* (New York: Longmans, Green, 1924).

5. For compilations of Follett's lectures, see L. Urwick, ed., *Freedom and Co-ordination: Lectures in Business Organizations* (London: Management Publications Trust, 1949); and Elliot M. Fox and L. Urwick, eds., *Dynamic Administration: The Collected Papers of Mary Parker Follett*, 2d ed. (New York: Pitman, 1973).

6. Follett, *Creative Experience*, xi, xii.

7. Ibid., 134.

8. Ibid., 135.

9. Follett, *New State*, 89.

10. Ibid., 25.

11. Ibid., 76.

12. Fox and Urwick, *Dynamic Administration*, 160.

13. Follett, *New State*, 23; and idem, *Creative Experience*, 303.

14. Follett, *Creative Experience*, 98.

15. Ibid., 47.

16. Follett, *New State*, 44–45.

17. Fox and Urwick, *Dynamic Administration*, 1–2.

18. Ibid., 2.

19. Follett, *Creative Experience*, xiv.
20. Ibid., 156, 163.
21. Ibid., 156.
22. From Introduction by Fox and Urwick to *Dynamic Administration*, xxv.
23. Follett, *New State*, 112.
24. Follett, *Creative Experience*, 150.
25. Ibid., 62.
26. Fox and Urwick, *Dynamic Administration*, 162.
27. Ibid., 165.
28. Follett, *New State*, 51.
29. Ibid., 34.
30. Ibid., 48.
31. Follett, *Creative Experience*, 163.
32. Fox and Urwick, *Dynamic Administration*, 16–19.
33. Ibid., 7–16.
34. From Introduction by Fox and Urwick to *Dynamic Administration*, xxx.
35. Follett, *New State*, 62, 65.
36. Ibid., 70.
37. Ibid., 52.
38. Ibid., 69.
39. Ibid., 72.
40. Follett, *Creative Experience*, 180, 189.
41. Fox and Urwick, *Dynamic Administration*, 70.
42. Ibid., 72.
43. Ibid., 70.
44. Follett, *New State*, 296–97.
45. Follett does not shrink from the extension of this logic to the international level. She contends that organized cooperation should be the basis for international relations and should reflect the interpenetration of the "rich content of widely varying characteristic and experience." See ibid., 345.
46. Ibid., 183.
47. Ibid., 312.
48. Ibid., 333.
49. Ibid., 52.
50. Ibid., 126.
51. Follett, *Creative Experience*, 278.
52. Fox and Urwick, *Dynamic Administration*, 260.
53. Ibid., 261–63.
54. Follett, *New State*, 165–67.
55. Follett, *Creative Experience*, 28.
56. Follett, *New State*, 220.
57. Ibid., 168.
58. Ibid., 74.
59. Follett, *Creative Experience*, 230.
60. Ibid., 216.
61. Follett, *New State*, 160.

62. Though emphasizing neighborhood groups, Follett would not deny a role for other groups, such as occupational groups. See ibid., 320.

63. Follett, *Creative Experience*, 212.

64. However, Follett proposes that the Senate might be composed of experts or representatives of occupational groups. See Follett, *New State*, 246.

65. Follett, *Creative Experience*, 253–54.

66. Follett, *New State*, 228.

67. Fox and Urwick, *Dynamic Administration*, 233.

68. Follett, *Creative Experience*, 21.

69. Ibid., 10–18.

70. Follett, *New State*, 175.

71. Fox and Urwick, *Dynamic Administration*, 112.

72. Ibid., 115.

73. Urwick, *Freedom and Coordination*, 63.

74. Fox and Urwick, *Dynamic Administration*, 172–73.

75. Ibid., 260.

76. Ibid., 70.

77. Urwick, *Freedom and Coordination*, 45–46.

78. Fox and Urwick, *Dynamic Administration*, 117.

79. Urwick, *Freedom and Coordination*, 43.

80. Ibid., 19–22.

81. From Introduction by Fox and Urwick to *Dynamic Administration*, xxvi, and 29–30.

82. Urwick, *Freedom and Coordination*, 31.

83. Fox and Urwick, *Dynamic Administration*, 23–24; and Urwick, *Freedom and Coordination*, 24.

84. Fox and Urwick, *Dynamic Administration*, 235.

85. Urwick, *Freedom and Coordination*, 58.

86. Fox and Urwick, *Dynamic Administration*, 249.

87. Ibid., 225–28.

88. Ibid., 225.

89. Urwick, *Freedom and Coordination*, 50–54.

90. Ibid., 59.

91. Fox and Urwick, *Dynamic Administration*, 51.

92. Urwick, *Freedom and Coordination*, 49.

93. Ibid., 54–55.

94. Fox and Urwick, *Dynamic Administration*, 176.

95. Urwick, *Freedom and Coordination*, 70.

96. Fox and Urwick, *Dynamic Administration*, 178.

97. Ibid., 38.

98. Urwick, *Freedom and Coordination*, 83.

99. Follett, *Creative Experience*, 20.

100. Fox and Urwick, *Dynamic Administration*, 139.

101. Ibid., 132–37.

102. Ibid., 79–80.

103. Ibid., 5.

104. Follett, *Creative Experience*, 180.

105. This approach might be contrasted with that of economics, which has

been called "the dismal science" because of its "worst-case" assumptions about human nature (i.e., man is motivated only by primitive self-interest) and its dire predictions.

106. Follett, *New State*, 363.

CHAPTER 5

Elton Mayo: The Human Relations Approach

With the work of Mary Parker Follett, we have seen the beginning of a dissent from the Classical view of the organization. Mayo's work continues some of those themes, adds new ones, and lends some empirical support to the dissenting view.

Mayo continues two of Follett's basic themes: the importance of the group process and the cumulative nature of authority in the organization. The group process is central to the analyses of both Follett and Mayo. For both, man is a social animal who finds a sense of identification and function in the group. Accordingly, individual behavior is largely determined by the group process and cannot be properly understood outside that process. There is also agreement on the cumulative nature of authority in the organization, although Mayo does not emphasize this facet of the organization as much as Follett did. For Mayo, the cumulative nature of authority is implied in his insistence that the needs of subordinates must be satisfied if they are to become productive members of the organization and in his assertion that the voluntary cooperation of all members of the organization must be secured if the organization is to be successful in achieving its objectives. Both Follett and Mayo temper their pronouncements on authority by acknowledging that elite leadership will be required, but the role of the elite is to establish the basis for proper group interaction, not to lead in an authoritarian manner.

Mayo extends Follett's perspective by adding a more general (and rather gloomy) sociological interpretation and elaborating on the role of the small group inside the organization. The more general sociological perspective is Mayo's assertion that the social disorganization attendant to the transition from a traditional to a modern society has led to personal disorganization. The linkage to organizational behavior comes in Mayo's contention that the problem of personal disorganization is exacerbated in the industrial setting. In industry, work has been reduced to a monotonous routine and the highly specialized procedures adopted have deprived work of a sense of social function. Routine and

121

monotonous work, in turn, lead to work being performed in a state of "reverie" with obsessions impairing work performance.

Follett's analysis is extended inward by Mayo's focus on the importance of the work group in the organization. The texture of the small-group experience, according to Mayo, will largely determine individual behavior in the organization. Whether that texture is such that it will produce spontaneous cooperation or hostility depends on the steps management takes to secure a spirit of cooperation and teamwork. A key actor in this scenario is the supervisor, who, operating at the point of human interface in the organization, is most likely to know of, and be able to respond to, the human needs of his or her subordinates.

Mayo also adds the important dimension of empirical research to his analysis. Although there is substantial controversy about the quality of his empirical analysis, Mayo's work did signal the importance of systematic, empirical investigation focusing on small groups within the organization. Indeed, the Western Electric research spurred a veritable deluge of empirical analyses, conducted under the general rubric of the Human Relations approach, which focused on the relationships among changes in the organization, worker satisfaction, and productivity.

There are also some points of disagreement between Follett and Mayo. A fundamental difference lies in the role of conflict in group interactions. For Follett, conflict should be recognized and used for productive purposes. For Mayo, conflict is pathological and is to be avoided. Spontaneous cooperation, not conflict, is the proper basis for relationships in the organization, and it is up to an elite to create the conditions for the emergence of spontaneous cooperation. Another point of difference is on the role of the state. For Follett, the state is a logical extension of the group process and, as such, the ultimate expression of the individual. For Mayo, the state is a potential instrument of tyranny, and its role should be subordinate to that of "peripheral" groups whose activities are crucial to social growth.

Elton Mayo is probably the most controversial author included in this volume (Taylor would run a close second). Much of that controversy swirls around the Western Electric research and, more particularly, Mayo's interpretation of that research. The controversy has shaped the structure of this chapter in three ways. First, Mayo's general sociological and political perspectives are examined in some detail, since it has been argued that these perspectives influenced his interpretation of the Western Electric study. Second, the Western Electric research itself is reviewed. This is done with apologies to those already familiar with that research; however, I thought it best to provide a summary for those who may not have had contact with the Western Electric research, since some knowledge is necessary to make sense of critiques of that work. Third, critiques of the Western Electric research are reviewed to give the reader at least a taste of the nature of that controversy. This I believe to be important because the Western Electric research and its critics raise some fundamental questions about the nature of the organization and the relationship between the organization and its members.

Life

George Elton Mayo was born on 26 December 1880 in Adelaide, Australia, the second child and the oldest son of seven children.[1] His father was an engineer, and several generations of the family had been prominent in the fields of medicine and law.

Mayo had something of a checkered educational experience. His early education was acquired at home. At age twelve, he entered Queen's College and, at age fourteen, St. Peter's College where he apparently performed capably, winning the Westminster Scholarship in 1895. In 1897 Mayo enrolled at the University of Adelaide to study medicine, but he soon became bored with the routine of medical studies. Mayo's parents then sent him to medical school in England. Mayo's interest in medicine was never truly kindled, however, and he left school. In the succeeding years, the restless Mayo sought to define his career interests, trying his hand at journalism and lecturing at the Working Men's College before returning to Australia in 1905 to become a partner in a printing firm. Still not satisfied, Mayo reentered the University of Adelaide in 1907 where he studied philosophy and psychology. This time, his interests crystallized, and Mayo went on to obtain both B.A. and M.A. degrees, graduating in 1910. On graduation, Mayo taught logic, ethics, and psychology, first at the University of Adelaide and then at the University of Queensland.

In the succeeding years, Mayo developed an interest in the relationship between society and individual problems, and became involved in the psychotherapeutic treatment of shell-shocked soldiers during World War I. Both the ideas and the experience acquired during this period were to have a significant influence on Mayo's subsequent work. The end of the decade saw the publication of Mayo's first book, *Democracy and Social Freedom*,[2] and his appointment to a newly created chair of philosophy at the University of Queensland.

In 1922 Mayo emigrated to the United States, attracted by the opportunity for continuing his studies of social and industrial problems. Mayo gained an appointment as a research associate at the Wharton School of Finance and Commerce of the University of Pennsylvania and received a grant from the Laura Spelman Rockefeller Foundation to study industrial problems. While at the University of Pennsylvania, Mayo did a study of a Philadelphia textile mill and published a series of articles in the *Personnel Journal* and in *Harper's Magazine*. The latter caught the eye of Wallace B. Donham, dean of the Harvard Business School, and in 1926 both Mayo and his Rockefeller grant moved to Harvard where Mayo was appointed associate professor of industrial research and director of the Department of Industrial Research. Mayo's work was to focus on the psychological, social, and organizational aspects of industry and serve as a complement to the physiological studies of Harvard's Fatigue Laboratory.

In 1927 a chance encounter and a casual conversation produced a collaboration that was to have a dramatic influence on the study of organizations. While in New York to speak at a meeting of the National Industrial Conference Board, Mayo met George A. Pennock, an engineer at Hawthorne Plant of the Western Electric Company.[3] On the basis of their conversation, Pennock invited Mayo to come to the plant to look over the puzzling results of a lighting experiment that the Western Electric engineers had been conducting. This visit was to eventuate in five years of experimentation, which have become known as "the Western Electric researches." Much of Mayo's efforts during the 1930s was concerned with the conduct of that research and a series of speeches and publications elaborating on the results of the investigations and extending Mayo's interpretation of their psychological and sociological import. In 1933, Mayo published *The Human Problems of an Industrial Civilization*, which constituted both a preliminary report on the Western Electric researches and a considerably broader interpretation of their implications.[4]

In the early 1940s, Mayo participated in a study of absenteeism and turnover in the aircraft industry in Southern California that echoed many of the findings of the Western Electric researches. In 1945 Mayo published his best-known, and perhaps most controversial, book, *The Social Problems of an Industrial Civilization*.[5] It was in *Social Problems* that Mayo attempted to synthesize the findings of his major empirical investigations and weave them into the broad tapestry of an analysis and critique of modern industrial society. In 1947 Mayo delivered two final lectures at Harvard, which were later published in the monograph *The Political Problems of an Industrial Civilization*.[6] Mayo retired from Harvard in the same year and returned to England where he resided until his death in 1949.

Mayo was a balding, bespectacled, chain-smoking man of slight build, but with an abundance of restless energy. Mayo's particular talent was in providing intellectual stimulation for, and integrating the activities of, a research team or working group. Described by his associate F.J. Roethlisberger as a "blithe spirit" and "an adventurer in the realm of ideas,"[7] Mayo was less a systematic thinker than a sower of "seeds to be cultivated."[8] His blithe spirit was manifested in something of a nonconformist attitude. During his association with the Western Electric Company, for instance, Mayo would arrive at the offices in midmorning and, instead of taking lunch with company executives, would frequent "joints" on Cicero Avenue near the plant. He reportedly treated the authorities at the Rockefeller Foundation as casually as those at Western Electric.[9]

As a scientific investigator, Mayo stressed "intimate, habitual, intuitive familiarity" with the subject of investigation rather than quantitative measurement and controlled experimentation.[10] Mayo believed the investigator should have a "knowledge-of-acquaintance" concerning human and social phenomena, not merely "knowledge about" those phenomena.[11] Accordingly, his methods were more those of clinical observation than laboratory experimentation. On a more general level, Mayo believed that philosophy is a good subject to engage in at the beginning and end of one's life. In the middle years, one should live it.[12] Mayo's own career was at least a rough approximation of that belief. Early in his career, Mayo was primarily concerned with general social, political, and philosophical questions. In the middle years, he engaged in scientific investigation based on direct observation. In the later years, he returned to his broader concerns, now conditioned by his observations and experience.

In discussing Mayo's work, I first consider his broader perspectives. This is followed by an examination of Mayo's empirical investigations. I conclude with a review of the criticisms of Mayo's work, a general assessment of that work, and an evaluation of Mayo's contributions to the study of organizations.

Mayo's Social, Political, and Philosophical Perspectives

Mayo's base assumption is that man is a social animal.[13] As such, he has a fundamental instinct for association with other humans and achieves a sense of meaning, purpose, and personal security in cooperative relationships. Society itself constitutes a cooperative system, and a civilized society is one in which cooperation is based on understanding and the will to work, rather than on force.[14] Thus, civilization is based on the spontaneous and voluntary cooperation of its members and is an "adventure in freedom" involving a struggle for both material control and individual expression.[15]

Although civilization is an adventure in freedom, Mayo also maintains that the "free life" must be based on social conditioning. Without the learned routines of social behavior, confusion would prevail.[16] Consequently, the intelligent development of civilization depends on "semiautomatic" routines of behavior learned in personal associations that make social collaboration both possible and effective. Logic and the immediate material interests of the individual are important, but they can be effective only in an existing social organization founded on established routines of social interaction. Mayo asserts that if the routines of society are disrupted, society will disintegrate into a "horde of individuals" seeking only self-preservation.[17] Mayo maintains that in a traditional society with established social routines, everyone understands economic activities and the social functions performed. The individual recognizes his or her social function and achieves adaptation when identified with that function.[18]

The Social Malaise

Mayo contends that modern society suffers from a breakdown of the social routines of traditional society. The breakdown began in the sixteenth century when the church lost authority.[19] Since then, there has been a progressive descent from "real civilization" toward mere cultures that change and pass. According to Mayo, we are now experiencing a condition of social disorganization. Modern society with its specialized logic and increased tempo of scientific and technological change has destroyed the social routines that fostered a sense of unity and the spirit of collaboration in traditional societies. The church has lost its authority. Work has been organized according to the dictates of mass production with the result that occupation has been divorced from social function. Ethnic diversity and geographical mobility have sundered personal ties. Even the family has become isolated and insignificant in the turbulent milieu of modern society.

Mayo asserts that the problem of social disorganization has been exacerbated by an economic theory that emphasizes competition in the pursuit of individual self-interest and a political system that heightens the level of social conflict by playing to the fears of the masses. Economic theory, based on the nineteenth-century concept of individualism, considers society to be a collection of unrelated individuals motivated by hedonistic interests.[20] Society is only a rabble of individuals competing for scarce resources; the worker is simply a cost of production; and economic logic produces a sense of human isolation and defeat. This all results in the formulation of a social code at a lower level in opposition to economic logic.[21]

Politics, instead of being a solution to the problem of social disorganization, has become part of the problem. Politics has succeeded only in dividing society into hostile camps, thereby rendering united action impossible and thwarting society's efforts to preserve its unity. This problem is most clearly evidenced, paradoxically, in democratic governments. Mayo contends that political parties were established to educate the public and thus give form to public opinion.[22] In actuality, they have merely become devices for winning elections as politicians appeal to the fears and hatreds of the masses. This has resulted in the debasement of the political function and a trend toward collective mediocrity.[23] In the process, the ideal of political liberty has been translated into the reality of "servitude to all that is intellectually futile and emotionally base."[24] The party system, based on class consciousness and the obsessions of hate and fear, has created a rift in the foundations of society and has exaggerated, not alleviated, the problem of social disorganization.

Social Disorganization and the Individual

Mayo argues that social disorganization leads to personal disorganization, since social disorganization deprives the individual of the traditional sense of social understanding and support.[25] Mayo contends that in modern society socialization has been subordinated to logic, but the logic developed has been inadequate to the task of promoting effective social relationships. Moreover, when an individual faces problems for which logic is inadequate and for which a code or tradition no longer exists, the likely response is irrationality.[26] The resort to irrationality is even more likely when the social situation is characterized by rivalry and complicated by mental obsessions.

As a result of these conditions of social and personal disorganization, Mayo asserts that individuals in modern society exist in a state of anomie or planless living, having been deprived of their sense of social function.[27] In this state of anomie, the individual is apt to be beset by reverie, or undirected thinking, which determines the individual's attitude toward life. According to Mayo, reverie normally illuminates and informs concentration, and the ability to shift rapidly back and forth from concentration to reverie is the achievement of the trained mind.[28] But reverie can also lead to the dominance of pessimism or melancholy, which may become virtually uncontrollable. These unacknowledged reveries are then manifested in strange ideas and eccentric behavior. Mayo asserts that no one is entirely free from the unreason produced by reverie and that the mentality of the average individual suggests a mild form of manic-depressive psychosis characterized by solitude and pessimism.[29] The search for amusement to avoid this reflective mood is merely an escape in which the individual seeks comfort in "artificial beauty, promiscuous adventure, or narcotic phantasies."[30] Long trains of unacknowledged reveries lead, in turn, to compulsions or obsessions in which individuals "overthink" situations and attribute their ills to a hostile environment. This obsessive state produces an incapacity to respond to present situations, especially social situations.

Mayo contends that there is a mutual interaction between social disorganization and personal obsessions. Consequently, the problems of social maladjustment and psychoneurosis cannot be separated. On the one hand, sociology has demonstrated a relationship between social and personal disorganization that breeds a tendency toward obsession.[31] From the sociological perspective, these morbid preoccupations are caused by a defective relationship between the family and the surrounding community. Thus sociologists maintain that psychoneurosis is a social rather than an individual phenomenon and results from the undue isolation of the family unit.

Psychologists, on the other hand, have shown that obsessive ills may be created by defective individual social conditioning.[32] Mayo argues that at the back of the infant mind is a repetition of primitive attitudes and beliefs. The infant feels impotent and afraid and, like the primitive, resorts to "magic" in the form of superstitions or taboos to reduce the feelings of impotence, fear, and ignorance.[33] To the extent that these attitudes and beliefs escape the synthesis of adolescence, they can reappear and dominate the life of an adult as childhood fears develop into adult obsessions. Alternatively, exercises of parental discipline may drive youths to obsessive conflict between the extremes of total acceptance or total rejection of authority.[34] Thus the psychological perspective suggests that social hostilities and obsessive behavior may not be primarily social ills but individual ills. Social ills may exacerbate individual ills, but Mayo contends that if the problem is attacked solely from the social end, the effort will be to no avail.[35]

Whatever the source, obsessions prevent fixed attention, and failure provokes a crisis of reverie in which victims of obsessional ideas are unable to rouse themselves from their evil dreams. These obsessions complicate individual and social situations through the intrusion of irrational motivations and delusions in human behavior. The irrational motives are not inherited or instinctual, but the product of defective social learning. Irrationality engendered by obsession makes the burden of decision the burden of possible sin, and, according to Mayo, life may be "made wretched and brought to nothing by irrationalities developed during a lifetime."[36]

Industry and Social Disorganization

Mayo asserts that the technological and scientific advances that contribute to social disorganization are most dramatically evidenced in industry and that conflict and class consciousness are magnified in the industrial setting. Mayo considers the industrial organization to be a fundamental social unit. The individual's sense of meaning comes primarily from a trade or profession that gives the individual worker the feeling that his or her work is socially necessary.[37] Yet in modern society, Mayo contends, occupation has become separated from social function, and social conflict has embittered relationships within industry.

Some blame for this bitterness can be assigned to both major parties to the dispute: management and labor. On management's part, a clear understanding of the technical and economic aspects of the organization is coupled with only rough guesswork about the human aspect of the organization. Work is so organized that it tends to lose, rather than gain, in interest as the imposition of highly systematized procedures destroys the traditions of work and craftsmanship. Mayo contends that the "great stupidity" of modern society is its disregard of the fact that the machine shop is a "potent agent of repression" and a "perversion of human energy."[38]

On labor's part, the response to changing industrial conditions has been unionization, which only increases the level of conflict. Mayo considers unions to be a reactionary attempt to conserve human values by "stalling" and thus resisting change.[39] Collective bargaining is similarly dismissed as a primitive squabble raised to a pseudo-scientific level that only perpetuates class conflict.[40]

Industry and Personal Disorganization

As social disorganization is magnified in the industrial setting, so too does the industrial setting further complicate the condition of personal disorganization. Machine production is monotonous and demands minimal concentration. As a result, work is likely to be performed in a mood of reverie, and personal ills are likely to inhibit work performance.

Mayo notes that this problem is often diagnosed as one of fatigue. Yet studies have indicated that fatigue, in a physiological sense, does not seem to be the problem.[41] The "fatigue" observed is not gradual in its onset, it is not related to a depletion of "fuel reserves," it is not associated with "oxygen debt," and it occurs long before the muscular system is exhausted. In short, the concept of physiological fatigue appears to be complicated by "mental fatigue" in the factory setting. Work continued after the appearance of mental fatigue is accompanied by an "oscillation of attention" and by pessimistic reflection or reverie,[42] and accentuates the individual's tendency to irrational thinking. This problem is most pronounced for work that is unskilled and for workers who are uneducated.[43]

Mayo contends that the alternative to these fatigue disabilities is the achievement of a "steady state" condition of equilibrium.[44] Without such an equilibrium, the worker will be unable to continue to perform effectively. Thus the strategic problem is to discover the sources of interference to the individual's state of equilibrium. That interference may be a function of the kind of work done and the intelligence of the worker. The temperament of the worker and social factors in the workplace are of at least equal importance, however. The individual reacts to a composite situation, although different individuals may react differently to the same situation.

The social setting of work is of particular importance to Mayo. He argues that work done in isolation becomes monotonous. Conversely, work gains in interest and dignity as an essential part of a social function.[45] Thus work is an exercise of skill best done in a social surrounding. Furthermore, Mayo contends that relationships among people in the workplace are more important than technical logic and the immediate material interests of the individual. Logic and incentives can work, but they are effective only in a supportive social organization.[46] If the social environment is not supportive, the interpersonal situation can produce "interferences" resulting in shifts in the individual's equilibrium and impaired performance.

Mayo argues that monotonous work, inadequate social conditions, and personal disorganization have combined to yield discontent in industry. Reveries born of imperfect adjustment to industrial conditions make the individual dissatisfied, restless, and unhappy, and encourage pessimistic thinking. Irrationalities produced by such thinking are like the unreason demonstrated by the shell-shock victims Mayo treated during World War I. The individual is dominated by reveries and is afraid to think out problems and thereby get rid of the fears. As a result, production suffers, and the individual becomes easy prey to the appeals of the politician and amusement promoters, which only worsens the situation.[47]

Mayo's argument, to this point, can be summarized as follows:

1. Civilization has moved from a society of established customs, an individual sense of social function, and accepted routines of personal interrelationships to a society marked by disruptive social, scientific, and technological change.

2. These changes have resulted in a condition of social disorganization in which logical responses to change have not been developed and irrational responses have been substituted for previous traditions.

3. The problem of social disorganization has been accentuated by an economic theory that promotes competition in the pursuit of self-interest and a political system that panders to the fears and superstitions of the body politic. Consequently, society has degenerated into class warfare, and there is a pervasive sense of anomie among individuals in society.

4. The social malaise is manifested in individual behavior in the form of uncontrolled reveries and irrational obsessions, which prevent proper adaptation to changing social conditions.

5. The problems are most acute in industry where technological change has robbed work of its social meaning and where uncontrolled reveries and obsessions have resulted in strained interpersonal relationships, labor unrest, and diminished work effectiveness.

The Solution

What is Mayo's solution to these maladies? It is perhaps instructive to start with what Mayo believes are *not* the solutions. Socialism, according to Mayo, is not the solution, since all the socialists can propose is a return to the "evil regime" from which laissez-faire theorists delivered us.[48] In addition, socialism gives rise to class consciousness and fosters the belief that society is composed of classes whose interests are naturally opposed. Mayo argues that this belief is both scientifically false and politically dangerous.[49] The issue, Mayo asserts, is not the ownership of property per se but the social use of property; Mayo contends that, if property is confiscated, all personal responsibility for its use will disappear.[50]

Nor are trade unions the solution to society's ills. Trade unions create the belief that there can be no harmony of interests between the employer and the employee—a belief that Mayo brands as "definitely obsessive."[51] For Mayo, the appropriate response to unionization is to anticipate its development and make it unnecessary.

Industrial democracy is not the cure, since neither the employer nor the employee knows what is wrong. Workers' democracy would only result in placing power in the hands of those least likely to be able to know what to do—the least skilled workers.[52]

Popular palliatives, such as revised incentive schemes, vocational adjustment, and new personnel systems, are also likely to be ineffective.[53] Such remedies are merely ad hoc responses to meet particular situations and fail to address the underlying problems. Indeed, Mayo argues that the demand for increased wages, for instance, may be simply a symptom of unrest, not its cause.[54]

Nor can improved family life or the better use of leisure effectively address the basic social problems. A happy family life is not enough. Social discipline beyond the family is required if individuals are to develop a capacity for fitting into a social situation and functioning properly in that situation.[55] Leisure time may be used to develop new stable relationships with other people. But seeking compensation in the "rose garden" cannot ease the sense of defeat at work.[56] Mayo argues that the right use of leisure is, and must be, subordinate to work actually done for the community.

Mayo's solution to the problems of social and personal disorganization lies in a combination of a restricted role for the state, the return of control to "peripheral" organizations, the creation of an administrative elite, the acquisition of scientific knowledge, and the development of an educational process appropriate to society's needs and problems. Mayo argues that the state is a subsidiary function of society whose first duty is to conserve the freedom of growth in the community. As such, the state cannot rightly do more than reflect social growth by recording the achievements of society, criticizing existing social relationships, and forbidding any contravention of established morality.[57] The state is simply an expedient to recognize social change. It cannot take the lead in creating change.

The problem with democratic government is that, in assuming that all authority derives from the state, it is likely to become tyrannical. Democracy must recognize that growth is a characteristic of social life, not the state, and that government should not exceed its moral function by undertaking social direction.[58] Democracy involves two phases: critical control from the top, and spontaneous and cooperative control from below. In emergencies, central control is required. After the emergency has passed, however, control must be transferred to peripheral groups such as informal groups in the workplace. Mayo contends that it is this transfer that distinguishes democracies from absolutist governments.[59] Continuation of central control inhibits the development of extrapolitical social activities, and these activities are crucial to social growth.

If the peripheral organizations are to function properly, Mayo argues that knowledge of human nature must be expanded, an informed administrative elite must be created, and the system of education must be improved. According to Mayo, societies suffer and die from ignorance. The particular ignorance of modern society is its ignorance of human nature.[60] The task of modern society is to substitute intelligent understanding for the integrative religious feelings of medieval times and to exorcise the current sense of social futility and hopelessness. Such understanding can come only from scientific analysis of the human situation based on direct observation. That is, we must initially develop what Mayo calls "knowledge-of-acquaintance," coming from direct experience, rather than mere "knowledge about," which relies on reflective and abstract thinking. Only then can we proceed to the development of appropriate skills, experimentation, and logic in the scientific quest.[61] Most critically, the industrial situation must be better understood. Industrial research must be concerned not only with the physiological and biochemical but also with the psychological and social factors of industry.[62]

The second requirement for effective democratic development, in its broader sense, is the creation of an informed administrative elite. Mayo contends that democracy has given too much attention to Rousseau and too little to Machiavelli. Rousseau relied too much on the "pious hope" that desires inimical to the general welfare would somehow be canceled in general discussion. Machiavelli recognized that administrators must set themselves to the task of understanding human motives, cultivating desirable social movements, and checking the undesirable.[63] Mayo asserts that civilization breaks down because of problems in administration and that democracy, in particular, has failed to realize the importance of administrative knowledge and skill. On morality, every individual must be judged equally. Scientific questions should be determined by skilled investigators, however, and the widest knowledge and the highest skills should be sovereign in these matters, not the opinion of "collective mediocrity."[64] Once again, the critical arena for the identification and development of an informed administrative elite is in industry. Industry should be guided by administrators who recognize the importance of the human factor and who can learn ways of adapting workers to the new industrial system by creating conditions that prevent an emergence of obsessive reverie.[65]

The final requirement for effective democratic development is to improve the system of education. Mayo asserts that the prime duty of education is to emancipate people from fear through understanding.[66] Education is a prelude to adventure and should light up the imagination of youth. Mayo contends that morbid adolescents of forty have had too much to say in the instruction of youth.[67] Youth scorns "dull compromises," and that spirit is the essence of civilization and morality.

The primary focus of education should be to develop a critical control of reverie thinking and to get the subjects of education into the reveries of students. This will eliminate dangerous reveries and demonstrate both the right use of reverie and the right relationship between reverie and concentration. Mayo argues that one can eliminate the eccentric from industry, but it is far better to eliminate eccentricities from otherwise normal persons in industry by better education.[68] In this way, we can reach the "nightmind" of the child and the savage surviving in the civilized adult and free humanity from the bonds of irrationality and superstition.

Mayo recognizes that we cannot return to the simplicity of traditional society.[69] Technical advance is required to establish the better standards of living vital to effective democracy. Nevertheless, securing collaboration in an industrial society cannot be left to chance. The state can play a role, but it is a necessarily limited role because compulsion has never succeeded in rousing eager and spontaneous cooperation. Mayo's vision is an "adaptive society" characterized by control from below by persons with skills in social relationships and communication.[70] The adaptive society would be based on an attitude of spontaneous cooperation, and would be free from irrationality and obsession. The path to the adaptive society is new knowledge and powers derived from scientific investigation. With this knowledge will come personal freedom, an end to industrial unrest, and the possibility of world peace as societies learn to cooperate in the tasks of civilization.[71]

Mayo's belief that society is not merely a horde of individuals, his conviction that knowledge of the human situation is vital to civilization, and his insistence on direct observation as a first step in the acquisition of that knowledge led him to a series of empirical studies designed to start the process of accumulating "knowledge-of-acquaintance" in the industrial setting.

Mayo's Empirical Studies

The Philadelphia Textile Mill

In 1923, while Mayo was still at the University of Pennsylvania, he was asked to undertake a study of turnover and morale in the spinning department of a Philadelphia textile mill.[72] The department was experiencing a turnover rate of 250 percent and the workers had a generally low level of morale. Previous experiments with a variety of incentive schemes had not been successful in either reducing turnover or improving morale.

The company itself was, according to Mayo, well organized with management that was both enlightened and humane. The president of the company was well regarded and generally inspired the loyalty of his workers. Paradoxically, conditions in the spinning department were not noticeably inferior to those in the rest of the mill. But the work in the department was repetitive and demanded constant vigilance as piecers walked up and down work alleys twisting together broken threads; and the work was essentially solitary. Mayo found workers in the department to be possessed of reveries that were "monotonously and uniformly pessimistic."[73]

Mayo decided to test the effects of rest periods on work attitudes and performance. Mayo also decided to adopt a research procedure that he was to employ throughout his empirical investigations. This approach combined direct observation of the work and working conditions and interviews designed to evoke the attitudes of the workers about their work.

The rest pauses produced beneficial results almost immediately. Labor turnover in the department was effectively eliminated, productivity increased, workers felt less fatigued, and melancholic reveries disappeared. Shortly thereafter, under heavy demands for production, rest periods were abandoned. The effects were a drop in productivity and a return of pessimistic reveries. Rest periods were then reinstituted, but this time they were to be "earned" according to level of production rather than be regularly scheduled. During this time, productivity increased, but did not attain the levels reached in the original rest-pause experiment. Spurred by these results, the president of the company ordered the reestablishment of regularly scheduled rest periods, which resulted in a 10 percent increase in production. Finally, rest periods were alternated among work groups in the department with the groups themselves determining the method of alternation. Again, the results were positive. Morale improved, fatigue was diminished, absenteeism decreased, and there was no labor turnover.

Mayo summarized his findings as follows:

1. Spinning produces postural fatigue and induces pessimistic reverie.

2. Rest pauses relieve these conditions and increase productivity by restoring normal circulation, relieving postural fatigue, and interrupting pessimistic reverie.

3. Rest pauses are more effective when they are regular and the workers have received instruction in the techniques of relaxation.

4. The life of the worker outside the mill is improved as workers become more interested in their families and more sober.[74]

More generally, Mayo interprets these findings in a manner consistent with his broader perspectives on the industrial environment. Mayo argues that the attitudes of workers in the spinning department were of paramount importance. The problem of turnover was not the result of an organic reaction to working conditions, but the result of an emotional response of the workers to the work performed. Furthermore, monotony per se was not the problem, but repetitive work done under a social condition of isolation that led to abnormal preoccupations.[75] Solitary and repetitive work done on a daily basis intensifies tendencies toward pessimistic or paranoid meditation, and this, Mayo argues, is the single most important factor in productive efficiency.[76] Thus unrest, manifested here in high rates of turnover and absenteeism, is a symptom of disturbances to the equilibrium between the worker and his work, accompanied by pessimistic preoccupations that determine the individual's attitude toward work.

Mayo asserts that the results of the institution of rest periods was as much a product of the mental interruption of obsessive reveries as it was the elimination of physical fatigue.[77] Mayo's explanation for the increase in work effectiveness goes beyond the rest periods themselves, however. He asserts that several changes had been introduced that combined to change the human atmosphere in the department, making it more "social" and lending dignity to the work performed.[78] Social interrelationships improved, workers welcomed the opportunity to express themselves freely to a trained interviewer, the experiment itself demonstrated management's interest in the workers, and the president of the company had helped transform a "horde of solitaries" into a social group by giving the workers control over the rest periods.[79]

The Western Electric Researches

Mayo's next major involvement in direct observation was in the famed Western Electric researches, conducted at the company's Hawthorne Plant near Chicago, which ran from 1927 to 1932.[80] The work of Mayo and his associates had been preceded by a series of experiments conducted by engineers at Western Electric concerning the effect of the degree of illumination on worker productivity.[81] In the first of these experiments, three departments were exposed to different levels of lighting. The results were inconsistent. In one department, output fluctuated with no direct relationship to the intensity of illumination. In the second department, output remained relatively stable over the period of the experiment. In the third department, output increased as the level of lighting increased, but failed to decline when the level of lighting was decreased.

Subsequent investigations did little to resolve these inconsistencies. In a second experiment, a test group and a control group were subjected to different levels of lighting. Output in the test group increased, as was expected; however, output also increased in the control group where the level of lighting was held constant. A third experiment involved just the use of artificial lighting to afford greater control over the degree of illumination. In this case, output suffered under decreased lighting only when the workers complained that they could barely see. Further informal experimentation served only to add to the confusion as two operators maintained their level of productivity even when the degree of illumination was reduced to the approximate level of moonlight.

Confounded by these results, company officials sought the advice of Mayo and his associates at Harvard. The Harvard group suggested that human response had defeated the purpose of the lighting experiments. The workers, they argued, had reacted to the experiments themselves, not to the level of lighting, and speculated that the implicit expression of management's concern in merely conducting the experiments had been a determining factor. This reaction was to become known as the "Hawthorne Effect."

At the outset, Mayo's involvement in the Western Electric researches was minimal. Indeed, Mayo never participated directly in the collection of data at the Hawthorne plant.[82] Mayo became more prominently involved later in the experiments when problems with the interpretation of the results arose.[83] From that point, Mayo visited the plant frequently, assisted in training interviewers, and participated in the interpretation of the results.[84]

Rest-Pause Experiments. The Harvard group's initial interest was in the effect of fatigue and monotony on work performance. Accordingly, the researchers decided to test for the effects of rest periods, and variations in the length of the workday and workweek. Since it was believed that the illumination studies had suffered from inadequate experimental controls, a small group was selected and was to be separated from the rest of the plant. Given the interest in monotony and fatigue, a repetitive task was decided on—the assembly of telephone relays. Two female relay assembly operators were chosen on the basis of their experience and cooperative attitude. These operators then were allowed to choose the three other participants. The operators were told about the nature of the experiment and were told specifically that the purpose of the experiment was not to increase productivity. It was only expected that they work at a normal pace.

An observer was assigned to the test room with responsibility for maintaining a friendly atmosphere in the room and for keeping records of conversations and group relationships. In addition, data were collected on such items as the quantity of output (recorded unobtrusively by a mechanical device), quality of output, reasons for temporary stops, time spent in bed every night, the medical condition of the operators, room temperature, outside temperature, and relative humidity. Finally, all the operators were periodically interviewed on a separate and individual basis.

Despite the researchers' efforts to establish rigorous experimental controls and the elaborate array of statistics collected, a number of changes in the relay assembly test room escaped control and went unmeasured. These changes, as we shall see, loomed large in the eventual interpretation of the experiment's results. Most critically, the payment system, the style of supervision, and the social environment were changed in the test room. Incentives in the test room were based on that group's productivity. Rewards were thus more closely linked to individual performance in the test room than in the larger group working in the regular plant. The method of supervision in the test room was also different, as the observer took over some supervisory functions and became responsible for maintaining a friendly climate. Finally, the social environment changed as the operators became members of a small group and were allowed to talk more freely than at their previous stations.[85]

There were five major periods in this study, which lasted from 1927 through 1932. In the first period, productivity records were established while the operators were still in their regular department. In the second period, the workers were moved to the test room to become familiar with their new surroundings, but no other changes were made. The third period involved the introduction of an incentive plan based on the productivity of the test group itself. The fourth and fifth periods were the central focus of the experiment with rest periods of varying duration and frequency instituted in period 4 and the length of the workday and workweek manipulated in period 5.

In a pattern that was to be characteristic of most of this research, the study of the relay assembly test room produced unexpected results and, as a consequence, raised more questions than it answered. In the rest-pause experiments, output generally increased regardless of the frequency and duration of the pauses. A problem did arise in regard to the amount of talking going on in the room. This resulted in a reprimand from the supervisor, an attempt to get the women to pay more attention to their work by requiring that they call out difficulties, and the return of two of the operators to the regular department because of the talking problem and "behavior approaching gross insubordination."[86] Variations in the length of the workday and workweek produced similar results. Only when the length of the working day was reduced by a full hour did output suffer. Of particular interest was a period in which the work group was ostensibly returned to its original working conditions. Output did diminish, but it did not fall back to its original level.

Several possible explanations of the increase in productivity in the relay assembly test room were considered by the research group. The increase could be attributed to improved materials and methods of work, fatigue reduction, the reduction of monotony, the small-group incentive plan, the changed method of supervision, or the altered social situation in the test room. Improved materials and methods of work were dismissed as being relatively insignificant.[87] The idea of fatigue reduction was examined more closely, but found wanting. This conclusion was based primarily on the finding that when conditions were supposedly returned to their initial state, production did not fall back to the pre-experimental level.[88] In addition, physiological tests indicated that the operators were working well within their physical capacities, and output did not follow the pattern predicted by a hypothetical "fatigue curve."[89] The monotony hypothesis was also rejected, but somewhat more equivocally. Output, again, did not follow the predicted "monotony curve," but it was felt that monotony might not be fully reflected in output measures.[90]

Thus the list of possible factors in increased productivity in the relay assembly test room was reduced to the incentive system, methods of supervision, and a changed social environment. To measure the possible effects of the incentive system, two more experiments were undertaken. In one, a second relay assembly test room, *only* the method of incentives was changed—that is, pay was based on small-group output.[91] In the other, involving the task of splitting sheets of mica into thinner strips, the conditions were to be the same as in the first relay assembly test room *with the exception* of the small-group incentive plan.[92] Comparisons of these two groups, it was believed, would permit an assessment of the relative impact of incentives versus other working conditions on output.

In the second relay assembly test room, five women were selected by the supervisor and paid separately from the rest of the department. The result was a 12.6 percent increase in output with a decline in productivity when the experiment ended. Thus the findings seemingly substantiated the incentive hypothesis. But the researchers believed that a rivalry between the first and second relay assembly test rooms had also contributed to the increase in productivity.[93]

The mica-room experiment was designed to replicate the conditions of the first relay assembly test room except for the incentive system. Two operators were selected by the research team, and those two chose the remaining three participants.[94] As in the first relay assembly test room, rest pauses and the length of the working day and week were varied.[95] The results were a moderate decline in output when the workers were first moved into the test room, a modest increase in output when rest pauses were introduced, a moderate decline after that point, and constant output over the final stages of the experiment. Thus, instead of a continuous increase, productivity showed little consistent relationship to the rest pauses and increased only after the initial introduction of the rest pauses. Undismayed, the researchers proceeded to explain away these seemingly perverse results. The decline in output after the introduction of the rest pauses was attributed to anxiety about possible cutbacks in employment, which constituted "interfering preoccupations."[96] Furthermore, the researchers concluded that the mica-room experiment was only a "story of individuals" without an incentive system designed to promote group solidarity.[97]

Based on these findings, it was concluded that incentives were not the sole explanation for the observed increases in productivity. The negative evidence of the mica-room experiment regarding manipulation of working conditions other than incentives was suspect because it fell short of experimental requirements. The positive findings on the relationship between incentives and productivity in the second relay assembly test room was attributed to a rivalry between the test rooms rather than the incentive system itself. Finally, it was observed that, though productivity had increased in the second relay assembly test room, the increase had not been as great as the 30 percent increase in the first relay assembly test room. This further reinforced the conclusion that something more than incentives were involved in the increase in productivity in the first relay assembly test room. In addition, the research group felt that whatever the effect of incentives may have been, that effect was dependent on other social factors.[98]

Thus, by a process of elimination, it was decided that the combination of a changed method of supervision and an altered social situation had been the primary factors in increasing output in the first relay assembly test room. Paradoxically, neither change had been intentionally introduced in the experiment itself. The new method of supervision had been the unplanned result of the research group assuming some of the functions of the regular supervisor. The new method of supervision was not necessarily less strict, but it had a different quality. Sympathetic listening replaced the giving of orders and personal criticism, and the operators felt that their new "supervisors" had a personal interest in their well-being. The work group was consulted about possible changes, it was not pushed to achieve higher output, and social conversation was permitted within the group. It was argued that these changes in the quality of supervision, as well as the segregation of the work group and the small-group incentive plan, had produced a new social situation in which the individual workers had become part of a team with a sense of comradeship among its members. A sense of social solidarity had thus been created that led to improved morale, relationships of confidence and friendliness, and enhanced work effectiveness. To Mayo, this meant that the supportive social structure had strengthened the "temperamental inner equilibrium" of the workers and allowed them to achieve a mental state that "offered a high resistance to a variety of external conditions."[99] In other words, the workers had developed a high and stable level of work effectiveness and were relatively unaffected by changes in working conditions, such as rest pauses and hours worked.

The Interviews. Given the importance attached to supervisory style and social conditions in the relay assembly test room, the next stage of the research began to focus more directly on those factors. This stage involved an interview program and was to eventually reach 21,000 of the 40,000 employees at the Hawthorne plant.[100] The interviews were originally designed to improve supervisory methods by gathering data on working conditions and workers' responses to supervision. That intention soon succumbed to the unanticipated consequences of the interviews themselves.

As a device for learning about conditions in the plant, the interviews were a notable failure. The comments on physical conditions expressed in the interviews were found to bear little relationship to the facts of the situation, criticisms addressed to persons or company policies were difficult to assess, and the interviewers had a hard time keeping the respondents to subjects the research team had intended to examine. Consequently, the interview format was changed to allow the respondents to comment on subjects of their own choosing. Under this revised format, it was soon learned that the interviews revealed more about personalities than the objective work situation and that the comments expressed in the interviews could be understood only in a context of the expectations and moods of the workers. This discovery led to a focus on the emotional significance of events and objects, as preoccupations or "obsessions" became a matter of central concern. Moreover, it was found that the interviews had a cathartic effect on the subjects and were thus of considerable therapeutic value. The welcomed opportunity to express themselves freely assisted the workers in getting rid of useless emotional complications, easing the sense of personal futility, learning to associate with others, and developing a desire to work better with management.[101]

The personal preoccupations revealed in the interviews were found to be partly a product of personal background and family environment. In a significant departure from Mayo's previous position, however, it was found that the obsessional preoccupations were also the result of the social environment in the workplace.[102] Individual attitudes were shaped by group sentiments, and those sentiments had a direct impact on work performance. This was often manifested in the form of a group concept of a "fair day's work" that was typically lower than management's expectations.[103] Thus it was concluded that the major difficulty in the work situation is not one of external influences or errors in supervision, but something more intimately human that was a product of group experience. Based on this conclusion, the focus of the research shifted once again, this time to an examination of the effect of informal social groups in the organization.

The Bank-Wiring Observation Room. The final stage of the Western Electric researches was designed to extend and confirm the observations of the interview program. In this stage, telephone bank-wiring operators were observed to study a shop situation from a sociological perspective. Fourteen men were selected for the experiment—nine wiremen, three soldermen, and two inspectors. The purpose of the experiment was explained to the men, and output records were kept prior to the beginning of the experiment. The workers were then moved to a separate room and an observer was assigned to act as a "disinterested spectator," looking for evidence of an informal group and attempting to understand the functions of such a group in regard to its members.[104] In addition, an outside interviewer was attached to the group to investigate individual attitudes. The group was considered a separate unit for payment purposes, and the incentive system was designed to tie individual earnings to group output. The study was conducted from November 1931 to May 1932.

The results of the experiment, in this case, conformed to the expectations of the research team. Group output remained at a constant level, and each individual in the group restricted his output in accordance with the group's concept of a fair day's work. In general, the social relationships within the informal group frustrated the pursuit of organizational interests as the group adopted its own performance standards and enforced them by social sanctions such as name-calling ("ratebusters," "chiselers," and "squealers") and "binging," or hitting a violator on the shoulder.[105]

The researchers concluded that the informal group had created fear about management's intentions and that the group performed the function of protecting its members from outside interference and internal indiscretions.[106] In that process, social considerations came to outweigh logical and economic considerations. Given the structure of the incentive scheme, logical and economic considerations should have led to an increase in output. Group norms took precedence over considerations of individual self-interest, however. Conformity to group norms determined whether the operator was accepted by the group and individual performance was a function of group status rather than ability.[107] According to Mayo, the informal group in the bank-wiring room was a means of resisting rapid changes in the environment that deprived work of its social meaning and over which the group had little control.[108] Thus, protection of the group became more important than spontaneous cooperation in the service of organizational objectives.

The Southern California Aircraft Industry

Mayo's final venture in direct observation was another study of absenteeism and turnover, this time in the Southern California aircraft industry during World War II.[109] Adopting a somewhat broader sociological perspective, Mayo and his associates first examined the community environment to look for possible causes of high rates of absenteeism and turnover in the industry. They concluded that the restless population movement characteristic of the area at that time was not the basic problem. The draft had withdrawn workers who had previously held work teams together. There had been similar occurrences elsewhere, however, and Mayo asserts that such external forces will have a major impact only when management has not been sufficiently attentive to the development of cohesive working groups in their organizations.[110]

Consequently, as had been the case at Western Electric, the study focused on social factors internal to the organization as probable determinants of absenteeism and turnover. The study also had a progressively narrowing perspective, moving from an industrywide focus to an examination of a single company, selected departments within that company, and, finally, a detailed analysis of a single work center that had a low rate of absenteeism.

The findings pretty much followed those of the Western Electric research. It was found that the rate of absenteeism and turnover was a function of the formation of work "teams." Absenteeism and turnover were lower when these teams created a condition of "active cooperation" with the company's policies and purposes.[111] Furthermore, team formation was found to be largely dependent on the quality of supervision and leadership—both formal and informal—in the work group. Successful supervisors were those who had been trained in the techniques of handling human relations; had assistants to take care of routine and technical problems, thus freeing the supervisor to respond to human problems; and allowed the workers to participate in the determination of working conditions.[112] Informal leadership was also found to be important. In one successful work center, the work was actually in charge of a leadman, and the foreman rarely visited the center. The leadman, a college man with considerable experience in the industry, facilitated the work of others by giving technical, personal, and social help to individual workers; seeing that adequate work materials were available; and handling contacts with the rest of the company.[113]

These findings were corroborated in interviews with workers who were irregular in their attendance. The "irregulars" were characterized by a condition of personal disorganization and discontent. Many left the job because their work had never become an integral part of their total life. This condition was traced to supervisors who were inconsiderate and showed "irritable impatience" rather than personal consideration and understanding.[114] As a result, the irregulars were simply a collection of unrelated individuals, not members of a cohesive group or team.

Mayo views the results of this study as being consistent with the findings of his previous investigations. The desire for association, he maintains, is deeply rooted, and informal social groups will inevitably exist. The only question is whether the attitude of the group will be one of hostility and wariness or one of wholehearted cooperation and friendliness.[115] The development of the social group should not be left to chance. Instead, management must be sensitive to the need for a meaningful social-group experience and create the conditions under which that need can be fulfilled in a manner compatible with effectiveness in the achievement of organizational objectives.

The Impact of Direct Observation on Mayo's Perspectives

Most of Mayo's thoughts about the nature of the "industrial problem" were pretty much in place before his empirical investigations. A consistent theme in his writings is that the problem is the maladjusted individual, besieged by evil reveries, dominated by obsessive preoccupations, and afflicted by irrational behavior. Whereas Mayo earlier viewed the problem in terms of personal history and a broader malaise of social disorganization, however, his empirical research led him to concentrate on the role of the social group within the organization in determining the individual's attitude toward work. These groups can either assist the organization in achieving its goals or can thwart those efforts.

Mayo argues that there are three persistent problems of management: the application of science and technical skill, the systematic ordering of operations, and the organization of teamwork or sustained cooperation.[116] Management, he charges, has paid too much attention to the first two elements and too little to the third. In particular, management has failed to perceive the importance of informal social groups, which, Mayo argues, are a response to a basic human need. Without a supportive social environment, workers become preoccupied by their personal situations and irrational in their behavior. This results in a sense of exasperation and futility and the likelihood of conflict between loyalty to the company and loyalty to the social group.

Accordingly, management must assume responsibility for creating conditions conducive to the development of a cooperative team spirit. Appeals to technical and economic logic are not sufficient. Technological change must be conditioned by an awareness of the limitations of, and consequences for, social change. Economic incentives can help to promote greater work effectiveness, but only in an otherwise healthy social situation. In short, management must learn to appeal to individual and social emotions and attitudes in a more intimately human way. Psychotherapeutic techniques can help individuals get rid of their obsessive preoccupations. Such techniques, however, must be coupled with a conscious effort to improve the social climate in the organization. A key ingredient in this effort is the supervisor, who, operating at the point of human interface in the organization, can play an important role in fostering supportive interpersonal relationships and team morale.

Mayo's Critics

Mayo's research, and more particularly his interpretation of that research, has raised a virtual firestorm of criticism. The criticism has been directed at both Mayo's philosophical values and his methodology and has centered on the most famous of his enterprises, the Western Electric researches.[117]

The ideological critiques have taken exception to Mayo's neglect of conflict in the organization and what is perceived to be Mayo's bias in favor of management. The critics charge that Mayo, blinded by his assumption of a natural harmony of interests in the workplace and his single-minded pursuit of spontaneous cooperation, has failed to recognize the inevitability, indeed desirability, of social conflict. It is argued that workers and management are fundamentally in conflict and that spontaneous cooperation and unanimity of purpose are, therefore, impossible.[118] Thus, industrial research should be directed at developing means for accommodating conflict rather than disregarding it. Central to this concern is the role of unions. Mayo, as we have seen, had little regard for unions and collective bargaining, and he conducted his research in organizations that had no unions. On this basis, Mayo is castigated for neglecting a major mechanism for conflict resolution, both by virtue of his personal bias and in his choice of research location.[119]

Furthermore, it is argued that where Mayo did observe conflict, he attributed it to workers' sentiments and attitudes rather than to objective working and social conditions. For instance, in the bank-wiring observation room experiment at Western Electric, Mayo stresses group sentiments and status as the determinants of output restriction as opposed to hostility to management bred of more concrete considerations, such as disputes over money, power, and control. The critics maintain that it is at least equally as plausible to interpret the group's restriction of output as a *collective* defense of economic interests in which the motivating impulse was resistance to change adversely affecting those interests, not simply as a primitive urge to form a tribal society in miniature.[120] Viewed in this light, worker resistance could even reflect worker solidarity that transcends individual psychological distinctions and immediate financial gain. In other words, industrial conflict, instead of being an irrational reaction to evil reveries, may well be the product of conflicts in values arising from the socioeconomic structure. As such, industrial conflict represents a power struggle between management and the workers over the division of the joint product and goes beyond the factory gate to a more general condition of class conflict.[121]

The critics also charge Mayo with a pro-management bias produced, in part, by his abhorrence of conflict. Mayo, it is argued, assumes that happiness and personal security are found in the subordination of the individual to a common purpose and rests his hopes on a managerial elite to rescue society from the ravages of personal independence. Thus the critics contend that Mayo's goal is, in fact, a static

145

society in which workers are to be manipulated by a benevolent leadership that requires that workers not only do the work but like it as well.[122] From this perspective, the organization is taken as a given, and the individual is expected to change. Little consideration is given to the possibility that management's orientation, not that of the worker, may be "defective."[123] Hence, the management techniques proposed by Mayo simply amount to new methods of social control designed to manipulate the worker's emotional and mental processes in order to build a harmonious organization. Exercises of managerial authority are simply disguised by the vocabulary of "human relations."[124]

Mayo's bias in favor of management is also said to be revealed in his emphasis on the skills of cooperation without reference to the aims of that cooperation. Although Mayo claims to be interested only in the efficiency of work performance, the concept of efficiency, it is argued, is empty without some notion of social value; and in the absence of an explicit statement of other social values, efficiency will be oriented toward the goals of management.[125] Thus, Mayo sees workers as "cooperating" only when they accept the goals of management.[126]

Finally, Mayo is charged not only with neglecting the inevitability of conflict but ignoring its desirability. Mayo's critics contend that a plurality of social relationships in which individuals are members of groups both within and outside the workplace produces divided loyalties, which are admittedly conducive to conflict, but also vital to freedom of choice.[127] This freedom is necessary to resist the totalitarian demands of any single organization; and conflict, within the rules of the game, protects the rights of the individual via-à-vis the organization.

Mayo's work has also been subjected to substantial empirical criticism. Two of the more prominent empirical critiques are those by Carey and by Franke and Kaul.[128] Both critiques concern the rest-pause experiments in the Western Electric study.

Carey challenges Mayo's interpretation of the results of the experiments in the two relay assembly test rooms and the mica-splitting room. He contends that Mayo and his associates understated the role of financial incentives and distorted the findings on supervisory style. On incentives, Carey notes that in the second relay assembly test room, where only the method of payment was changed, output increased while the incentive system was in force and decreased thereafter. This, Carey argues, would normally be taken as evidence of a direct and favorable influence of incentives on output. Mayo chose to disregard this conclusion and attributed the increase in output to an alleged rivalry between the first and second relay assembly groups. In addition, in the mica-splitting room where there was no change in the incentive system, individual rates of output increased, but total group output declined because of a shortening of the workweek. Mayo suggests that "friendly supervision" led to an increase in productivity. The individual increase, Carey contends, may have been due simply to fatigue reduction from a shorter workweek. Moreover, there was a *decline* in group productivity, thus casting doubt on the importance of new modes of supervision. Furthermore, since a combination of incentives and friendly supervision in the first relay assembly test room led to a substantial increase in total output and friendly supervision alone led to no increase in total output in the mica-splitting room, Carey maintains that all of the increase in output in the first relay assembly test room could logically be attributed to financial incentives alone.

Carey also challenges Mayo's interpretation of the role of supervisory style in the first relay assembly test room. He argues that supervision was not as consistently "friendly" as Mayo suggests. Operators were required to call out their mistakes as a means of keeping their minds on their jobs, were subjected to numerous reprimands for talking too much, and were warned about the loss of their free snacks if their performance did not improve. These threats culminated in the dismissal of two operators from the test room for insubordination. Carey maintains that there were actually three phases of the experiment identified by the kind of supervision exercised. In the first phase, supervision was generally friendly, casual, and low pressure. But there was no substantial increase in productivity in this phase. The second phase was marked by increasingly stern and close supervision, with no change in output. In phase 3, which followed the replacement of the two operators, supervision again became free and friendly, and output increased sharply. Carey suggests that the increase in output in phase 3 may have been the result of an exercise of supervisory discipline in phase 2 (the dismissal of the operators) and the higher productivity of, and leadership roles assumed by, the replacement operators. In addition, the relaxation of supervisory control in phase 3 may have been the *result* of higher productivity, not its cause.

Carey asserts that the Western Electric research was characterized by "gross error and incompetence." [129] The researchers misinterpreted the data, failed to establish sample groups representative of some larger population, ignored the systematic use of control groups, and rested their conclusions on the statistically unreliable findings of a study of only five operators. As a result, Carey contends, "The limitations of the Hawthorne studies clearly render them incapable of yielding serious support for any sort of generalization whatever." [130]

Franke and Kaul offer a somewhat more dispassionate and systematic critique than that of Carey. Franke and Kaul focus on the measured variables of the first relay assembly test room—rest pauses, hours of the working days, days in the working week, and the small-group incentive plan—plus the inadvertent changes caused by the replacement of two operators (conceptualized à la Carey as an exercise of managerial discipline) and the onset of the Great Depression. These variables are used in time-series regression analysis to determine their explanatory power regarding the quantity and quality of work for both the group and individual members of the group.

For group productivity, the variables listed account for 97 percent of the variance in hourly and weekly output, with the exercise of managerial discipline bearing the strongest relationship to both measures of group output. For the quality of group output, a measure of the quality of the materials provided to the work group was added, and the resulting equation accounted for 92 percent of the variance. Similar results were found for individuals, with the percentage of variance explained ranging from 66 to 90 percent for hourly output, 89 to 95 percent for weekly output, and 56 to 98 percent for quality of output.

The authors conclude that managerial discipline, the depression, and the rest pauses account for most of the variance in the quantity and quality of output in the first relay assembly test room.[131] These equations, the authors argue, are so strong that the impact of other factors, such as the social conditions emphasized but not measured by the Western Electric researchers, was likely to have been negligible.[132] Indeed, the findings suggest that it was not a relaxation of oppressive supervision but its reassertion that was the primary factor in improving the performance of the workers.[133]

To summarize, the critics charge that the research at Western Electric was superficial, missed the point, originated in the personal biases of the researchers, was deliberately formulated to favor one group over another, and was methodologically naive.[134]

Assessment and Conclusion

These critiques constitute a potentially devastating attack on Mayo's work. Nevertheless, the critiques themselves are not definitive, and rejoinders are both possible and appropriate.

In regard to the ideological critiques, it is clear that Mayo assumed a harmony of interests in the community and in the organization. Mayo's critics merely propose an alternative assumption—an inevitable conflict of interests—rather than present evidence to contradict Mayo's assumption. Mayo may have been unfair in branding the assumption of a conflict of interest as "obsessive." Indeed, his own stance, and the tenacity with which he maintained it, would appear to be no less obsessive. But the burden of proof regarding this critical assumption is as great for his critics as it is for Mayo.

Mayo would also deny that he had a bias in favor of management. Mayo repeatedly stated that he had no intrinsic interest in increased productivity.[135] Productivity is only a measure of the worker's capacity to sustain interest in work under a variety of conditions and an indicator of the performance of the human organism. Thus, Mayo's concern was human behavior in general, not its particular manifestation in productivity.

Turning to the empirical critiques, the critics first argue that Mayo understates the role of financial incentives in motivating behavior. But Mayo did not claim that financial incentives were unimportant. He did say that such incentives will have the expected effect only when acting on an appropriate social situation. The differing results in the first relay assembly test room and the bank-wiring room would seem to support this assertion. In the relay assembly test room, financial incentives were associated with higher output in a supportive social environment. In the bank-wiring room, incentives failed to elicit higher productivity without supportive social norms. In addition, subsequent research supports Mayo's position that the effect of financial incentives is mediated by psychological and social "filtering" processes.[136] Finally, it should be noted that Franke and Kaul failed to find evidence of a substantial independent influence for incentives on performance in the relay assembly test room.[137]

The empirical critique related to supervisory style is more troublesome. It is apparent that supervision in the relay assembly test room was not as benign as Mayo and his associates suggested. Yet Mayo was more concerned with the broader social environment of the work than with supervision per se. This is evidenced, for instance, by the fact that the Western Electric researches shifted in emphasis from supervision to the social group in the interview period and maintained that focus in the bank-wiring room study. Nor is Franke and Kaul's assertion that the explanatory power of their "measured" variables precludes a role for other social factors convincing. If the regression model is insufficiently specified and excludes variables closely related to the variables included, the observed relationships may be spurious, or the variables examined may simply be "intervening" variables (i.e., they are effective only on prior conditions). In short, Mayo may have been wrong about supervision in this particular instance, but right on the effects of supportive social conditions, which he thought could be created by friendly and sympathetic supervision.

The more general empirical critique of Mayo's work is that it did not fulfill the requirements of controlled experimentation. This criticism must be considered in the broader context of Mayo's approach to scientific investigation and his objectives in the investigations he conducted. Mayo considered his work, including the research at Western

Electric, to be exploratory in nature.[138] In addition, his approach was more one of "clinical observation" than laboratory experimentation. Experiment and logic, according to Mayo, must follow, not precede, observation by which one acquires the appropriate "knowledge-of-acquaintance."

The effort at controlled experimentation in the Western Electric researches was abandoned during the rest-pause experiments at about the time that Mayo became more involved in the studies. From that point on, the research no longer focused on single variables but moved to the broader constellation of social factors in the work environment. The investigations lost some precision in the process, but Mayo believed this to be inevitable. Discussing his later study in Southern California, Mayo states: "Our concern was with significant approximations rather than complete accuracy; complete accuracy can be had only in mathematics; in factual determination an approximation is the best that can be achieved."[139] With his emphasis on "habitual, intuitive familiarity with the data," Mayo was impatient with what he considered to be a vain pursuit of quantification and experimental controls. In Mayo's words, "the poor observer ... continues dogmatically onward with his original thesis, lost in a maze of correlations, long after the facts have shrieked in protest against the interpretation put upon them."[140] In short, Mayo was prepared, when necessary, to sacrifice illusory precision for real understanding.

Nevertheless, the foregoing considerations do not entirely absolve Mayo of his scientific responsibilities. The weaknesses in the research design and methodology employed by Mayo throughout his empirical investigations make his work subject to question and his speculative interpretations of that work subject to controversy. The Western Electric researches, in particular, embodied a progression of unanticipated outcomes and interpretations based on mere surmise as to why the expected did not occur. What ended up being the primary concern in the investigations—conditions in the social group—were never systematically examined.

These methodological ambiguities, in turn, leave Mayo open to the charge that he merely discovered what he was looking for in his empirical studies, based on previously held beliefs. Thus Mayo may have fallen prey to his own criticism of the "crowd psychologists," of whom he wrote: "Their opinion of humanity is determined before the discussion begins; they seek only indications that fortify or 'rationalize' their preconceived ideas."[141]

Mayo also remains vulnerable to the charge that his work has a pro-management bias, regardless of his intentions. Although Mayo's emphasis changes from the individual to the social group in his empirical investigations, the "maladjusted" individual remains the source of the industrial problem. Thus it is the individual who is to be "cured" under the benevolent and informed guidance of an administrative elite. Mayo's story of an encounter with a young radical is, perhaps, instructive in regard to the nature of the cure. The radical "suffered" from resistance to authority, which was the product of an unhappy relationship with his drunken father. After therapeutic counseling, the young man lost interest in his radical activities, abandoned his former associates, took a clerical position, and kept it.[142] In short, the cure was an accommodation to authority, which some might consider obeisance. One is reminded of Clark Kerr's protest that management should buy the labor power of the worker and leave his psyche alone.[143]

For Mayo, the question is not who is to control, but whether control will be exercised on a rational basis.[144] But this pronouncement simply evades a fundamental issue and admits the possibility of the manipulation of the individual to serve the purposes of management. Mayo's primary concern may not have been improved productivity, but the techniques he offers have a substantial manipulative potential, whether for ill or for good.

Despite these reservations, Mayo's ideas have had an undeniable impact on the study of organizations. Mayo's attention to defining his underlying assumptions and exploring the broader implications of his studies is refreshing in a field that has become dismayingly bereft of such considerations. One does not have to agree with Mayo's position to appreciate the fact that critical issues are raised and examined in his works. Moreover, Mayo's work was largely responsible for a major shift in the study of organizations. His concern with the attitudes and sentiments of the worker, the importance he attached to the social group in determining individual behavior, and his search for "knowledge-of-acquaintance" based on direct observation, all served as an inspiration for a succeeding generation of scholars.

Notes

1. Information on Mayo's life, except where otherwise noted, is taken from George F.F. Lombard, "George Elton Mayo," in *Dictionary of American Biography*, supplement 4, 1946–50 (New York: Scribner's, 1974), 564–66.

2. Elton Mayo, *Democracy and Freedom: An Essay in Social Logic* (Melbourne, Australia: Macmillan, 1919).

3. "The Fruitful Errors of Elton Mayo," *Fortune* 34, no. 5 (November 1946): 181.

4. Elton Mayo, *The Human Problems of an Industrial Civilization* (New York: Viking, 1960).

5. Elton Mayo, *The Social Problems of an Industrial Civilization* (Boston: Graduate School of Business Administration, Harvard University, 1945).

6. Elton Mayo, *The Political Problems of an Industrial Civilization* (two lectures delivered at a conference on Human Relations and Administration, Harvard University Graduate School of Business Administration, 10 and 11 May 1947).

7. F.J. Roethlisberger, *The Elusive Phenomenon* (Boston: Division of Research, Harvard Graduate School of Business Administration), 50 and 51.

8. Mayo, *Human Problems*, ix.

9. Roethlisberger, *Elusive Phenomenon*, 50–52.

10. Ibid., 30.

11. Mayo, *Social Problems*, 16.

12. Roethlisberger, *Elusive Phenomenon*, 36.

13. Elton Mayo, "The Great Stupidity," *Harper's Magazine* 151 (July 1925): 230–31.

14. Mayo, *Political Problems*, 6.

15. Elton Mayo, "Civilization—The Perilous Adventure," *Harper's Magazine* 149 (October 1924): 590.

16. Elton Mayo, "Routine Interaction and the Problem of Collaboration," *American Sociological Review* 4, no. 3 (June 1939): 335.

17. Mayo, *Social Problems*, 41.

18. Elton Mayo, "The Maladjustment of the Industrial Worker," in *Wertheim Lectures on Industrial Relations, 1928* (Cambridge, Mass.: Harvard University Press, 1929), 172.

19. Mayo, *Political Problems*, 20.

20. Mayo, *Democracy and Freedom*, 5.

21. Mayo, *Human Problems*, 116.

22. Mayo, *Democracy and Freedom*, 65.

23. Ibid., 20.

24. Ibid., 27.

25. Mayo, *Human Problems*, 123–24.

26. Ibid., 158.

27. Ibid., 125.

28. Elton Mayo, "Irrationality and Revery," *Personnel Journal* 1, no. 10 (1923): 481.

29. Elton Mayo, "Great Stupidity," 230.

30. Ibid., 233.

31. Elton Mayo, "Psychiatry and Sociology in Relation to Social Disorganization," *American Journal of Sociology* 42 (May 1937): 830.

32. Ibid.

33. Elton Mayo, "Civilization," 594.

34. Elton Mayo, "Sin with a Capital 'S,'" *Harper's Magazine* 154 (April 1927): 544.

35. Elton Mayo, "Civilized Unreason," *Harper's Magazine* 148 (March 1924): 530.

36. Ibid.

37. Mayo, *Democracy and Freedom*, 37.

38. Mayo, "The Great Stupidity," 231.

39. Mayo, *Human Problems*, 174.

40. Mayo, "Civilization," 591.

41. Mayo, "Maladjustment of Industrial Worker," 170; and idem, *Human Problems*, 162.

42. Mayo, "Maladjustment of Industrial Worker," 171.

43. Ibid., 194.

44. Mayo, *Human Problems*, 162.

45. Elton Mayo, "What Every Village Knows," *Survey Graphic* 26, no. 12 (December 1937): 696.

46. Ibid., 697.

47. Mayo, "Great Stupidity," 233.

48. Mayo, *Democracy and Freedom*, 47.

49. Ibid., 38.

50. Ibid., 12.

51. Mayo, "Maladjustment of Industrial Worker," 167.

52. Mayo, *Democracy and Freedom*, 58; and idem, "Great Stupidity," 229, 231.

53. Mayo, "Great Stupidity," 231.

54. Mayo, "Irrationality and Revery," 481.

55. Mayo, "Psychiatry and Sociology," 829.

56. Mayo, "Great Stupidity," 230.

57. Mayo, *Democracy and Freedom*, 73.

58. Ibid.

59. Elton Mayo, "Research in Human Relations," *Personnel* 16, no. 4 (1941): 267–68.

60. Mayo, "Civilization," 590–91.

61. Mayo, "Social Problems," 19.

62. Mayo, "Maladjustment of Industrial Worker," 191.

63. Mayo, "Great Stupidity," 226.

64. Mayo, *Democracy and Freedom*, 57.

65. Mayo, "Maladjustment of Industrial Worker," 195.

66. Mayo, "Civilization," 593.

67. Mayo, "Sin with a Capital 'S,'" 545.

68. Mayo, "Irrationality and Revery," 483.

69. Mayo, *Social Problems*, 9.

70. Ibid., 11.

71. Mayo, *Democracy and Freedom*, 70.

72. This research is reported in Elton Mayo, "Revery and Industrial Fatigue," *Personnel Journal* 3, no. 8 (December 1924): 273–81.

73. Ibid., 274.

74. Ibid., 281; Mayo, "Maladjustment of Industrial Worker," 184.

75. Mayo, "Revery and Industrial Fatigue," 280.

76. Ibid., 279.

77. Ibid., 281.

78. Mayo, "What Every Village Knows," 696.

79. Mayo, *Social Problems*, 67.

80. For a comprehensive report of this study, see F. J. Roethlisberger and William J. Dickson, *Management and the Worker*, (Cambridge, Mass.: Harvard University Press, 1939).

81. Ibid., 14–18.

82. Roethlisberger, *Elusive Phenomenon,* 48, 49.

83. Ibid., 48.

84. This association was never very formal. True to Mayo's personal predilections, the collaboration was spontaneous with no formal contracts or agreements. See ibid.

85. Ibid., 39.

86. Ibid., 54.

87. Ibid., 87.

88. Ibid.

89. Ibid., 127, 117.

90. Ibid.

91. Ibid., 129–34.

92. Ibid., 134–58.

93. Ibid., 158.

94. In this case, random selection of the participants was attempted. However, only two of those selected wished to participate in the experiment. Ibid., 136.

95. The interpretation of the results of this experiment was complicated by the fact that the operators were also required to work overtime. Ibid., 134.

96. Ibid., 153.

97. Ibid., 156.

98. Ibid., 160.

99. Mayo, *Human Problems,* 92.

100. Ibid., 83.

101. Mayo, *Social Problems,* 84.

102. Roethlisberger and Dickson, *Management and the Worker,* 314.

103. Ibid., 379.

104. Ibid., 390.

105. Ibid., 522.

106. Ibid., 523.

107. Ibid., 520.

108. L.J. Henderson, T.N. Whitehead, and Elton Mayo, "The Effects of Social Environment," in *Papers on the Science of Administration,* eds. Luther Gulick and L. Urwick (New York: Institute of Public Administration, 1937), 156.

109. This research is reported in Elton Mayo and George F.F. Lombard, *Teamwork and Labor Turnover in the Aircraft Industry of Southern California,* vol. 31, no. 6, Business Research Studies no. 32 (Boston: Harvard University Graduate School of Business, Bureau of Business Research, October 1944).

110. Ibid., 6.

111. Ibid., 17.

112. Mayo, *Social Problems,* 100–101.

113. Mayo and Lombard, *Teamwork and Labor Turnover,* 19.

114. Ibid., 24.

115. Ibid., 28.

116. Ibid., 1.

117. See Henry A. Landsberger, *Hawthorne Revisited: Management and the Worker, Its Critics, and Developments in Human Relations in Industry*

(Ithaca, N.Y.: New York State School of Industrial and Labor Relations, 1958), for an extensive review of these critiques.

118. See, for instance, Herbert Blumer, "Sociological Theory in Industrial Relations," *American Sociological Review* 12, no. 3 (June 1947): 273; and Reinhard Bendix and Lloyd H. Fisher, "The Perspectives of Elton Mayo," *Review of Economics and Statistics* 31 (1949): 318.

119. Landsberger, *Hawthorne Revisited*, 43–46, 51.

120. Georges Friedmann, "Philosophy Underlying the Hawthorne Investigation," *Social Forces* 28, no. 2 (December 1949): 208.

121. Landsberger, *Hawthorne Revisited*, 63.

122. Clark Kerr, "What Became of the Independent Spirit?" *Fortune* 48 (July 1953): 111.

123. W.A. Koivisto, "Value, Theory, and Fact in Industrial Psychology," *American Journal of Sociology* 58, no. 6 (May 1953): 570.

124. Bendix and Fisher, "Perspectives of Elton Mayo," 317.

125. Koivisto, "Value, Theory, and Fact in Industrial Psychology," 567.

126. Bendix and Fisher, "Perspectives of Elton Mayo," 316.

127. Clark Kerr, "What Became of the Independent Spirit?" 134.

128. Alex Carey, "The Hawthorne Studies: A Radical Criticism," *American Sociological Review* 32, no. 3 (June 1967): 403–16; and Richard Herbert Franke and James D. Kaul, "The Hawthorne Experiments: First Statistical Interpretation," *American Sociological Review* 43, no. 5 (October 1978): 623–43.

129. Carey, "Hawthorne Studies," 416.

130. Ibid.

131. Franke and Kaul, "Hawthorne Experiments," 636.

132. Ibid., 636–37.

133. Ibid., 636.

134. Adapted from Landsberger, *Hawthorne Revisited*, 46.

135. See, for instance, Mayo, "Revery and Industrial Fatigue," 275–76; Henderson, Whitehead, and Mayo, "Effects of Social Environment," 146; and Elton Mayo, "Changing Methods in Industry," *Personnel Journal* 8, no. 5 (1939): 327.

136. Jon M. Shepard, "On Alex Carey's Radical Criticism of the Hawthorne Studies," *Academy of Management Journal* 14, no. 1 (March 1971): 30.

137. Franke and Kaul, "Hawthorne Experiments," 636.

138. Mayo, *Social Problems*, 128.

139. Ibid., 91.

140. Ibid., 116.

141. Mayo, "Civilized Unreason," 529.

142. Mayo, "Routine Interaction and Problem of Collaboration," 337–38.

143. Kerr, "What Became of the Independent Spirit?" 136.

144. Mayo, *Human Problems*, 174.

CHAPTER 6

Chester Barnard: Organizations as Systems of Exchange

With the works of Chester Barnard we reach the culmination of the trend noted in the writings of Follett and Mayo in which authority is considered to be cumulative in nature (i.e., it arises from below) rather than emanating from the apex of the organizational pyramid. At the same time, Barnard provides a conceptual justification for Mayo's assertion that the organization must learn to respond to the needs of subordinates as they perceive them if the organization is to be effective in accomplishing its objectives. Both considerations are rooted in Barnard's conceptualization of the organization as a system of exchange.

Taking them in reverse order, the idea that subordinates' needs must be satisfied as they perceive them is derived directly from Barnard's idea that the relationship between the individual and the organization constitutes a free contractual arrangement. The terms of the contract are expressed in an implicit or explicit agreement about what the organization will offer in the form of inducements and what will be expected of the individual in the form of contributions. This contract is subject to termination by either party if it believes the terms of the contract are not being fulfilled. On the individual's side, participation will continue only as long as he (or she) perceives that he is receiving more from the organization than he is required to contribute. Moreover, the balance of inducements and contributions is a matter of personal and subjective evaluation by the individual. From this perspective, it is clear that the organization must respond to the individuals' needs as they perceive them. Otherwise the individual will refuse to further participate in the organization.

The assertion that authority is cumulative in nature is similarly derived from Barnard's conceptualization of the organization as a system of exchange. Barnard takes the argument a step further by asserting that the individual's response to organizational directives is a function of incentives in the organization. In brief, he asserts that the greater the perceived balance of inducements over required contributions, the more likely it is that the individual will accept organizational directives. And, once again, that balance is a matter of personal and subjective evaluation. This, in turn, leads Barnard to define authority as "the character of a communication (order) in a formal organization by virtue of which it is accepted by a contributor to, or member of, the organization as governing the action he contributes." This definition suggests that authority resides, not in a position, but in a relationship between a superior and a subordinate and that authority is not exercised on issuance of a command but on its acceptance. Thus authority ultimately arises from the bottom, it does not descend from the top. This formulation helped establish one of the basic items on the research agenda of the Behavioral approach: the problem of securing compliance to organizational authority.

There are at least two other major contributions from Barnard. One is his assertion that organizations are, by their nature, cooperative social systems. As we shall see, Barnard derives this proposition from a series of assumptions about human nature and the reasons for association in formal organizations. A second is Barnard's specification of the functions of the leader. In a literature in which leadership would soon come to be defined as little more than supervision, Barnard charges the leader with responsibilities of more heroic dimensions. Among these is the responsibility for establishing and observing a moral code in the organization and adjudicating disputes arising therefrom.

Even these items fail to exhaust the list of Barnard's contributions to the study of organizations. Others would include the systems concept of the organization, the focus on informal organizations, the emphasis on decision making, the attention given to nonlogical thought processes, and the focus on executive organization as a communication system.[1] This is, indeed, an impressive list, and Barnard's works remain among the most widely cited in the literature.

Life

Chester Irving Barnard was born in Malden, Massachusetts, on 7 November 1886.[2] Barnard's family was one of modest means, and the home environment was "frugal but intellectual." Barnard's father, a machinist, raised young Barnard and his brother after the death of his wife. Although Barnard had little formal religious training (the family was only loosely associated with the Congregational church), the family often had philosophical discussions, and Barnard was imbued with a New England mentality stressing "independence of mind, pragmatism, respect for the individual, and industriousness." These traits would later be reflected in both Barnard's career and his writings.

Barnard was born nearsighted and had poor balance. Consequently, his involvement in the usual boyhood sports and other physical activities was limited. Instead, Barnard became a voracious reader and an accomplished pianist and was generally something of a loner. Because of limited family finances, Barnard was forced to go to work after completing grammar school, and he continued to work throughout his school years. While awaiting enrollment at Mount Hermon prep school, Barnard worked at the school's farm; later, he supported his studies at Harvard by conducting a dance orchestra and typing theses. At Harvard, Barnard majored in economics and completed three years of study. His efforts were cut short of a degree because of his lack of training in science and his consequent inability to master chemistry. Although Barnard never had an "earned" degree in higher education, he was eventually awarded honorary degrees by such prestigious universities as Brown, Princeton, Pennsylvania, and Rutgers.

In 1909 Barnard left Harvard to embark on what would prove to be a long and distinguished career with the Bell Telephone Company. Barnard began in the statistics department translating German, French, and Italian to make studies of foreign rate systems, and he soon became an expert on rate systems. In 1922 Barnard moved to Pennsylvania to become assistant to the vice-president and general manager of Bell Telephone Company of Pennsylvania. He was promoted to vice-president after four years. In 1928, at the age of forty-one, Barnard became president of Bell Telephone Company of New Jersey. Barnard left the Bell System in 1948 to assume the position of president of the Rockefeller Foundation where he served until 1952 when he reached mandatory retirement age. Barnard subsequently served as chairman of the National Science Foundation and in a variety of public capacities until his death on 7 June 1961.

While pursuing his main career interests, Barnard also compiled an impressive record of public service. Barnard served as director of the New Jersey Emergency Relief Fund in the 1930s. During World War II, Barnard was president of the United Service Organization, director of the National War Fund, and served as a member of the Naval Manpower Survey Committee. Barnard was also assistant to the secretary of the treasury, a consultant to the director of the Federal Office of Science Research and Development, a member of the Atomic Energy Committee, and a consultant to the American representative to the United Nations' Atomic Energy Committee. In addition, Barnard was a founder of the Bach Society of New Jersey, participated in various youth activities, was a member of the boards of several companies, served as director of the National Bureau of Economic Research, and maintained memberships in the American Association for the Advancement of Arts and Sciences, the American Academy of Arts and Science, the American Philosophical Society, and the Institute of World Affairs.

Barnard has been described as reserved, dignified, and somewhat awesome.[3] Unlike several of the authors discussed in this volume, Barnard never acquired a circle of personal devotees. He believed service, which requires "fortitude" and "adherence to principles," to be more important than popularity.[4] Barnard's record at New Jersey Bell brought only mixed reviews from his contemporaries.[5] Although he accepted several honorary degrees, he turned down a number of others, deeming them empty distinctions. Overall, one gets the impression of a somewhat distant and aloof man with a strong sense of propriety and dedication to his work. As we shall see, these are some of the attributes Barnard ascribed to the effective executive.

With Barnard's level of activity in other areas, it is not surprising that his publications were somewhat limited in number. Barnard started writing in the 1920s and over the course of his lifetime produced some thirty-seven published articles and one book, *The Functions of the Executive*.[6] It is the latter for which Barnard is best known and in which he made his most important contribution to the understanding of organizations.

The genesis of *The Functions* is somewhat ironic given its subsequent importance. Barnard had no original intention of writing a book. The manuscript was drawn from a series of eight lectures Barnard gave at the Lowell Institute at Harvard. Publication apparently came as a result of the desire of Harvard University Press to do something with the Lowell lecture series rather than the content of Barnard's lectures.[7] At the request of Harvard University Press, Barnard undertook the arduous task of producing a publishable manuscript. Barnard attacked the problem with characteristic care and vigor. He ended up writing sixteen drafts of the manuscript and later claimed that there is "scarcely a word that has not been thoroughly weighed."[8]

Barnard has disclaimed any specific intellectual parentage for the ideas and concepts in *The Functions*. He has stated that he did not draw ideas directly from his extensive readings nor is *The Functions*, according to Barnard, an attempt to put together a collection of his personal observations. In particular, Barnard has denied the intriguing possibility that there was some connection between his writing of *The Functions* and Elton Mayo's work at Western Electric. Despite the facts that Barnard and Mayo were acquaintances at Harvard, that Barnard worked at Bell Telephone Company and Mayo did his research at one of Bell's subsidiaries, and that there are some strong parallels between Barnard's ideas and those of Mayo, Barnard says he knew nothing of the Western Electric researches.[9]

Whatever the source of his ideas, the impact of *The Functions* is indisputable. The book is one of the most widely cited in the literature on organizations and continues to have substantial influence.[10]

The Origins and Development of Organizations

Although Barnard's book is entitled *The Functions of the Executive*, his objectives in writing the book were far broader than the title would imply. Barnard sought to join the theory of the state and the theory of organizations and to elaborate a theory of human behavior that would go beyond its economic aspects.[11] Accordingly, Barnard starts with some fundamental observations about the nature of human behavior and the genesis and nature of organizations in society that provide the context for his discussion of the role and functions of the executive in the organization.

Human Nature

Barnard begins with some fundamental assumptions about the nature of human beings. According to Barnard, human beings are physically and biologically limited, social, active and purposeful, and possess a limited degree of free will. The first three characteristics lead to cooperative behavior in organizations. Physical and biological limitations raise the necessity of cooperation if individuals are to achieve purposes beyond their own capacities. The social nature of the human being leads to cooperation with other persons to achieve those purposes. Indeed, Barnard argues that human organisms are incapable of functioning except in conjunction with other human organisms.[12] Finally, Barnard asserts that passive associations among humans are not durable—that they are impelled to do something. This need for purposeful activity leads to the organization of cooperative activities to achieve joint purposes. In short, given these assumptions, Barnard argues that organizations are, *by their nature*, cooperative endeavors.

Barnard's characterization of humans as possessing free will shapes his conception of the relationship between the individual and the organization. Although Barnard assumes that humans have the power of choice, that power is limited. Indeed, the *limitations* on choice make choice possible, since the individual would likely be overwhelmed if confronted by a large number of alternatives.[13] Consequently, the processes of choice are, in part, techniques for narrowing the range of alternatives. The limitations on choice are imposed by physical, biological, and social factors. For instance, some alternatives may be excluded because they are simply physically impossible; others may be excluded by psychological conditioning. A major limiting factor in the organizational setting is the definition of the organization's purpose, which helps to identify relevant alternatives. These limitations are necessary to choice in that they describe an area in which choice can take place. Nevertheless, an irreducible minimum of free will still exists, and this characteristic makes human behavior something more than merely conditioned response.[14]

The organization attempts to influence individual behavior either by narrowing the limitations on choice or by expanding the opportunities of choice. In the first instance, the individual is regarded as an object to be manipulated; in the second, as a subject to be persuaded.[15] In either case, the individual's response is not totally predetermined. Instead, the individual has an area of choice that both grants the individual a degree of freedom and imposes a measure of responsibility for his actions. As we shall see, both implications are integral to Barnard's formulation of the organization and the individual's role in it.

Cooperative Activity

Based on these assumptions about the nature of human beings, Barnard traces the development of cooperative activity in organizations. According to Barnard, cooperation originates in the need to accomplish purposes that cannot be accomplished individually. Cooperation is thus a means of overcoming limitations imposed by the physical environment or the biological characteristics of the individual, depending on one's perspective.[16] These limitations can be overcome by cooperation or the joining of an individual's efforts with those of others to accomplish a purpose. In short, cooperation arises from the existence of a purpose and the experience of limitations, and the limiting or strategic factor to be overcome is physical or biological in nature.

Once cooperation has been decided on, the limiting factor is social relationships. To survive, the system must not only be effective in achieving the cooperative purpose but also efficient in satisfying individual motives. In addition, the satisfactions received by each individual must be greater than the burdens imposed by the cooperative effort. The balancing of satisfactions and burdens is the method by which the system induces cooperative social relationships. Barnard notes that successful cooperation is not the normal situation. Few cooperative ventures have withstood the ravages of time, and, at any given point in time, only a small minority of society is willing to partake in a particular cooperative enterprise.[17]

Informal Organization

The next stage in the development of an organization is the informal organization.[18] Barnard describes informal organizations as transitory in character, rather structureless in form, and involving interactions that occur without any specific joint purpose. Barnard contends that informal organizations serve an important function, however, by establishing general understandings, customs, habits, and institutions, and thus create conditions favorable to the rise of formal organizations.[19] Furthermore, since informal organizations are essentially passive associations, and since Barnard maintains that human beings are by nature active and purposive, informal organization virtually compels some amount of formal organization.

Formal Organization

Formal organizations are distinguished from informal organizations in that cooperative efforts are conscious, deliberate, and purposeful. Barnard thus defines the formal organization as "a system of consciously coordinated activities or forces of two or more persons."[20] It should be noted that Barnard defines formal organizations in terms of "activities" or "forces" rather than people. Barnard reasons that since no individual is vital to the organization (i.e., one person may be freely substituted for another as long as the activity is maintained), the organization is not a group of people but a series of actions designed to achieve a goal or goals. Furthermore, the activities constituting the organization are not limited to those of employees. Instead, the activities also include those of investors, customers, clients, and suppliers. Barnard does reserve the term "organization" for that part of the cooperative system from which the physical environment and the broader social environment have been excluded. Nevertheless, social elements *within* the organization are included, and, Barnard asserts, these elements are the strategic factor in the formal organization.[21]

Complex Formal Organization. The final stage of organizational development is the complex formal organization. Barnard maintains that complex organizations grow out of simple formal organizations whose size is restricted by limits on communication.[22] Growth requires the creation of new units, but overall purpose serves as the unifying element in the complex organization. The limits of communication shape the structure of the complex organization by requiring that the subunits be specialized and relatively autonomous. The necessity of coordinated communication in a complex organization requires the location of executive functions in a single body that directs the activities of those relatively autonomous subunits by acting as a communication center. Consequently, although relatively autonomous, organizational subunits must act within the limits imposed by the larger organization.

Characteristics of Complex Formal Organizations. Barnard ascribes four basic characteristics to complex formal organizations: they are "systems," they are depersonalized, they are specialized, and they contain informal organizations. As systems, complex formal organizations possess a number of significant properties. They are composed of subsidiary or partial systems and are themselves part of a larger social system that creates a series of mutual interdependencies. The organization qua system is also dynamic because of changes in the environment and the evolution of new purposes. Finally, in a point vital to Barnard's analysis, the organization as a system is more than simply a sum of its parts.[23] This is important for two reasons. First, the posited distinction between the system and its component parts allows Barnard to distinguish between the objectives of the cooperative system as a whole and the "motives" of individuals in the system. The distinction is also important because Barnard argues that each participant in the organization must receive more in inducements (rewards) than is given in contributions to the organization. Since individual contributions are the source of organizational inducements, each individual can receive more than is contributed only if something additional is created by the operation of the system per se. This additional element is the result of cooperative activity in the organization.

A second characteristic of complex formal organizations is that organizational activities are depersonalized. As noted earlier, Barnard claims the significance of any given individual to the organization is limited. This, in turn, leads Barnard to define organizations in terms of forces or activities rather than persons. Barnard acknowledges that, outside the organization, a person is a unique individual. On joining a cooperative system, however, a person's efforts are "depersonalized" in the sense that the individual's activities must be determined by the needs of the system, not individual motives.[24] Persons are thus agents, but their actions are not personal. Instead, organizational activities are guided by an acquired organizational personality, and individual motives are satisfied by the distribution of rewards in the organization.

A third characteristic of complex formal organizations is specialization. Barnard's categorization of the bases of specialization is similar to that of Gulick. Gulick listed purpose, process, clientele (materiel), and place (geography) as the bases for organizational specialization.[25] Barnard adds time and persons to Gulick's list and cautions that the several bases of specialization are mutually interdependent. Specialization by person, or "associational specialization," as Barnard calls it, is the most important addition from Barnard's perspective with his emphasis on the social factors in organizational behavior. Barnard argues that specialized units should be composed of socially compatible persons to foster cooperation and minimize conflict.[26]

Nonetheless, Barnard felt that purpose is the primary aspect of specialization. Specialization by purpose involves the progressive breakdown of the overall organizational purpose or purposes into intermediate or more detailed objectives that actually constitute means of achieving the ultimate objectives of the organization. The intermediate objectives serve as a basis for organizational specialization as they are assigned to subunits and become the purpose of those subunits. Barnard contends that it is important that each member of an organizational subunit understand the purpose of that unit in order to be properly motivated. It is not necessary that each individual understand the purpose of the overall organization, however, since a requirement of intellectual understanding may be divisive.[27] It is only necessary that each individual in the organization have a belief in the ultimate purpose of the organization.[28]

A fourth characteristic of complex formal organizations is the existence of informal organizations. Barnard states that informal organizations always exist in formal organizations and describes them as "areas of special density" for interactions that occur without any specific joint purpose.[29] According to Barnard, informal organizations should not be viewed as simply an unavoidable evil. On the contrary; Barnard claims that if informal organizations did not exist, they would probably have to be created, since they perform a number of functions for the organization. Informal organizations assist communication, help to maintain cohesion in the formal organization, and foster a feeling of personal integrity in the largely depersonalized environment of the formal organization.[30] In addition, informal groups create and maintain the "fiction of superior authority" (i.e., the belief that authority comes from the top of the organization). Barnard does not mean by this that hierarchical authority is not real. He uses "fiction" in the sense of an explanation for overt acts with the fiction being a belief fostered by informal group processes. The fiction of superior authority does two things. First, it serves as a justification for delegating organizational decisions upward. Second, it signals that the good of the organization is at stake in the exercise of authority.[31]

To summarize, Barnard makes the following points regarding the nature of the individual, the genesis of complex formal organizations, and the characteristics of complex formal organizations:

1. Humans are, by nature, physically and biologically limited, social, active, and purposeful in their behavior, and possess an irreducible minimum of free will.

2. The existence of a purpose and the experience of individual limitations leads to cooperative activity.

3. When cooperative activity is undertaken, the strategic or limiting factor to be overcome is social in nature.

4. To survive, the cooperative system must be both effective in accomplishing its purposes and efficient in satisfying individual motives.

5. Initially, cooperation may be informal. Given the individual's active and purposeful nature, however, formal organizations are likely to arise in which cooperative activity is deliberate, conscious, and purposeful rather than spontaneous.

6. Complex formal organizations are created from simple formal organizations with the simple organizations constituting the relatively autonomous component parts of the complex formal organization.

7. Complex formal organizations are characterized by their systemic nature, depersonalized activity, specialization, and the existence of informal groups.

This formulation serves as a prelude to the heart of Barnard's creative contribution to the theory of organizations: the dynamics of organizational behavior.

Organizational Dynamics

Barnard identifies three basic organizational activities: inducing a willingness to cooperate on the part of organizational participants, establishing and defining organizational purpose, and communication.[32] Inducing a willingness to cooperate involves the system of incentives in the organizations and is a function of inducements offered by the organizations and contributions required of the participants. Its result is deference to organizational authority. Purpose is divided into two elements. The first is what Barnard calls the "cooperative aspect," which is concerned with the interests of the organization as a whole. The second is the "subjective aspect," which involves individual motives.[33] Accordingly, the subjective aspect of purpose is related to the incentive system, while the cooperative aspect is related to organizational decision making. Communication is the third essential element of organizational activity and is important both in conveying the purpose of the organization and in the exercise of authority. With the preceding relationships in mind, willingness to cooperate is discussed under the headings of incentives and authority, establishing and defining purpose are discussed under the headings of decision making (objective aspect) and incentives (subjective aspect), and communication is discussed under the heading of authority and in the section on executive functions.

The Incentive System
Barnard conceives of the organization as a system of exchange between the organization and each of its participants. The decision by any individual to participate in the organization involves an immediate cost: the loss of control over one's personal actions. As Barnard puts it: "The ethical ideal upon which cooperation depends requires the general diffusion of a willingness to subordinate immediate personal interests for both the ultimate personal interest and the general good."[34] Consequently, willingness to cooperate involves a personal cost-benefit calculation that is dependent on individual purposes, desires, and impulses of the moment (Barnard calls these "motives"). Participation in the organization is a function of the net inducements (inducements

minus costs) offered by the organization compared to the net induce-ments afforded by alternative activities. Evaluations of inducements and costs are personal and subjective for each individual and are based on the "egotistical" motives of self-preservation and self-satisfaction.[35] Furthermore, Barnard argues that these evaluations are seldom a matter of logical thought. Having made the decision to participate in the or-ganization, the individual's willingness to cooperate is contingent on the continuing perception of a net positive balance of inducements over required contributions. The organization is in equilibrium when all participants perceive that they are receiving more from the organiza-tion in the form of inducements than they are required to contribute.

Incentives are related to personal motives and are thus associated with personal efficiency and effectiveness and with organizational effi-ciency as defined by Barnard. Personal efficiency is achieved when the unsought consequences of personal behavior are unimportant or triv-ial—that is, if the behavior satisfies the motives of the behavior.[36] Personal behavior is effective when a specific desired end is accom-plished.[37] In either case, behavior is evaluated in terms of personal pur-poses and motives. Organizational efficiency is also defined in terms of individual motives. Organizational efficiency is achieved when the mo-tives of individuals in the organization are fulfilled and is a function of the capacity of an organization to offer inducements in sufficient quan-tity to maintain the system. Organizational effectiveness, in contrast, is not related to personal motives. Organizational effectiveness is the degree to which the purposes of the organization have been fulfilled and, as such, has no direct relevance to personal motives.[38] This defini-tion of organizational effectiveness is predicated on Barnard's position that organizational activities are depersonalized and, consequently, that the purpose of those activities is "removed" from the individual.

Barnard's listing of inducements or incentives is quite broad and includes a number of nonmaterial incentives that he felt had previously received too little attention. Barnard divides incentives into two cate-gories: objective incentives, which he calls the "method of incentives"; and subjective incentives, which he calls the "method of persuasion." Objective incentives may be specific or general in character. Specific objective incentives include material incentives, personal incentives, nonmaterial opportunities, physical working conditions, and "ideal benefactions" or the capacity of individuals to satisfy personal ideals such as pride of workmanship or altruistic service. General objective incentives include associational attractiveness (i.e., the avoidance of personal aversions based on nationality, color, or class); adaptation of working conditions to habitual methods and attitudes; the opportunity of enlarged participation (i.e., a feeling of greater participation in the course of events or a sense of mission); and a "condition of communion," or a feeling of solidarity, social integration, and comradeship.[39]

Barnard notes that different individuals are likely to be motivated by different incentives. Consequently, organizations are never able to offer all of the objective incentives and are usually unable to offer sufficient levels of incentives even among those they command. One possible organizational response is growth, which allows the organization to increase its range and level of incentives, and Barnard identifies the desire to increase available incentives as the primary cause of growth. Another response is persuasion.[40] Barnard argues, in effect, that if the organization does not have what the participants want, it should try to make them want what it has. The subjective aspect of incentives (persuasion) is, once again, divided into a number of categories. Somewhat anomalously, Barnard includes the creation of coercive conditions among the methods of persuasion. Nevertheless, he maintains that no complex organization can operate for any length of time on the basis of coercion. A second method of persuasion is propaganda, which may entail general justifications for the organization as a whole or specific appeals in recruiting. The final method of persuasion is what Barnard terms the "inculcation of motives" by which the organization directly attempts to condition the motives of individuals and their emotional response to organizational incentives.

One aspect of the incentive system which Barnard singles out for special attention is the status system.[41] Barnard asserts that a hierarchy of positions with a gradation of honors and privileges is an important nonmaterial incentive in the organization. Barnard defines status as "that condition of the individual that is defined by a statement of his rights, privileges, immunities, duties, and obligations in the organization and, obversely, by a statement of the restrictions, limitations, and prohibitions governing his behavior."[42] Barnard sees status systems as arising from differences in individual abilities, difficulties in performing jobs, the importance of the job performed, credentialing, and the need for the protection of the integrity of the individual. Status may be of two kinds: functional status, which is based on competence in the job performed; and scalar status, which is based on position in the organization.

Barnard recognizes the disruptive tendencies of status systems. He acknowledges that status systems may lead to distorted evaluations of individuals, restrict the circulation of elites because of a reluctance to deprive a person of existing status, distort the system of distributive justice by according some more than their due measure of perquisites, exaggerate the importance of administrative matters over leadership, exalt the symbolic function of status, and generally limit the adaptability of the organization. But Barnard emphasizes the positive functions that the status system can perform for the organization. Not only is the status system a form of incentive in the organization, it can also encourage a sense of responsibility and assist organizational communications by establishing that they are authentic (i.e., they are organizationally approved), authoritative (i.e., they came from an appropriate source), and intelligible (i.e., they employ language suitable to the status of the individual addressed).

Authority

If incentives provide the basis for the willingness to cooperate, authority is its expression. It is in regard to the concept of authority that Barnard makes perhaps his most significant contribution. As I noted earlier, Barnard defines authority as "the character of a communication (order) in a formal organization by virtue of which it is accepted by a contributor to, or 'member' of, the organization as governing the action he contributes; that is as determining what he does or is not to do so far as the organization is concerned."[43] In other words, authority resides in a relationship between a superior and a subordinate, not in a position; and it is effectively exercised only when accepted, not on issuance of a command. This definition of authority springs directly from Barnard's conceptualization of the organization as a system of exchange. Since continuing participation is contingent on the assessment of a net positive balance of inducements over required contributions, the participant has the alternative of refusing to accede to organizational authority, based either on the threat of withdrawal or actual withdrawal from the organization. As Barnard puts it: "The existence of a net inducement is the only reason for accepting *any* order as having authority."[44]

Barnard posits four conditions for the effective exercise of organizational authority, all of which emphasize the role of the subordinate in the authority relationship and the importance of effective communication.[45] First, the subordinate must understand the directive. Second, at the time of the decision regarding whether or not to accept authority, the subordinate must believe the directive to be consistent with the purpose of the organization. Third, the subordinate must believe the directive to be consistent with his or her personal interests as a whole. Fourth, the subordinate must be mentally and physically capable of complying with the directive. Given this emphasis on subordinate perception, communication will perform a key role in the exercise of authority.

Barnard's assertions that acceptance is the critical act in the exercise of authority, that acceptance is contingent on net inducements, and his listing of the conditions for the effective exercise of authority emphasize the subjective nature of the exercise of authority and underline the possibility that authority may not be accepted. Indeed, Barnard notes that attempted exercises of authority are often ineffective and that disobedience under certain conditions may well be a moral responsibility. All of this suggests that the subordinate's response to organizational directives is not predetermined. Instead, Barnard indicates that the subordinate's response may take any of three forms: acceptance of a directive without consideration of its merits, acceptance only after consideration of the merits, and rejection.[46]

The first of these potential responses describes what Barnard calls the "zone of indifference" and is of particular importance to the organization. The zone of indifference involves acceptance without consideration of merits and thus constitutes an area in which orders are automatically obeyed. That is, the subordinate, in this case, does not pause to examine whether the directive satisfies the conditions stated for the effective exercise of authority. Instead, directives falling within the zone of indifference involve activities that reside in a domain described by the individual's "contractual agreement" with the organization and thus will be performed without hesitation. Barnard argues that a sizable zone of indifference among subordinates is necessary to facilitate the smooth operation of the organization.

Although Barnard emphasizes the subjective aspect of authority and admits the possibility that orders may, and in some cases should, be disobeyed, he does not gainsay the importance of the objective aspect of authority, and he acknowledges that organizational authority is usually effective. Objective authority, or authority based on position or competence, is both present and important in the organization; and when authority of position is combined with authority of competence, it can be a very effective force. There are several reasons why organizational authority is usually effective.[47] First, the organization can increase the size of the zone of indifference and the overall zone of acceptance (and correspondingly reduce the zone of rejection) by judiciously manipulating organizational incentives and employing persuasive techniques. Second, to the extent that directives fall within the range of duties anticipated at the time the individual joined the organization, those directives are likely to be in the individual's zone of indifference and perceived as a "contractual obligation." Third, orders are not usually given unless they conform to the four conditions outlined by Barnard. Finally, informal group attitudes tend to buttress the exercise of organizational authority. Since authority is necessary to organizational survival, Barnard argues that all participants have a stake in preserving organizational authority. Consequently, informal group influences are likely to maintain and stabilize the individual's zone of indifference. In addition, informal group attitudes foster the previously mentioned "fiction of superior authority," or the belief that authority comes down from above.

Decision Making

Decision making is an integral function in the organization, being both the means by which the purpose of the organization is related to the organization's environment and the means by which purpose is translated into organizational action. Barnard defines decisions as "acts of individuals ... which are the result of deliberation, calculation, and thought ... involving the ordering of means to ends."[48]

According to Barnard, there are two major categories of decisions: personal decisions and organizational decisions. Personal decisions are decisions about whether or not to participate in the organization and have already been discussed in reference to the incentive system.[49] Barnard says personal decisions are made outside the organization and cannot be delegated, since they are subjective in nature. Furthermore, as indicated earlier, personal decisions are not likely to be the product of logical thought.

Organizational decisions, in contrast, are decisions dominated by organizational purpose, not personal considerations. As such, Barnard argues that organizational decisions can, and should, be delegated. Organizational decisions are best made at communication centers by executives who specialize in organizational decision making. This assures both that requisite information is brought to bear on the decision and that organizational decisions are appropriately coordinated. Organizational decisions, in contrast to personal decisions, are also the product of logical thought. This does not mean that organizational decisions are necessarily correct. Factual premises and reasoning may be faulty. But Barnard argues that the logical processes of discrimination, analysis, and choice are required. Indeed, Barnard maintains that the deliberate adaptation of means to ends is the essence of formal organization.[50]

Organizational decisions consist of two elements: the organization's purpose, or the "moral" element; and the "opportunistic" element, which involves finding what circumstances are significant with reference to the organization's purpose. Barnard takes the moral element or purpose of the organization as given at the time of the decision.[51] As such, organizational purpose is part of the "environment" of decision making, which also includes the physical world, the social world, external things and forces, and circumstances of the moment. Organizational decisions are intended to adjust the purpose of the organization to the other aspects of the decision environment with purpose enabling the decision maker to discriminate between the relevant and irrelevant elements of the decision environment.

The relevant elements of the decision environment consist of strategic factors and complementary factors. The identification of these factors constitutes the opportunistic element of organizational decision making. Strategic factors (or limiting factors) are those conditions of the environment that, if changed or absent, would permit the organization to accomplish its purposes.[52] Complementary factors are environmental conditions that would have to remain unchanged for the manipulation of strategic factors to accomplish the purposes of the organization.[53] Strategic factors are the key to organizational decision making. The act of decision entails choosing an appropriate action or set of actions to manipulate the strategic factors. Once a strategic factor has been identified and action has been chosen to deal with it, the organizational purpose is reduced to a more specific level, and a search is instituted for a new strategic factor and a new decision process is initiated. This process continues until all strategic factors have been identified and decisions have been made to deal with them. Thus the opportunistic element of decision making consists of constructing means-ends chains in which purpose is defined and redefined with increasing degrees of specificity and selecting means to accomplish the organizational purposes.

The processes of decision making in the organization are, according to Barnard, necessarily specialized. Decisions made at the upper levels of the organization relate more to the ends of the organization, and those at the lower level more to means to achieve those ends. In addition, executive communication centers are established in the organization that specialize in decision making. Consequently, the efforts of most individuals in the organization are guided by decisions that, in part, are made by organizational executives who, according to Barnard, act "impersonally" (i.e., their decisions are dominated by organizational objectives).[54] As a result, although the decision processes of the organization are logical, they are not necessarily the product of the logical processes of all individuals in the organization. Many of the actions of individuals in the organization are habitual and repetitive responses to the design of the organization and decisions made elsewhere.

Though Barnard emphasizes the logical character of organizational decision making, he also recognizes the necessity of what he calls "nonlogical processes," particularly in regard to executive decision making. Logical processes involve "conscious thinking" or reasoning that "could be expressed in words, or other symbols".[55] Nonlogical processes, in contrast, cannot be expressed in words or as reasoning and are made known only by judgment, decision, or action.[56] The process employed in organizational decision making depends on three factors: the purpose of the decision, the speed required in making the decision, and the quality of the information available to the decision maker. Barnard maintains that if the purpose of the decision process is to ascertain truth, the process itself must be logical. If the purpose of the decision is to determine a course of action, Barnard argues that too many intangibles are likely to be involved and thus the process cannot be totally logical. If the purpose of the process is persuasion, the process requires rationalization but is ultimately nonlogical in character. The second factor determining the decision process employed is the speed required in making the decision. If time is short, logical processes cannot be employed. Finally, the process of decision making used is a function of the quality of the information available to the decision maker. Precise information permits the use of logical processes. In the opposite limiting case, uncertainty necessitates the use of nonlogical processes. Thus organizational decision making, to the extent that it is involved with choosing courses of action or persuasion, must be performed in a short time frame, and is based on imprecise information, will require varying degrees of nonlogical processes.

Executive Functions

Having established the groundwork by discussing the genesis of complex formal organizations, their basic characteristics, and their dynamics, Barnard next turns to his primary topic: the functions of the executive in the organization. Barnard identifies the fundamental executive functions as the performance of processes that deal with the relationships between the system of cooperation and its environment and processes concerned with the creation and distribution of satisfactions to organizational participants.[57] The adjustment of cooperative systems to changes in the environment and new purposes requires the development of an executive organization; in complex organizations, the necessities of communication require the location of executive functions in a single body. The creation and distribution of satisfactions involves altering individual behavior by the inculcation of motives and the construction of incentives to achieve organizational objectives. Executives occupy centers of communication in the organization and maintain the organization's operations in a fashion analogous, according to Barnard, to the relationship between the brain and the rest of the body.

More specifically, Barnard identifies three executive functions: providing a system of communication, securing individual effort, and formulating and defining organizational purposes.[58] In order for executive decisions to be implemented, they must be appropriately communicated. Barnard posits several requirements for effective communication in the organization.[59] First, the channel of communication should be definitely known. Second, a definite formal channel of communication to each individual is required. Third, the line of communication should be as short as possible to avoid time lags. Fourth, the complete line of communication usually should be used to avoid conflicting communication. Fifth, persons serving as communication centers must have adequate competence. Sixth, the line of communication should not be interrupted when the organization is functioning. Finally, every communication should be authenticated with status playing an important role by appropriately identifying the issuer of the communication. The provision of communication is partially a function of formal organizational design and personnel. Of even greater importance is the establishment of an informal executive organization. The establishment of an informal executive organization both avoids the necessity of formal orders on routine matters and expands the available means of communication through informal contacts.

Securing essential services requires both bringing people into the organization by use of the techniques of propaganda and persuasion, then eliciting their contributions. The latter involves the maintenance of morale, the maintenance of a system of inducements, the maintenance of a scheme of deterrents, supervision, control, inspection, education, and the provision of appropriate training.

The formulation and definition of purpose, although primarily an executive function, is a shared responsibility. Overall objectives are initially established at the executive level. But the process of formulating objectives, according to Barnard, is an iterative process in which communication passes up and down the chain of command reporting difficulties and accomplishments. Accordingly, purpose may be redefined and modified throughout the organization. In this sense, organizational purpose is less a formal statement than an aggregate of actions. In Barnard's words, organizational purpose is a "residuum of decisions ... resulting in closer approximations to concrete acts."[60] Responsibility for general long-run decisions is delegated upward, while responsibility for definition and action resides at the base of the organization within the constraints imposed by executive decisions.

To perform these functions adequately, the executive must have a sense of the total organization and the organizational environment. This, Barnard argues, is more a matter of art than science, more aesthetic than logical. In his responsibility for the total organization, the executive must be concerned with both organizational effectiveness and efficiency. At the organizational level, effectiveness is primarily a matter of integrating technologies so that the organization achieves its objectives. Organizational efficiency is more personal than technological. The executive must coordinate four economies in the organization: the material economy, social relationships external to the organization, internal social relationships, and personal economies.[61] The sum of these four economies is the organizational economy, and a statement of the organizational economy cannot be captured in a mere financial statement because it ignores the personal and social considerations vital to the organization. The only statement of the status of the organizational economy is the success or failure of the organization itself. The maintenance of the organizational economy is the responsibility of the executive because only the executive has the necessary perspective to accomplish the task.

Leadership

Because one is an executive does not necessarily mean that he or she is a leader. The former rests on position, the latter on function. Barnard defines leadership as "the power of individuals to inspire cooperative personal decisions by creating faith,"[62] or, "the quality of behavior of individuals whereby they guide people or their activities in organized effort."[63] Since Barnard maintains that executive capacity in the form of leadership is the most general strategic factor in human cooperation, a major task of the organization is to see that those in executive positions are indeed leaders.

Barnard lists five qualities of leaders: vitality and endurance, decisiveness, persuasiveness, responsibility, and intellectual capacity. Of these, Barnard singles out two— responsibility and intellectual capacity—for special attention.[64] Intellectual capacity is interesting because Barnard purposely relegates it to fifth place on his list of qualities. Barnard apparently has fairly low regard for intellectuals, who, he alleges, tend to be irresponsible (i.e., absentminded and nonpunctual), nondecisive, and nonpersuasive (i.e., a little "queer" and not interested in people).[65] In short, intellectual preparation tends to inhibit the development of the very qualities deemed indispensable to leadership. Consequently, Barnard argues that leaders are more found than trained. As for the education of leaders, it should be general in nature and aimed at teaching the individual how further to educate himself.[66] Education should also convey an understanding of human relations, an appreciation of nonlogical behavior, and an appreciation of formal organizations as evolving organic systems.[67]

Responsibility, in contrast to formal education, is vital to leadership. Barnard asserts that responsibility derives from the existence of a moral code; he defines morals as "personal forces or propensities of a general and stable character which tend to inhibit, control, or modify inconsistent, immediate, specific desires, impulses, or interests, and to intensify those which are consistent with those propensities."[68] But morality by itself does not imply responsibility. Responsibility comes when a moral code actually governs individual behavior. Thus it is possible for a person to be moral but not responsible, although a person cannot be responsible without a moral code.[69]

Barnard argues that organizations create their own moral codes. An individual code for organizational behavior derived from the organization's moral code is one aspect of the organizational personality. A condition of organizational responsibility is present when the organization's moral code governs the individual's behavior in the organization. Barnard notes that individual and organizational moral codes sometimes conflict, and, more frequently, there is conflict among the several moral codes of the organization itself. Furthermore, moral complexity with a high potential for internal conflict is likely under conditions of high physical and social activity.

Executive Responsibility

This brings us to executive responsibility. Barnard contends that executives are necessarily highly active. As a result, the executive, faced with a condition of moral complexity, must have a high capacity for responsibility. In addition, the executive must possess a faculty for creating moral standards and resolving conflicts among moral codes. Accordingly, Barnard defines executive responsibility as the capacity of leaders to establish ideals by which "they are compelled to bind the wills of men to the accomplishment of purposes beyond their immediate ends, beyond their times."[70] This depends on the ability of the executive to establish an organizational moral code that guides individuals in the pursuit of organizational objectives. The creation of moral codes for the organization and the adjudication of moral conflicts are thus key functions of the executive. An internalized sense of organizational morality counteracts the centrifugal forces of individual interests in the organization, and organizations survive in direct proportion to the extent to which individual behavior is governed by a sense of organizational morality. Morality and a condition of responsibility are not substitutes for the other elements of the organization; rather, morality and responsibility in organizational behavior are necessary for those other elements to be effective. As Barnard puts it, "the quality of leadership, the persistence of its influence, the durability of its related organizations, the power of the coordination it incites, all express the height of moral aspirations, the breadth of moral foundations."[71]

Conclusion

Barnard's observations on complex formal organizations may be summarized as follows:

1. The complex formal organization constitutes a free contractual arrangement between the organization and each of its participants.

2. The system of incentives serves to satisfy individual motives and wed individual efforts to the accomplishment of organizational objectives.

3. Since the organization constitutes a free contractual relationship from which participants may withdraw if they perceive that the terms of the contract have not been fulfilled, authority resides in the relationship between a superior and a subordinate and is exercised only on consent of the subordinate.

4. Communication plays a key role in the organization both in terms of the exercise of authority and in conveying the purpose of the organization.

5. Organizational, as opposed to individual, decision processes are necessarily logical in character. Furthermore, decision making is a specialized activity with primary responsibility assigned to the executives who act as communication centers.

6. Executive organization is a natural outgrowth of organizational development. Executives are responsible for providing a system of communication, securing individual efforts, and defining organizational purposes.

7. Organizational leadership requires both the adoption of a personal moral code that governs the behavior of the executive and the creation and inculcation of an organizational moral code that serves as a standard of behavior throughout the organization.

Barnard's impact on the study of organizations is undeniable. Nonetheless, his writings have been a source of some controversy. That controversy centers on the role of management in the organization. Barnard has been accused both of suggesting the repeal of traditional managerial prerogatives and of being an apologist for management.[72] Substantial arguments can be marshaled on both sides of the dispute.

On the one hand, it is clear that Barnard's conceptualization of the organization as a system of exchange, the definition of authority derived from that conceptualization, and the dynamics of the organizational process impose constraints on the arbitrary exercise of hierarchical authority. The exchange model embodies the notion of a contractual arrangement between the organization and its participants that is subject to termination by either party if its terms are not fulfilled. The value of the inducements and contributions involved in that exchange is determined by the personal and subjective assessment of each participant in the organization. In this context, authority does not reside in a hierarchical position but in a relationship between a superior and a subordinate, and it is not exercised on issuance of a directive but on acceptance by a subordinate. The exercise of authority is further limited by the condition that the subordinate perceive the directive to be compatible with his or her own interests and the interests of the organization. Furthermore, the specification of organizational objectives is an iterative process involving communication traveling up and down

176

the chain of command with hierarchical controls and centralized planning limited by constraints on information and analytical capabilities. As a consequence, nonhierarchical controls in the form of multilateral, spontaneous coordination are a fundamental requirement for the effectiveness of the organization, and Barnard counsels that maximum practical decentralization be exercised in the organization.

On the other hand, Barnard exalts the organization beyond any individual in it, and cooperation is to be in the service of organizational objectives. Actions are to be determined by the needs of the organization, not individual motives, and decisions are to be dominated by organizational objectives. Organizational behavior is "depersonalized," and an organizational personality is to be substituted for an individual identity. Executives are assigned primary responsibility for formulating organizational objectives, while subordinates are expected only to believe in the existence of a common purpose, not possess an "intellectual understanding" of that purpose. Conflict is seen as short-term and nearsighted and is to be controlled by grouping like-minded individuals. Individuals are ascribed a measure of free will. Individuals are seldom rational, however, and the techniques of persuasion are to be employed to encourage participants to value the inducements the organization has to offer, and coercion can be employed for short periods of time, if necessary. Although organizational directives can be rejected, the organization is to do what it can to enlarge the subordinate's zone of indifference so that directives will be accepted without question. Informal groups, instead of being a necessary evil, can support the exercise of hierarchical authority through a belief in the "fiction of superior authority."

In sum, while Barnard argued that managers cannot manage in an authoritarian manner, he did not argue that managers cannot manage. The organization may be system of exchange, but it is an asymmetrical exchange in which hierarchical superiors maintain a position of *primus inter pares*. Nevertheless, hierarchy confers only relative, not absolute, advantage in the superior-subordinate relationship, and, like Machiavelli's prince, the superior must operate within boundaries, however loosely imposed, by the necessity of securing consent. Rather than deny the existence, and desirability, of hierachical authority, Barnard is concerned with the preconditions for the effective exercise of hierarchical authority, which requires obtaining the consent of the governed to be governed.

Though governance entails an element of consent, Barnard did not believe that this requires the adoption of democratic procedures in the organization. In Barnard's words: "The dogmatic assertion that 'democracy' or 'democratic methods' are (or are not) in accordance with the principles here discussed is not tenable. . . . No doubt in many situations formal democratic processes may be an important element in the maintenance of authority, i.e., of organizational cohesion, but may in other situations be disruptive and probably never could be in themselves sufficient. On the other hand, the solidarity of some cooperative systems ... under many conditions may be unexcelled, though requiring formally autocratic processes."[73] Indeed, Barnard expressed significant reservations about democratic processes, which, he contended, are time-consuming, conflict ridden, incapable of dealing with complex issues, and ineffective in selecting leaders on the basis of merit. To the extent that "democracy" is required in the organization, it is a "silent democracy" of behavior in the form of consent and cooperation and rests on an "aristocracy of leadership" to be effective.[74]

Barnard does not attempt to resolve the apparent paradoxes in the relationship between man and the organization. Instead, he accepts the inevitable tensions in that relationship while seeking a balance between the needs of the individual and the needs of the organization. In Barnard's words:

> free and unfree, controlling and controlled, choosing and being chosen, inducing and unable to resist inducement, the source of authority and unable to deny it, independent and dependent, nourishing their personalities, and yet depersonalized; forming purposes and being forced to change them, searching for limitations in order to make decisions, seeking the particular, but concerned with the whole, finding leaders and denying their leadership, hoping to dominate the earth and being dominated by the unseen—this is the story of man in society told in these pages.... I believe that the expansion of cooperation and the development of the individual are mutually dependent realities, and that a due proportion or balance between them is a necessary condition of human welfare.[75]

Notes

1. See William B. Wolf, *The Basic Barnard: An Introduction to Chester I. Barnard and His Theories of Organizational Management*, ILR Paperback no. 14 (Ithaca, N.Y.: New York State School of Industrial and Labor Relations, Cornell University, 1974), 3–4.

2. Material on Barnard's life is taken from Wolf, *The Basic Barnard*, chap. 2.

3. Kenneth R. Andrews, "Introduction," in Chester I. Barnard, *The Functions of the Executive* (Cambridge, Mass.: Harvard University Press, 1968), ix.

4. Wolf, *Basic Barnard*, 48.

5. Ibid., 44.

6. Ibid., 23.

7. Ibid., 18.

8. Ibid., 19.

9. William B. Wolf, *Conversations with Chester I. Barnard*, ILR Paperback no. 12 (Ithaca, N.Y.: New York State School of Industrial and Labor Relations, Cornell University, 1973), 16.

10. Andrews, "Introduction," vi.

11. Barnard, *The Functions*, xxix, xxx.

12. Ibid., 10.

13. Ibid., 14.

14. Ibid., 38.

15. Ibid., 40.

16. To use Barnard's example, an individual's inability to move a large stone may be viewed as a result of the size of the stone (environment) or the physical limitations of the individual (biological). See ibid., 23, 24.

17. Ibid., 84.

18. Though Barnard discusses informal organizations as one stage of organizational development, it is not clear whether he considers it a necessary stage.

19. Barnard, *The Functions*, 116.

20. Ibid., 73.

21. Ibid., 60.

22. Ibid., 104.

23. Ibid., 79.

24. Ibid., 77.

25. See chapter 3.

26. Barnard, *The Functions*, 131.

27. Ibid., 137.

28. In this stance, Barnard has been both praised as being an early exponent of "management by objectives" and castigated as being pro-management in his orientation.

29. Barnard, *The Functions*, 114–15.

30. Ibid., 122.

31. Ibid., 170–71.

32. Ibid., 82.

33. Ibid., 86–89. This separation between organizational purpose and individual motives continues Barnard's theme that the purpose of the organization has no direct meaning to the individual. Barnard asserts that organizational purpose and individual motives are seldom identical. All that is required is that there be no significant divergence between the individual's perception of the organization's purpose and the actual purpose of the organization, and that the individual believe that a common purpose exists.

34. Ibid., 293.

35. Ibid., 139.

36. Ibid., 19.

37. Ibid.

38. Ibid., 43.

39. Ibid., 142–49.

40. Ibid., 149–53.

41. Chester I. Barnard, "Functions and Pathology of Status Systems," in

Organization and Management (Cambridge, Mass.: Harvard University Press, 1962), 207–44.

42. Ibid., 208.

43. Barnard, *The Functions*, 163.

44. Ibid., 166.

45. Ibid., 165.

46. Ibid., 167.

47. Ibid., 167–71.

48. Ibid., 185.

49. Ibid., 187.

50. Ibid., 186. Barnard also notes that organizational decisions are not always positive in character. An important category of organizational decisions is the decision not to decide. In Barnard's words: *"The fine art of executive decision consists in not deciding questions that are not now pertinent, in not deciding prematurely, in not making decisions that cannot be made effective, and in not making decisions that others should make."* Ibid., 194.

51. Ibid., 195.

52. Ibid., 203.

53. Ibid.

54. Ibid., 210.

55. Ibid., 302.

56. Ibid.

57. Ibid., 60–61.

58. Ibid., 217.

59. Ibid., 175–81.

60. Ibid., 231.

61. Ibid., 241–42.

62. Ibid., 259.

63. Chester I. Barnard, "The Nature of Leadership," in *Organization and Management*, 83.

64. Ibid., 93.

65. Ibid., 98.

66. Chester I. Barnard, "Education for Executives," in *Organization and Management*, 195–96.

67. Ibid., 198–99.

68. Barnard, *The Functions*, 261.

69. Ibid., 263.

70. Ibid., 283.

71. Ibid., 284.

72. See, for instance, Charles Perrow, *Complex Organizations: A Critical Essay* (Glenview, Ill.: Scott, Foresman, 1972), 95, on the "apologist position"; and John M. Pfiffner and Robert Presthus, *Public Administration*, 5th ed. (New York: Ronald Press, 1965), 213, for the other side.

73. Barnard, *The Functions*, 167–68.

74. Barnard, "Dilemmas of Leadership in the Democratic Process," in *Organization and Management*, 24–50.

75. Barnard, *The Functions*, 296.

CHAPTER 7

Herbert A. Simon:
A Decision-Making Perspective

With authors such as Follett, Mayo, and Barnard, I have dealt with figures probably best considered transitional in the shift from the Classical to the Behavioral perspective in the study of public administration in the United States. In turning now to Herbert Simon, I present an author whose works are commonly considered a watershed rather than simply a transition. Simon's works are firmly entrenched in the Behavioral perspective, and his work, in general, represents a radical departure from the Classical approach to public administration. Yet there are a number of similarities between Simon's positions and those of the authors who preceded him. In short, Simon's work is a combination of disjunctures and continuities, impressive in the evolutionary, rather than revolutionary, character of the views he advances.

Let us consider first the similarities between Simon and his predecessors in the field. Simon's most obvious intellectual debt is to Chester Barnard. Simon adopts, in toto, Barnard's conceptualization of the organization as a system of exchange and the definition of authority suggested by that conceptualization. He also adopts Barnard's notion that complex formal organizations evolve from, and consist of, simple formal organizations (Barnard ascribing the development to limits on communication, while Simon attributes it to the necessity of simplifying decisions), as well as Barnard's emphasis on decision making, although that emphasis is accentuated in Simon's works. But Simon's intellectual indebtedness is not limited to Barnard. At the most general level, Simon shares with the Classical approach the objective of developing a science of administration, an effort to describe a value-free domain for the construction of that science, a quest for general principles of administration, the acceptance of efficiency as the criterion for decision making, and an emphasis on hierarchy as well as its justifications (coordination, superior rationality, and the location of responsibility). Indeed, Simon's assignment of responsibilities to the hierarchy —the construction of decision premises and, later, system design—is reminiscent of Taylor's charge to management. Simon's assertion that the harshness of hierarchical directives can be mitigated if determined by the "logic of the situation" echoes Follett's reliance on the "law of the situation" and Gulick's admonition that hierarchy must rely on "coordination through ideas" as well as the structure of authority. Simon also shares with Gulick concern for the adequacy of the politics-administration dichotomy as the basis for the construction of a science of administration. They even agree on the general definition for an appropriate scientific domain. For Gulick, it is relationships between actions and outcome (statements of "variations and interrelationships"); for Simon, it lies in the relationship between alternatives and their outcomes (the "factual" element of decisions). Finally, there is agreement between Weber and Simon that the organization (for Weber, the bureaucratic organization) provides a broader context of rationality for individual decision making.

Nevertheless, this specification of similarities should not blind us to the fact that important differences also exist between Simon's work and his predecessors'. Although Simon agrees with Gulick on the politics-administration dichotomy, that stance was in opposition to the dominant stance, and Simon is considerably more determined than Gulick in pressing the fact-value dichotomy as the appropriate substitute in defining the domain for the construction of a science of administration. Although Simon adopts Barnard's exchange model of the organization and his definition of authority, he substantially elaborates the former and draws an important distinction on the latter consideration. But the truly distinctive feature of Simon's work lies in his preoccupation with decision making in the organization. Here, Simon proposes a new unit of analysis for scientific investigation (decision premises); a different methodological approach (an inductive approach based on the tenets of logical positivism); and a revised concept of the decision maker as, in Simon's hands, Economic Man is translated into the more modest dimensions of Satisficing Man. All this is cast in terms of routinized decision making in an organizational environment as Simon attempts to develop a descriptive model of organizational decision making and remake administrative theory in the process.

This chapter focuses on Simon's elaboration of decision making in an organizational environment, since this perspective is the most pertinent to the considerations raised in this book. That means that I concentrate on Simon's earlier work and, of necessity, am not able to do full justice to Simon's more recent work in the field of individual decision making and artificial intelligence.

Life

Herbert A. Simon was born in Milwaukee, Wisconsin, on 15 June 1916.[1]

Simon earned B.A. (1936) and Ph.D. (1943) degrees from the University of Chicago and has received honorary degrees from Yale University, Case Institute of Technology, Lund University (Sweden), McGill University (Canada), and the Netherlands School of Economics. Simon began his professional career in 1936 as an assistant to Clarence E. Ridley of the International City Managers' Association. In 1939 Simon became director of Administrative Measurement Studies at the Bureau of Public Administration of the University of California at Berkeley. In 1942 Simon took a position at the Illinois Institute of Technology and was chairman of the Department of Political and Social Sciences from 1946 to 1949. He moved to Carnegie-Mellon University in Pittsburgh in 1949 as professor of administration and psychology and has remained there since that time. At Carnegie-Mellon, Simon has been head of the Department of Industrial Management, associate dean of the Graduate School of Industrial Management, and Richard King Mellon Professor of Computer Science and Psychology.

During his career, Simon has compiled a substantial public service record. He has worked for the U.S. Bureau of the Budget, the Census Bureau, and the Economic Cooperation Administration. In addition, Simon has served as a member of the President's Science Advisory Committee, chairman of the Pennsylvania Governor's Milk Inquiry Commission, chairman of the Board of Directors of the Social Science Research Council, and chairman of the Division of Behavioral Sciences of the National Research Council. Simon has also acted as a consultant to a variety of governmental and business organizations.

Simon's distinguished career has been marked by a number of honors and awards including the Administrator's Award of the American College of Hospital Administrators, the Distinguished Scientific Contribution Award of the American Psychological Association, and the A.M. Turing Award of the Association for Computing Machinery. In 1978 Simon received the Nobel Prize in Economics.

Simon's career has been distinguished by the breadth of his concerns. His interest in the study of man, originating in high school, was spurred by his uncle, who had studied economics at the University of Wisconsin.[2] Simon notes that many of the ideas contained in his first book, *Administrative Behavior*, were drawn from the Institutionalist school of economics.[3] Simon's interests expanded to include almost all the social sciences. Perhaps the breadth of his interests is best illustrated by looking at the progression of Simon's career. Simon began with a Ph.D. in political science and a major field in public administration. He has spent much of his career teaching in a school of industrial management. He is a professor of computer science and psychology. He received the Nobel Prize for his work in the field of economics.[4] His articles have appeared in the professional journals of every branch of the social sciences except anthropology.[5] He has maintained memberships in professional associations in the fields of political science, economics, psychology, sociology, computer science, management sciences, and philosophy. In sum, Simon is a man of catholic interests and a "social scientist" in the truest sense of that term.

Nevertheless, there has been a common theme in Simon's interests—a central focus on human decision making. This central theme is evidenced in all his major works, although the perspective changes over time. Simon describes his first book, *Administrative Behavior*, as a "prolegomena to theory" with the objectives of establishing decisions as a focus of analysis and constructing a common operational language for the literature of organization theory.[6] *Public Administration*, written with Donald Smithburg and Victor Thompson, is an attempt to synthesize various perspectives on public administration, but with emphasis on organizational decision making.[7] *Organizations*, written with James March, elaborates the theoretical framework presented in *Administrative Behavior* and marshals a wide array of empirical evidence pertaining to that theory.[8] In *Models of Man*, a collection of his articles, Simon presents a formalization of some basic elements of his decision theory.[9] With *The New Science of Management Decision* comes a computer-based perspective and an assessment of the computer's consequences for organizational decision making.[10] In *The Sciences of the Artificial* Simon expands his scope to artificial systems in general (only one of which is an organization) and a model of man as an information-processing system.[11] *Human Problem-Solving* and *Models of Thought*, two more compilations of articles, written by Simon and his associates, are concerned with the processes of human cognition with the ambitious aim of presenting "a unified explanation of human cognition in all of its manifestations."[12]

The common focus on human decision making is clear. The changing perspective is marked by a progression in which the emphasis on the organizational environment as it influences decision making is replaced by an increasingly specific concentration on individual decision-making processes. Though my primary concern in this chapter is decision making in an organizational environment, I consider Simon's works in a broader frame of reference, starting with an examination of Simon's objective of establishing a "science of administration," proceeding through an analysis of individual decision-making processes, and ending with an examination of organizational decision making.

A Science of Administration

Simon, like the authors of the Classical period who preceded him, sought to construct a science of administration. But Simon differs from the Classical authors in several respects. Simon focuses on decisions or, more precisely, decision premises as his unit of analysis; he designates the factual component of administrative decisions as the appropriate scientific domain; and he adopts a procedure that emphasizes systematic, empirical investigation.

A Unit of Analysis: Decision Premises

Simon contends that the logic and psychology of choice is the heart of administration, and, at times, he uses the terms "decision making" and "managing" synonymously. Nevertheless, Simon considers "decisions" to be too broad to serve as a unit of analysis in a science of administration, since they are not unitary events (i.e., pieces of a decision may be made at different points in time and more than one actor may be involved) and involve the processes of alerting, exploring, and analyzing, which precede the act of choice.

Consequently, Simon adopts decision premises rather than decisions as his unit of analysis.[13] Decision premises provide the basis for the process of decision making, while decisions themselves are conclusions drawn from these premises. Stated in the form of an analogy to the computer, premises are represented by data input and a program of instruction, whereas a decision is the product of applying the program to the input. Simon contends that decisions are best analyzed by examining their underlying premises, discovering the sources of those premises, and tracing the channels of communication and influence by which premises are transmitted in an organizational setting.

The Domain of a Science of Administration

Simon also differs from the Classical authors in defining the area in which a science of administration can, and should, be constructed. Following Wilson, the search for a science of administration in the Classical period was founded on a proposed institutional separation between policy functions and administrative functions (the policy-administration dichotomy).[14] Policy matters or objectives were to be decided by elected officials, whereas administrative decisions were to be limited to "the systematic and detailed execution of public law" or the selection of means to achieve those objectives.[15] By limiting administrative activity to the selection of means rather than ends, Wilson believed that a value-free domain was defined for the construction of an empirically based science of administration. The objective of this science of administration was to make the conduct of government business more efficient. Fidelity to the policy intentions of elected officials was to be ensured by the establishment of appropriate hierarchical controls.[16]

Simon rejects the policy-administration dichotomy on both descriptive and normative grounds. Descriptively, Simon contends that policy and administrative functions, as defined by Wilson, are performed by both political and administrative officials.[17] Political officials are often involved in the selection of means, and, more important, administrators are integrally involved in the policy function both in the initiation of policy and in the exercise of discretion in the execution of policy.[18] Consequently, the policy-administration dichotomy fails to define a value-free domain required for the development of a science of administration, since administrators are involved in policy functions and thus value considerations.

Simon also rejects the policy-administration dichotomy on normative grounds. Although he concedes that the dichotomy may have been a normative standard appropriate to the historical context in which Wilson wrote, Simon contends that political institutions and the normative and practical problems they pose have changed since that time.[19] Resistance to the hierarchical controls required by the policy-administration dichotomy has increased. Moreover, governmental operations have expanded, imposing severe limits on the ability of political officials to exercise adequate oversight and control over bureaucrats. Finally, the increasing role of science in government has complicated the problem of establishing controls by generalists over professionals who have specialized expertise.[20] Simon argues that it is unrealistic to attempt to establish strict, external, hierarchical controls over the bureaucracy and undesirable to separate administrators from policy functions. Instead, we must discover ways of using the technical knowledge of administrators in the policy process.[21]

In place of the policy-administration dichotomy, Simon proposes the fact-value dichotomy, which, he argues, provides a better basis for a science of administration and a more appropriate standard for administrative conduct. Simon divides decision premises into two categories: value premises and factual premises. Value premises are ethical statements about what should be done. As such, they may be good or bad, but they cannot be true or false.[22] Factual premises, in contrast, are statements about the observable world. Consequently, it can be determined whether factual premises are true or false.[23]. The factual premises of decisions are the perceived relationships between alternatives and their consequences. Factual premises are true if the alternative selected leads to the predicted set of consequences.[24] They are false if it does not.

Simon maintains that propositions about administrative processes are scientific only to the extent that their truth or falsity can be assessed. Therefore, a science of administration must be based on the factual premises of administrative decisions and cannot deal with value premises. Thus, Simon substitutes a conceptual distinction—the fact-value dichotomy—for what he considers to be a descriptively invalid institutional distinction—the policy-administration dichotomy—to define a value-free domain for the development of a science of administration.

The substitution of the fact-value dichotomy for the policy-administration dichotomy also suggests a different standard for administrative behavior. The policy-administration dichotomy requires policy neutrality on the part of administrators and the establishment of hierarchical controls to ensure the responsiveness of administrators to the policy directives of their political superiors. Simon contends that public administrators are not, and should not be, neutral concerning policy. Instead, public administrators should be predictable in regard to the value premises entering into their decisions.[25] The value premises of the administrator are predictable, within limits, because of the processes of recruitment, socialization, and professional identification. Simon argues that predictability is superior to neutrality because a group of value-free professionals would be the most corruptible of all bodies, or a "force of janissaries."[26] In addition, since the bureaucracy is controlled by controlling its decision premises, and since the premises entering into any decision are so complex that it is impossible to control more than a few, external controls by political officials cannot be the sole guarantee of administrative responsibility. Instead, internalized professional standards must guide administrative behavior.

Although inevitably limited, external controls are still required. Facts and values cannot be entirely separated, and the administrator's value premises may not be the same as those of political officials. Therefore, procedural devices should be formulated to assign value-laden decisions to elected officials and to hold administrators responsible to community values.[27] More important, automation of decision making can assist in clarifying value premises and, by making those premises more explicit, render review and evaluation both easier and more likely.[28]

The Scientific Process

Finally, Simon differs from the Classical authors with respect to the procedures to be employed in the development of a science of administration.[29] For Simon, a science of administration should be based on systematic, empirical analysis rather than casual observation; it should be inductive in nature, not deductive, with "principles" the result of an accumulation of empirical evidence rather than intuition; and at least at the outset, it should be descriptive rather than prescriptive.[30]

Simon suggests that two kinds of administrative science can be established: a "pure" science and a "practical" science. A pure science seeks to describe ways in which humans behave in organizations with the objective of discovering and verifying empirical propositions.[31] A practical science attempts to develop propositions about how decision makers would behave if they sought to achieve more efficient performance.[32] A practical science of administration can assist the administrator in making decisions. Administrative decision making can be based only partly on scientific knowledge, however, since a science of administration can deal only with efficiency in the achievement of values, not with the selection of values themselves.

Simon believes a science of administration would be applicable to both public and private organizations. He contends that public and private organizations have more similarities than differences, and the differences that do exist are more differences in degree than in kind. Public organizations differ from private organizations in that they are characterized by more legalism, they are subject to congressional scrutiny, they have less discretion in interpreting the relationships between organizational welfare and the general welfare, and they are more likely to be seen as inefficient and corrupt than are private organizations.[33] Nonetheless, Simon argues that there are fundamental commonalities in human behavior in public and private organizations and that the findings of a science of administration are applicable in both settings.[34] In emphasizing the similarities between public and private organizations, Simon is in agreement with the Classical authors, although he would counsel substantially different techniques of administration from those of the Classical authors.

In sum, Simon's objective is to construct a science of administration focusing on decision making, with decision premises as the unit of analysis and the factual component of those premises constituting the scientific domain. This science is to be based on systematic empirical investigation, it is to be inductive and primarily descriptive, and its findings would be generally applicable to both public and private organizations. Simon's efforts to develop a science of administration have led him to a reconceptualization of existing models of man as a decision maker and the interaction between man and the organization in making decisions in an organizational environment. These considerations are the subject of examination in the remainder of this chapter with primary emphasis on decision making in an organizational context.

Individual Decision Making

In discussing Simon's view of decision-making processes, it is useful to begin at the end. That is, I reverse the chronological ordering of the development of Simon's interests, as outlined earlier, and work from individual decision processes to decision making in the organization.

Simon starts his analysis by proposing a new model of decision-making man. Simon refers to this model as "Satisficing Man," that is, a decision maker who, because of the limits on his cognitive and analytical abilities, accepts alternatives that are merely satisfactory or sufficient in regard to his aspiration levels.[35] Simon notes that there are several alternative models of man as a decision maker. The psychological model of man as a decision maker emphasizes affective (i.e, emotional) considerations in decision making.[36] The sociological model emphasizes role playing with little room for choice and, consequently, rationality.[37] Probably the best known of the models of man is Economic Man, which emphasizes cognitive and analytical, as opposed to affective, processes and embodies maximizing assumptions about the decision-making behavior.[38]

In proposing the model of Satisficing Man, Simon seeks a middle ground among these alternatives. Thus, Satisficing Man is distinguished from Psychological Man in the former's emphasis on cognitive and analytical elements of decision making. Satisficing Man is distinguished from Sociological Man in that his decision making is not totally determined by social roles. He is distinguished from Economic Man by being limited in his cognitive and analytical capabilities.

Though Simon recognizes that a mature science must accommodate both affective and cognitive elements of human behavior, his central concerns are cognitive elements. He defines his task as the reconstruction of theory to provide an explanation of rational human behavior with some pretense of realism.[39] Given this emphasis on the cognitive elements of the decision-making process, Simon is primarily concerned with distinguishing Satisficing Man from Economic Man.

Economic Man

Simon argues that the field of economics has concentrated on only one aspect of man, his reason, and the application of that reason to the problem of allocation in the face of scarcity. In this context, Economic Man is viewed as a value maximizer who can deal effectively with uncertainty. The model of Economic Man is based on the following assumptions:

1. The decision maker knows all the relevant aspects of the decision environment.

2. The decision maker knows all the alternative courses of action.

3. The decision maker knows all the consequences of those alternatives with certainty, or he knows the probability distribution of the occurrence of the consequences (risk).

4. The decision maker has a known, and temporally stable, preference function for all sets of consequences. That is, he knows how he

values the sets of consequences, he can rank-order the sets of consequences, and that ordering will remain stable over time.

5. The decision maker has the required computational skills.

6. The decision maker maximizes the satisfaction of his values by choosing that alternative which is followed by the most preferred set of consequences.[40]

Given this set of assumptions, Economic Man employs a relatively simple decision procedure. First, he arrays all the alternatives. Second, he determines all the consequences attached to each alternative. Third, he makes a comparative evaluation of each set of consequences. Fourth, Economic Man selects the strategy that is followed by the preferred set of consequences.

Simon does not gainsay the importance of the economics model. He considers it an appropriate normative model of decision making and one that provides a precise definition of rationality.[41] Nevertheless, Simon charges that the economic model of man is an inadequate description of actual decision-making behavior and is based on an overly restrictive view of rationality.

The basic descriptive problem of the economic model is its neglect of uncertainty in most phases of the decision-making procedure and its failure to deal effectively with uncertainty where it attempts to do so. Simon argues that uncertainty pervades the decision process.[42] Thus the decision maker is likely to be uncertain about objectives, the range of possible alternatives, the consequences of those alternatives, and the relationships between the alternatives and their consequences. The economic model ignores uncertainty about objectives, alternatives, and consequences. The model deals with uncertainty only in regard to the relationships between alternatives and their consequences; even there, it does so unsuccessfully, since it provides no generally acceptable criterion for the selection of an alternative under conditions of uncertainty.

The descriptive inadequacies of the economic model limit its predictive capabilities. Simon argues that economists who insist on maximization in their model of man become satisficers in evaluating their own theories.[43] By this, he means that economists require only that their model be good enough to render satisfactory predictions and ignore the actual processes of choice. Although a model should be limited in its required assumptions, however, it should also incorporate all the assumptions necessary to account for behavior. Simon contends that the economic model cannot sufficiently account for behavior and, consequently, cannot effectively predict decision-making outcomes. Furthermore, he argues that the model of Satisficing Man is a better description of decision-making behavior and thus has better predictive power.[44]

In regard to rationality, Simon contends that almost all behavior has a rational component, but not necessarily in terms of "economic" rationality (i.e., value-maximizing behavior).[45] Consequently, he argues that the definition of rationality should be expanded to incorporate a wider range of human behavior.

Satisficing Man

Satisficing Man represents Simon's effort to provide a suitable descriptive model of human decision making in a broadened context of rationality. Simon's reformulation casts the decision maker in the modest role of one who is intendedly rational but who satisfices because he has "not the wits to maximize."[46] In making decisions, Satisficing Man does not examine all possible alternatives, he ignores most of the complex interrelationships of the real world, and he makes decisions by applying relatively simple rules-of-thumb or heuristics.[47] In short, Satisficing Man simplifies and satisfices because he operates in an area of "bounded rationality" with bounds imposed by the limits on available information and his own computational abilities.

Can such a decision procedure be considered rational? Simon's answer is a qualified yes, with the qualification being that it depends on how one defines *rationality*—and Simon proposes a rather broad definition. Simon imposes two requirements on the definition of rationality. The definition must accommodate the extent to which appropriate courses of action are actually chosen (outcomes), and the definition should address the effectiveness and limitations of the procedures used to make decisions (process). Accordingly, Simon defines rationality as "the selection of preferred behavioral alternatives in terms of some system of values whereby the consequences of behavior can be evaluated."[48] Furthermore, Simon distinguishes among several kinds of rationality that, taken together, serve to expand substantially the compass of the term.[49] Objective rationality is, in fact, the correct behavior for maximizing given values in a given situation. Subjective rationality is maximizing value attainment relative to the actual knowledge of the decision maker. Conscious rationality is a conscious adjustment of means to ends, but the adjustment of means to ends may also be subconscious in nature.[50] Deliberate rationality is a process by which the adjustment of means to ends is deliberate, but the adjustment of means to ends may also be nondeliberate in character. Organizational rationality is oriented toward the organization's objectives, whereas individual rationality is oriented toward individual goals.

In short, Simon would have rationality range across a continuum bounded on one end by subconscious and nondeliberate adaptations of means to ends based on incomplete knowledge and on the other by conscious and deliberate adaptations based on complete knowledge. Most decision-making behavior, of course, would fall somewhere between these extremes. In addition, the system of values by which alternatives are chosen may be either organizational or individual. I return to this point in examining organizational decision-making processes.

This enlarged definition of rationality is consistent with Simon's claim that all human behavior has a rational component and his insistence that we look beyond the rather narrow bounds of economic rationality in analyzing and assessing human behavior. Simon would extend the reach of rationality even to psychoanalytic theory, which explains behavior in terms of the functions performed for the individual; Simon notes that "even madness has its methods."[51]

Individual Decision Processes

Much of Simon's most recent work has been concerned with elaborating the ways in which Satisficing Man goes about making decisions. At the broadest level of generalization, the decision maker can be conceptualized as an artificial system, that is, a system that adapts through goals and purposes to the environment in which it exists.[52] More specifically, Simon conceives of the decision maker as an information-processing system and maintains that there are broad commonalities among humans as information-processing systems engaging in the task of making decisions.

As an information-processing system, the decision maker is limited in his capacities and deals with alternatives sequentially. That is, the decision maker can process only a few symbols at a time, and those symbols are held in memory structures of limited access, capacity, or both.[53] As a result, the decision maker is forced to deal with one or a few alternatives at a time rather than deal with all alternatives simultaneously. Problem-solving activities involve interaction between the decision maker and the decision environment, and the behavior of the decision maker is determined by his internal state, stimuli from the decision environment, and the interaction between the two. The internal state of the decision maker is a function of his previous history with information from his history stored in a memory. Nonetheless, any specific decision-making activity can involve only a small part of the information contained in the memory. Thus decision making is a mutual product of a process for evoking some portion of the information contained in the memory and the limited information evoked. Therefore, decision-making behavior is influenced either by changing the active determiners of current behavior (evocation) or by altering the information contained in the memory (learning).[54] In sum, the decision maker as an information-processing system is a problem solver who can do only a few things at a time and can attend to only a small portion of the information contained in his memory and presented by the task environment at any given point in time.

Stimuli. The first basic element in individual decisions is a stimulus from the decision environment. Simon distinguishes between two kinds of stimuli: repetitive and novel.[55] Repetitive stimuli evoke routinized or habitual responses. Novel stimuli evoke problem-solving responses and prompt search activity that may be either routinized or creative. Creative search activity, if necessary, proceeds until a solution is discovered or until some routinized response becomes applicable.

Given his limited capacities, the decision maker is not likely to be aware of, nor will he be able to respond to, all the stimuli emanating from the decision environment. Instead, there is likely to be selective attention to stimuli that is reinforced by the existence of a mutual interaction between environmental stimuli and the information evoked from the memory. That is, not only do environmental stimuli influence what information will be drawn from the memory, but also the information drawn from the memory will influence what environmental stimuli will be perceived.[56]

Memory. The second basic element in individual decisions is the memory. Information stored in the memory consists of criteria that are applied to determine preferred courses of action (values or goals); the alternative possible courses of action; and beliefs, perceptions, and expectations regarding the relationships between alternative courses of action and their outcomes.[57] The memory consists of two components: short-term and long-term. The short-term memory is characterized by a limited capacity and relatively quick access. The long-term memory has a virtually unlimited capacity, but a relatively long period is required to transfer information from the short-term memory to the long-term memory, and vice versa.

Simon notes that the most serious limits on the decision-maker's ability to employ appropriate decision-making strategies are the limited capacity of the short-term memory and the amount of time required to store information in the long-term memory.[58] Given the difficulties of attention and access, only a small part of the information stored in the long-term memory plays an active role in problem solving at any given time. Nevertheless, one element of the long-term memory may activate other elements based on prior learning and increase the amount of information brought to bear on the decision problem. In the case of habitual response, the connecting links between the stimulus and response and among elements of the memory may be suppressed from the decision-maker's consciousness.[59]

Problem-Solving Process. The problem-solving process begins with what Simon refers to as a "problem space."[60] The problem space is the decision-maker's subjective and simplified representation of the decision environment. The problem space determines the possible programs or strategies that will be used for problem solving as the individual extracts information from the decision environment and uses that information to make a selective search for a solution to the problem as defined. The effectiveness of problem-solving activity is thus a function of how well the critical features of the decision environment are reflected in the problem space.

Having defined the problem space, the decision maker proceeds to scan that space for viable alternative solutions. Search activity is simplified in a number of ways. First, search takes place only in the area defined by the problem space. Second, search is patterned, rather than random, with the pattern determined by simplified rules-of-thumb (heuristics) suggesting which path should be followed. Selectivity in search is made possible by trial-and-error experimentation and, more important, by learning from previous experience.[61] Third, search is sequential rather than simultaneous in nature. By this, Simon means that all alternatives are not considered at once. Instead, alternatives are scanned one at a time, evaluated, and accepted or rejected. Only when a given alternative is rejected does the decision maker move on to another alternative. Fourth, the decision maker will attempt to reduce the problem to one already solved with creative search limited to bridging the gap between the new problem and the old solution. Finally, search will be limited, and consequently simplified, by feasibility considerations. Search cannot extend beyond the boundaries imposed by the amount of resources available to conduct the search.

The decision maker may employ any of several strategies in searching the problem space. When there is a standardized response (routine), search is minimal or nonexistent, and the decision maker simply applies the routine. If a routine is not applicable, search may be standardized and based on a pattern or rule stored in the memory to calculate successive moves. Simon calls this "pattern-driven" search. If neither a routine nor a patterned search procedure is applicable, search will take one of two forms: stimulus-driven search, which uses visual cues to determine successive moves; or goal-driven search, which employs a goal or subgoal structure to determine successive moves.[62] Heuristic search in its pattern-driven, stimulus-driven, and goal-driven forms proceeds by finding the difference between current and desired states, finding an operator relevant to each difference, and applying that operator to reduce the difference.[63]

The final step in the individual's decision process is choice. The decision maker will choose the first alternative that satisfices in terms of an aspired level of performance along each relevant dimension. In evaluating alternatives the decision maker operates with what Simon calls "simple payoff functions" that are "partially ordered."[64] By this he means that the decision maker will examine the consequences of a given alternative in terms of the presence or absence of a particular attribute (a simply payoff function) and will compare alternatives on the basis of at least minimal satisfaction of aspirations in regard to each relevant attribute (a partial ordering of the payoffs). In this way, the decision maker both simplifies the problem of choice and deals with the potential noncomparability of outcomes.

The discovery of a satisficing alternative will normally terminate search and result in a choice. An exception to this rule occurs when a satisficing alternative is discovered too easily. In this case, the aspiration level will be raised, and search will continue. If a satisficing alternative is not discovered and the cost of additional search is considered to be excessive (i.e., greater than the potential benefits), the decision maker will lower his aspiration level to accommodate alternatives already discovered.[65]

Decision Making in an Organizational Environment

Having outlined the individual's decision process, we can now consider that decision process in an organizational environment and, more particularly, the impact of organizations on individual decisions. Simon states that formal organizations are organizations in which roles are highly elaborated, relatively stable, and well defined; transactions among organizational participants are preplanned and precoordinated; and the processes of influence are specific. As an environment for decision making, Simon says the organization can be considered a complex network of decision processes oriented toward influencing individual behavior.[66] The organization creates stimuli that determine the focus of attention for specific decisions, provides premises for those decisions, and maintains stable expectations about the actions and reactions of other participants in the organization. The organization also creates personal qualities and habits in the individual (an organizational personality) and provides those in positions of responsibility with the means for exerting authority and influence. In short, Simon states that the organization takes from the individual some of his or her decision autonomy and substitutes for it an organizational decision process.[67]

The behavior of the individual acquires a "broader context of rationality," however, through the environment of choice provided by the organization. In this, Simon agrees with Weber, who contended that the organization can overcome the computational limits of man by such devices as specialization and the division of labor, which bring expert knowledge to bear on organization decisions and limit the required focus of attention. In Simon's words, "The rational individual is, and must be, an organized and institutionalized individual."[68] The behavior of the individual acquires a broader context of rationality as the organization places the individual in a psychological environment that adapts individual decisions to organizational objectives and provides the individual with information to make decisions correctly.

Although Simon is in basic accord with the Classical authors in this formulation, he differs in respect to his assessment of the degree of control that the organization can exercise over individual decisions. Simon argues that the Classical model is not sufficiently attentive to the character of human organism. It ignores the wide range of roles that participants perform simultaneously and does not treat the coordination of those roles effectively. As a result, the Classical model fails to recognize that only some influences on individual decision making in the organization are under the control of the organization and that individual behavior is manipulable only within limits imposed by potential or actual individual and/or group resistance.[69]

Accordingly, Simon takes as his objective the construction of a model of the organization that more fully accounts for human nature and the relationship of the individual to the organization. In so doing, Simon addresses what he believes to be the two central concerns of any theory of organizations: (1) why people join, remain in, or leave organizations (the decision to participate), and (2) behavior while people are in the organization (the decision to produce).

The Decision to Participate

In addressing the question why people decide to participate in the organization, Simon adopts Barnard's basic framework in which the organization is viewed as a system of exchange involving inducements for participation offered by the organization and the contributions required by the organization of each participant—or, more precisely, the utilities attached to those inducements and contributions. Each participant will agree to participate, and will continue to participate, in the organization only as long as that individual perceives that he or she is receiving a net positive balance of inducements over required contributions. The organization is in equilibrium when all participants perceive that they are receiving such a balance, and it is solvent as long as the inducements offered by the organization are sufficient to elicit required contributions from the participants.

Simon refers to the perceived utility of inducements and contributions as the Inducement-Contribution Utility Scale.[70] Positions on the Inducement-Contribution Utility Scale are a function of two considerations: the perceived desirability of moving from the organization and the perceived ease of such movement. The perceived desirability of moving from the organization depends on the individual's satisfaction with his or her participation. Satisfaction, in turn, is conditioned by a broad range of personal, social, and economic considerations. The perceived ease of movement is a function of the availability of alternatives to participation in the organization and the participant's awareness of those alternatives.

The nature of the "contractual" relationship between the participant and the organization varies among classes of participants. For most participants, the contract is in the form of a "sales contract" in which specific considerations (inducements and contributions) are exchanged. For one class of participants—employees of the organization—the contract is in the form of what Simon calls an "employment contract" in which the employee makes a general agreement to accept organizational authority rather than exchange specific considerations with the organization.[71] Simon argues that the employer is willing to enter into an employment contract, and pay additional compensation, because he is likely to be uncertain about the specific task requirements of a position. The employee is willing to enter into an employment contract because he is "substantially indifferent" about the specific tasks to be performed. The result of this contractual arrangement, according to Simon, is that the employee signs, in effect, a "blank check" giving the employer authority over the employee's behavior in the organization.

The nature of the employment contract has important consequences for both the organization and the employee. From the organization's viewpoint, the employee's willingness to sell his services and, consequently, to become a neutral instrument in the performance of those services means that the importance of personal motives is reduced or eliminated and that the employee will accept criteria unrelated to personal values as the basis for his organizational decision making. From the viewpoint of the employee, acceptance of the terms of the employment contract reduces the cognitive demands on his decision-making capacity by restricting his attention to organizational decision-making criteria. These criteria then determine both the alternatives scanned and the alternative selected in a decision situation. In short, the decision environment is simplified.

There are also significant consequences for Simon's theory of the organization. By positing an employment contract, Simon can ignore personal values and the affective components of an employee's behavior in the organization and focus on the cognitive aspects of individual behavior. It should be noted that Simon does not deny the importance of personal values and motives. Instead, he relegates these considerations to "boundary decisions," that is, decisions influencing the decision to participate in the organization, not to decisions made once the individual has agreed to participate. Simon admits this is an oversimplified view, but it is an analytical simplification that plays an important role in the elaboration of his theory.[72]

Consonant with his notion of the employment contract, Simon distinguishes between motives and goals and between individual goals and organizational goals.[73] Motives are forces that lead individuals to select some goals rather than others as decision premises. Personal motives, as implied by the employment contract, pertain only to the decision to participate in the organization. Goals are the result of motives and serve as value premises for decisions. Individual goals in the organization are selected by reference to organizational roles, not personal motives. Since individual goals act as constraints on the behavior of others in a mutually interdependent organizational setting, Simon defines organizational goals as "widely shared constraint sets" or, and not necessarily equivalently, the constraint sets and criteria of search that define the roles of persons in the upper levels of the organization.[74] Thus, personal motives determine the decision to participate in the organization, but organizational roles determine the selection of organizational goals and the selection courses of action to achieve those goals.

The Decision to Produce

According to Simon, once the individual has decided to participate in the organization, he or she takes on an organizational personality. In so doing, the individual adopts a generalized deference to organizational authority and is "substantially indifferent" regarding the specific tasks to be performed. It then becomes the strategic task of the organization to translate that generalized deference to authority into specific deference to organizational directives. This raises two central, and related, concerns: employee motivation and compliance.

Whereas the decision to participate in the organization is a function of the Inducement-Contribution Utility Scale, Simon argues that the motivation to produce in the organization is a function of the Satisfaction Scale.[75] The two scales are related, since a higher perceived net positive balance of inducements over required contributions is associated with higher levels of satisfaction. The scales are different in that the Inducement-Contribution Utility Scale, as noted earlier, is a function of both the desire to move and the perceived ease of movement, whereas the Satisfaction Scale is a function of the desire to move only. In other words, the Inducement-Contribution Utility Scale includes opportunity cost calculations, and the Satisfaction Scale does not. This means that, though functionally related, the scales differ in the location of their zero points.[76] If it is perceived that alternative employment is available and that the employment possibility is superior to the individual's current position, a satisfied employee may leave the organization. In contrast, if alternative employment opportunities do not seem to be available, an employee who is not satisfied may remain in the organization.

Although arguing that one's position on the Satisfaction Scale is related to the decision to produce, Simon rejects the suggestion that there is a simple and direct causal relationship between satisfaction and productivity. Indeed, Simon would reverse that causal ordering. Simon argues that the motivation to produce stems from a present or anticipated state of discontent and a perception that there is a direct connection between individual productivity and a new state of satisfaction.[77] Thus, the employee produces more to achieve a state of greater satisfaction; he is not more productive simply because he is more satisfied. Nevertheless, the organization must arrange incentives so that the employee perceives a linkage between work effort and rewards.

On compliance, Simon starts with Barnard's concept of authority. Simon agrees with Barnard that authority resides in a relationship between a superior and a subordinate, not in a position, and that the critical act in the authority relationship is the acceptance of a directive, not its issuance. But Simon proposes an important revision of Barnard's concept of authority. Barnard's position is that authority is exercised when the subordinate either accepts a directive without examining its merits or accepts a directive after examining its merits and being convinced that it is appropriate. In the first case, the directive falls within the subordinate's "zone of indifference." In the latter case, the directive falls outside the zone of indifference but within the "zone of acceptance." Simon defines authority as the power to make decisions in the form of a directive or a command that guide the actions of another and, in contrast to Barnard, he contends that authority is exercised *only* when the subordinate holds his critical faculties in abeyance.[78] Thus Simon argues that authority is exercised only in the zone of indifference and in those instances where the subordinate examines the merits of a directive and accepts the directive *despite* the fact that he is not convinced of its merits or thinks the directive is wrong. Instances where the subordinate is convinced of the merits of a directive and accepts the directive fall within the domain of influence or persuasion rather than authority.

The questions of motivation and compliance are joined in Simon's consideration of why subordinates defer to organizational authority. Broadly speaking, employee deference to organizational authority is a function of the perceived balance between inducements and contributions required. The larger the perceived net positive balance of inducements over required contributions, the more likely is it that an employee will accept an organizational directive. More specifically, Simon identifies four bases of organizational authority that both derive from, and reinforce, the operation of the organizational incentive system. *Authority of confidence* is based on functional status and/or the charismatic qualities of the person issuing the directive. *Authority of identification* is the product of the acceptance of a directive by a group with which the individual identifies. *Authority of sanctions* is derived from the anticipation that a sanction will be applied. The *authority of legitimacy* springs from the beliefs, mores, and values of a society establishing the right of the superior to command and the duty of the subordinate to obey.[79]

Decision Premises

When the individual has decided to participate and produce, the organizational problem is reduced to one of providing the appropriate premises for individual decision making in the organization. For Simon, the primary responsibility for the provision of decision premises lies with the hierarchy. In this, Simon echoes Taylor's injunction that management first make itself efficient before expecting efficiency from its subordinates. The executive's responsibility is both to make decisions and to see that other individuals in the organization make decisions effectively.[80]

Simon offers a number of justifications for his emphasis on hierarchical control in organizational decision making. In a traditional vein, hierarchy is seen as a means for securing coordination, specialization, and accountability.[81] Coordination is achieved as hierarchy synchronizes the disparate elements produced in the process of horizontal specialization in complex organizations.[82] In addition, hierarchy is a method of *vertical* specialization that affords those with greater expertise greater authority in the organization and, consequently, assures that technical experts will play a commanding role in organizational decision making. Finally, by making relatively precise assignments of authority and jurisdiction, hierarchy is a means for assigning responsibilities in the organization and thus locating accountability.

In addition to these traditional arguments, Simon argues that hierarchy simplifies the decision-making task. Indeed, Simon contends that hierarchy is *the* adaptive form for finite intelligence to take in the face of complexity.[83] Simon maintains that complex hierarchical organizations evolve from relatively stable subsystems that are largely independent units of the overall organization. In this "room-within-rooms" structure, complexity is independent of size, since interdependencies are minimized. The result is that a complex hierarchical organization requires less information transmission, and, consequently, the decision-making process is simplified.[84]

Simon assigns a wide range of critical functions to superiors in the organizational structure. Management sets goals. Management allocates work by establishing the overall structure of the organization and assigning tasks to its subunits. Management is responsible for innovation and long-range planning. Management settles disputes. Most important, from the perspective of decision making, management establishes decision premises for the organization. Broad premises (policy) are framed at the upper reaches of the hierarchy. More specific premises are developed as one descends the hierarchy and standard operating procedures are constructed for organizational decision making.

The criterion of efficiency serves as a standard for decision making throughout the organization and, indirectly, as means for hierarchical control. Simon defines efficiency as the maximization of the ratio of net positive results (i.e., positive results minus negative results) to opportunity costs.[85] In other words, efficiency is getting the greatest possible results with the lowest possible opportunity costs. Simon argues that the criterion of efficiency should become an internalized standard of performance for each organizational employee. Though each individual seeks efficiency in terms of his or her own values, those values should be the product of an organizational role and, to the extent that management has been successful in establishing organizational objectives, efficiency will be measured in reference to the goals of the management group.[86]

The organizational hierarchy has a variety of means at its disposal for performing its functions. The most important is transmitting the right decision premise to the right person at the right time. The exercise of authority is a central means of establishing decision premises by formal directive. Communication in forms other than formal directives also serves to establish decision premises by influencing which decision stimuli will be encountered and how forcefully particular courses of action will be brought to the attention of the decision maker. Selection processes allow management to choose employees whose values and skills are consistent with the needs of the organizations. Once the individual is in the organization, training can assist in translating general values and skills into specific organizational values and skills as the employee develops a sense of loyalty to the organization.

Organizational Decision Making
To this point, the role of decision premises in organizational behavior and mechanisms for establishing decision premises have been discussed. The next concern is the actual processes of decision making in the organization. Simon deals with two basic kinds of decision proce-

dures: programmed and nonprogrammed. Before discussing these decision procedures, some characteristics common to both can be elaborated.

First, both programmed and nonprogrammed decision making start with what Simon calls a "definition of the situation." This is a simplified model of reality constructed to reduce the complexities of the actual decision environment. The definition of the situation includes the decision-maker's perception of the likelihood of future events, the range of alternatives seen as possible, expectations regarding the consequences of those alternatives, and rules for ordering the consequences according to the preferences of the decision maker.[87]

A second characteristic common to the two decision procedures is that some form of means-ends analysis is conducted to link specific actions with the ultimate objectives of the organization. The means-ends chain has both factual and value elements. The factual element is the relationship between alternatives and their consequences. Since lover-level objectives in the means-ends chain are both the ends of lower-level means and the means to achieve higher-level objectives, a factual element exists at all levels except the highest of the means-ends chain. The value element of the means-ends chains is the selection of the ultimate objective or objectives of the organization. Since the ultimate objective of the organization is, by definition, not a means to a higher end, there is no factual element involved in its selection.[88]

The means-ends chain is characterized by increasing uncertainty about the relationship between alternatives and their consequences as one ascends the chain. This has two important implications. First, uncertainty introduces a level of indeterminateness in the decision process and forces the use of judgment regarding relationships between alternatives and consequences that though knowable, are not known.[89] Second, uncertainty means that the decision maker will likely use "value indicators" rather than ultimate objectives to choose among alternatives. The value indicator is the highest-level objective in the means-ends chain that can be stated operationally, that is, in such a way that the steps required to meet the objective can be elaborated and that the objective can be measured to determine whether it has, in fact, been achieved.[90]

A third characteristic common to both programmed and nonprogrammed decision making is that decisions (problems) are factored or divided into nearly independent parts and assigned to organizational subunits.[91] The upper levels of the hierarchy make broad determinations and delegate more specific considerations to subordinate units. It is likely that this will result in what Simon calls a "loosely coupled" system in which the objectives of the organization and its subunits are only imperfectly reconciled. But since organizations typically operate under conditions of organizational "slack" (i.e., resources in excess of the amount required for survival), the organization can tolerate some inconsistency among its objectives.[92]

A fourth common characteristic is that "satisficing" rather than "optimizing" criteria are used in choosing among alternatives. Simon distinguishes satisficing from optimizing criteria on the following basis: For optimization, one posits a set of criteria that permits all alternatives to be compared. The optimizing decision maker selects the alternative preferred, by these criteria, to all other alternatives. For satisficing, one posits a set of criteria that describes minimally satisfactory alternatives. The satisficing decision maker simply selects an alternative that meets or exceeds all these criteria.[93]

A fifth common characteristic is that the decision-making process is likely to involve uncertainty absorption. Uncertainty absorption entails drawing conclusions from data that themselves take on an aura of unwarranted certainty. The conclusions become decision premises for the rest of the organization and points of uncertainty absorption are thus critical locations of power in the organization.[94]

A final common characteristic is that decision making in the organization is routinized. The degree of routinization ranges from specified responses in programmed decision making to routinized search procedures in nonprogrammed decision making.

Simon identifies four phases of the decision-making process that will be used to compare programmed and nonprogrammed decision making in the organization.

1. Finding occasions to make decisions
2. Finding alternative possible courses of action
3. Choosing among alternatives
4. Evaluating past choices[95]

Programmed Decision Making. Programmed decision making occurs when a decision stimulus is repetitive, and the organization has developed a definite procedure for handling the situation. The procedure is embodied in what Simon calls a "performance program" that determines the sequence of responses to a task.[96] Performance programs vary in regard to their degree of specificity. Organizational routines are the most specific of the performance programs. Decisions are made by reference to approved practices rather than by consideration of alternatives on their merits. Thus, choice is fixed, and no search activity is involved. Simon compares organizational routines to individual habit and, perhaps more aptly, to computer programs. For performance strategies, as opposed to routines, the responses are not fixed. Search is restricted to the contingencies and alternatives specified by the strategy, however. In either case, the performance program deals with a restricted range of situations and consequences, and each program is executed in relative independence from other programs.

Performance programs can be constructed at various levels of the organization. In general, higher levels of the organization are more concerned with coordinating programs developed elsewhere than with the development of new programs. Once the organization has established a repertory of standard responses, it develops a classification of program-evoking situations and a set of rules to determine the appropriate response for each class of situations to guide the individual decision maker.

Simon identifies a number of techniques for making and/or influencing programmed decision making in the organization.[97] Traditional methods have been habit, clerical routines, and organizational structure. Habit is the most pervasive technique and is established by such mechanisms as educational and training systems maintained by society and the selection and training processes within the organization. Clerical routines or standard operating procedures are explicit statements used to formalize habitual patterns. The organizational structure influences programmed decision making by dividing decisions, providing a common set of presuppositions and expectations regarding role behavior, establishing a structure of goals and subgoals, and instituting a well-defined communication system. Modern techniques include operations research and simulation.[98] Operations research relies on mathematical analysis and model construction to establish programs for organizational decisions. Simulation replicates, in simplified fashion, system operations under a variety of conditions and stipulates appropriate decision rules for those situations.

Returning to the phases of the decision process cited previously, programmed decision making is a truncated process in which search activity is either severely restricted or nonexistent. Repetitive stimuli serve as a means for identifying occasions for making decisions. Performance programs, in the limiting case of organizational routines, determine the alternative of choice. For performance strategies, the range of alternatives scanned is restricted, and the criterion of choice is defined. Evaluation is relevant only to the extent that, over time, the performance program produces noticeably unsatisfactory outcomes.

Nonprogrammed Decision Making. Nonprogrammed decisions are made in response to novel stimuli for which no structured response exists. Consequently, nonprogrammed decision making requires some search activity. That search will follow predictable and prescribed patterns.

Search activity is prompted by the perception of a "performance gap" or a deficiency in the actual as opposed to the aspired level of performance. The performance gap may be the product of unsatisfactory performance in regard to previous aspiration levels, heightened aspirations resulting from factors such as encounters with new opportunities, or a combination of those factors.[99] The size of the performance gap generally determines the intensity of the search effort (i.e., the larger the gap, the more intense will be the search). If the gap is too small, however, it may produce apathy; if too large, it may produce frustration. In those cases, a performance gap will not stimulate search activity. Simon refers to points between these extremes as "optimum stress," and performance gaps in that range lead to the initiation of an action program to eliminate the gap.[100] The goals of the search procedure are determined by aspired levels of performance in the organization that are stated in satisficing rather than optimizing terms. The aspiration levels, in turn, are determined by factors such as the past performance of other similar organizations, changes in the organizational environment, and/or accidental encounters with opportunities.

The search activity of the organization is both sequential and routinized in character. Search is sequential in that one alternative at a time is examined rather than a range of alternatives being scanned simultaneously.[101] Search is routinized in that it follows predictable and prescribed patterns. Variables under the direct control of the organization are examined first. If a satisfactory alternative is not generated, search proceeds to variables not under the direct control of the organization. If the search procedure still has not produced a satisfactory alternative, the aspiration level is lowered, and the search procedure returns to its initial phase. Search activity continues until an alternative is found that closes the performance gap, either in terms of the original or the revised level of aspiration.[102]

As with programmed decision making, Simon identifies a number of procedures that have been employed in nonprogrammed decision making. Traditionally, organizations have relied on judgment, rules-of-thumb, and the selection and training of executives to cope with nonprogrammed decision situations.[103] Simon indicates that these techniques can be improved somewhat by training in orderly thinking, the assignment of primary responsibility for nonprogrammed decision making to top executives, and the designation of a specific unit in the organization to deal with nonprogrammed decisions. More recently, Simon believes that major advances have been made in developing techniques for dealing with nonprogrammed decision making.[104] These techniques fall under the general rubric of heuristic problem solving, which involves looking for simplifying clues or hints for right directions to follow in addressing problems. Modern techniques of heuristic problem solving are based on computer simulations of actual decision makers as they engage in problem-solving tasks. This simulation is intended to expose, evaluate, systematize, and routinize the traditional techniques of judgment, intuition, and creativity.

Returning once again to the phases of the decision process, in nonprogrammed decision making the occasion of choice is identified by the perception of a performance gap. The alternatives scanned are limited by previous organizational practices with the range of alternatives being incrementally expanded only in the absence of the discovery of a satisfactory alternative. Choice is determined by an encounter with the first satisfactory alternative. Evaluation takes place at each stage of a sequential search process. The major difference between programmed and nonprogrammed decision making is that whereas in programmed decision making the organization determines the alternative of choice either in the form of an organizational routine or a performance strategy, in nonprogrammed decision making the organization merely provides the parameters for the search procedure and the criterion of choice embodied in an organizationally determined aspiration level.

Rationality and Organizational Decision Making. We can raise the same question here that was raised in regard to Simon's model of individual decision making: Can the organizational decision procedures just described be considered rational even within the expanded boundaries of Simon's definition of "rationality"? To the extent that subordinates accept organizational decision premises in the form of routines, such behavior would fall toward the unconscious and nondeliberate end of Simon's rationality continuum but could nonetheless be rational for organizational objectives in terms of the outcomes of the decisions. The employment of performance strategies and nonprogrammed decision procedures represent conscious and deliberate processes in the pursuit of organizational objectives, but processes likely to fall in the realm of subjective rationality, that is, bounded by the limits on the informational resources and analytical capabilities of the decision maker. In short, although not likely optimal, Simon would not summarily dismiss the organizational decision-making procedures described as "nonrational."

Nevertheless, although Simon would expand the compass of the term "rationality," he would not contend that all organizational decisions are necessarily rational, even in that expanded context. Available information and analytical capabilities may not be used to the fullest extent. The definition of the situation used in problem solving may not be a sufficiently accurate representation of the decision environment, and, consequently, the problem itself may not be formulated correctly. The process of uncertainty absorption may also lead to nonrational outcomes if the inferences drawn from the raw data are not appropriate to the information received and thus provide faulty premises for subsequent decision making in the organization. Indeed, the very nature of routinized decision making may result in nonrational outcomes if the routines employed are not appropriate to the accomplishment of organizational objectives. This is a particular problem when, as is likely, the application of the routine falls within the individual's zone of indifference and, consequently, is applied without evaluation.

A major concern for Simon regarding the rationality of organizational decisions is the phenomenon of displacement of goals, a process in which instrumental values or goals are either substituted for the ultimate objectives of the organization or become valued because they have desirable consequences that were not originally anticipated.[105] Simon notes two major sources of possible goal displacement: loyalty to organizational subgoals and the use of value indicators in constructing means-ends chains.

Loyalty to organizational subgoals may develop as problems are factored and assigned to subunits in the organization. The result is that members of the subunits may concentrate on the goals of the subunit and lose sight of broader organizational objectives. Loyalty to subunit objectives is, in turn, generally the product of cognitive limits on rationality. That is, given the inability to think of everything at once, members of the subunit concentrate on considerations limited to the goals of the subunit rather than broader organizational goals. Thus, selective perception may lead to concentration only on information relevant to subgoals. Communication within the subgroup may shape the focus of information and exclude information seen as unrelated to subgoals. The formal division of labor in the organization may limit the information received by the subunit to that considered appropriate to the subgoals of the unit. Finally, professional identification may restrict the focus of attention as professionals emphasize information consistent with their calling.[106]

Displacement of goals may also result from the use of value indicators in the decision process. It will be recalled that value indicators are the highest-level operational objectives in the means-ends chain. Value indicators are employed because of uncertainty at the upper levels of the means-ends chain and the consequent inability of organizational decision makers to fully elaborate the chain. If pursuit of the objectives represented by the value indicators leads to the accomplishment of the ultimate objectives of the organization, no displacement of goals occurs. If it does not, then a displacement of goals does occur as instrumental values (the value indicators) replace the terminal values (ultimate objectives) of the organization.[107] Moreover, the displacement of goals is likely to go unnoticed, since, of necessity, the ultimate objectives of the organization cannot be stated operationally, and the organization will have no way of determining whether its ultimate objectives have been achieved.

In summary, the decision-making processes described by Simon are likely to be rational only in a subjective and bounded sense, and they may not be rational even in that sense.

Conclusion

In reviewing Simon's work, three primary considerations have been raised: Simon's objective of constructing a science of public administration, processes of individual decision making, and decision making in an organizational environment. Simon's proposed foundation for the construction of a science of public administration is the fact-value dichotomy. In proposing the fact-value dichotomy, Simon sought to describe a value-free domain in which scientific investigation could be conducted. That domain is the factual premises of administrative decisions defined as the relationship between alternatives and their consequences. Since that relationship is empirically observable, it is amenable to systematic (i.e., scientific) investigation. Simon proposes that two kinds of science be developed: a practical science with the objective of developing more efficient administrative procedures and a pure science, which is to examine the basic processes of human behavior as they relate to decision making.

There are problems with Simon's proposed fact-value dichotomy as a basis for either a practical or a pure science of administration. The acceptance of the standard of efficiency, the selection criterion of a practical science of administration, is in itself a value judgment.[108] Thus a practical science cannot be totally "scientific." Moreover, the fact-value dichotomy defines a rather narrowly circumscribed area for the construction of a practical science of administration. Values are involved in the selection of the ultimate objectives of the organization and, accordingly, fall outside the province of a practical science of administration. But values may also be present at other points in the means-ends chain. The selection of means is not valuationally neutral. That is, whether a means will accomplish a given objective is a factual (i.e., empirically observable) consideration, but the selection of the means is not necessarily value free (one does not rob a bank to provide funds for a charity even if that alternative leads to a desired consequence). Even an assessment of the relationship between an alternative and its consequences may be contaminated by values if uncertainty exists about the relationship, if judgment therefore must be exercised, and if that judgment is conditioned by the values of the observer. In sum, values may be present throughout the means-ends chain and limit the area of applicability of a practical science of administration.

The fact-value dichotomy also fails to describe fully the scientific domain for a pure science of administration. Decisions do not constitute the entirety of administrative behavior, and more is empirically observable than the relationship between alternatives and their consequences. Group relationships, styles of supervision, levels of satisfaction, and even whether particular values are held are only a few examples of empirically observable phenomena falling beyond the purview of a science based on facts as defined by Simon.

The second major component of Simon's work is his description of individual decision processes. Here, Simon substitutes the concept of Satisficing Man for the omniscient and lightning-quick calculator of utilities of economic theory. This view of the decision maker prompts Simon to expand the definition of rationality with rational decisions ranging from conscious and deliberate adaptations of means to ends based on complete information to subconscious and nondeliberate adaptations based on incomplete information.

The concept of Satisficing Man and the associated concept of rationality raise troublesome questions. Simon would seem to stretch the definition of rationality to the point of breaking when including all forms of functional adaptation, particularly functional adaptation to psychotic disturbances. This raises the question whether rationality as defined by Simon provides a basis for distinguishing between rational and nonrational behavior. Simon contends that all human behavior has a rational component, but the logical implication of that contention is that human behavior also has a nonrational component, and Simon's definition of rationality provides little basis for distinguishing between the two.

In addition, the model of Satisficing Man has limited predictive value. The model, as is acknowledged by Simon, does not provide unique solutions and, therefore, precise predictions. In particular, the level of aspirations is an elusive concept Simon is unable to fully explain. Without a prior definition of the level of aspirations, the theory has a tendency to degenerate into ex post facto explanations rather than be a predictive construct. Moreover, the model requires a great deal of information to make any predictions; that is, it is not parsimonious. The question here is how much precision we require of prediction. Simon may be right that the model of Satisficing Man yields different behavioral predictions than does the model of Economic Man, but he gives us no criteria to assess whether the difference in prediction is worth the cost of acquiring the required information.

The third major component of Simon's work is the description of organizational decision making, which raises two concerns. The first is

Simon's emphasis on the cognitive, as opposed to affective, elements of organizational behavior. The second is the intent of Simon's analysis. Is his intent descriptive, prescriptive, both, or neither?

Throughout his analysis, Simon stresses the cognitive aspects of organizational behavior while admitting that a mature science must ultimately deal with both the cognitive and affective dimensions of behavior in the organization. Several key elements of Simon's theory illustrate his relative emphasis on cognitive, as opposed to affective, dimensions of organizational behavior. Most basic, of course, is the employment contract under which, according to Simon, the employee agrees to be a neutral instrument with affective considerations held in abeyance in regard to behavior in the organization. Simon's assertion that the criterion of efficiency should be the standard for organizational performance is also based on the assumption that the employee is affectively neutral about the means selected to achieve organizational objectives. The exercise of authority itself is characterized as "an abdication of choice" in which the employee is either indifferent about an organizational directive or sets aside his disagreement with the directive. In regard to informal groups, the focus of many discussions of affective considerations, Simon simply advises that the formal organization should set limits on informal relationships and encourage the development of informal groups in ways compatible with the accomplishment of organizational objectives. The displacement of goals is interpreted in terms of cognitive limits on rationality rather than its affective dimensions.[109]

Even conflict in the organization is reduced by Simon to its cognitive dimensions. Simon does not deny that differences exist between organizational and individual interests. On the contrary, he explicitly rejects the assumption that there is some preordained harmony of interests in the organization.[110] Nevertheless, Simon contends that when the individual decides to participate in the organization, an organizational role is assumed and organizational loyalties are adopted. Thus, potential conflict between individual and organizational interests is resolved. What remains is potential conflict stemming from cognitive limits on rationality.[111] One such source of conflict is the nature of organizational goals themselves. Simon argues that conflict regarding organizational goals is likely to be the product of a cognitive inability to find courses of action satisfactory to the multiple constraints embodied in goals that are only loosely coupled and probably imperfectly reconciled. Another source of potential conflict is parochial loyalties, which Simon attributes to the cognitive inability to elaborate fully means-ends chains for organizational decision making. Finally, potential conflict may derive from such cognitive factors as lack of an acceptable alternative, incomparability of the consequences of alternatives examined, differing perceptions of reality used in constructing the definition of the situation, and/or uncertainty about the relationship between alternatives and their consequences.

Where Simon does deal with affective considerations, he simply argues that affective needs will be well served in the organizations he describes. Simon contends that individuals are uncomfortable in unstructured situations. Accordingly, organizations are most humane (i.e., they best serve affective needs) when they strike a balance between freedom and constraint.[112] For lower-level employees, service of affective needs does not mean an absence of hierarchical constraints. It simply means that those constraints should be reasonable and understandable. Furthermore, if a person is motivated to work for organizational objectives, appropriate behavior can be determined by the "logic of the situation" rather than by personal impositions of hierarchical authority.[113]

For middle management, the primary benefits stem from increased centralization, made possible, in part, by the application of computer technology. Centralization allows middle management to concentrate on overall objectives, since subgoal formation is discouraged; it reduces the amount of nonprogrammed decision making with which middle management must contend as hierarchically prescribed performance programs are developed; and it substitutes machine-paced for man-paced operations, which, Simon argues, is less grating on the individual.[114]

There are also benefits for top management. The development of programmed decision-making procedures relieves top management of the tedium of dealing with routine matters and frees them to deal with critical functions such as system design and innovation.[115]

Simon's emphasis on cognitive, as opposed to affective, considerations is clear. Whether such an emphasis is justified is a more difficult matter. There is a considerable body of literature indicating that affective considerations do influence organizational behavior. The *relative* importance of cognition and affect in the organization, although an empirical question, is one that, despite Simon's insistence on systematic empirical analysis, he fails to address. Simon admits that his formulation of the employment contract, for instance, is at least suspect on descriptive grounds. Nevertheless, he disregards evidence indicating that affective considerations are not abandoned once the employee crosses the threshold of the organization. Thus the employment contract and all that it implies for organizational behavior stands more as an analytical simplification than an empirical finding.

This suggests a broader question about Simon's intent: Is his work meant to be descriptive, prescriptive, both, or neither? The apparently anomalous, but nonetheless appropriate, response is probably *all of the above.* Simon's original intent was clearly descriptive in nature. In *Administration Science,* Simon faults the Classical authors for concentrating on prescriptions for the allocation of functions and the establishment of an appropriate formal structure of authority. Simon argues that "the first task of administrative theory is to develop a set of concepts that will permit the description, in terms of a relevant theory of administration, of administrative situations."[116] Simon's discussions of individual decision processes and at least some aspects of organizational behavior would appear to be primarily descriptive.

Simon also argues that description alone is not sufficient. Instead, description should provide the foundation for prescription. In Simon's words, "Until administrative description reaches a higher level of sophistication, there is little reason to hope that rapid progress will be made toward the identification and verification of valid administrative principles."[117] In other words, the derivation of principles and prescriptions based on those principles should be the result of an accumulation of descriptive, empirical findings. Simon goes even further in the direction of prescription in *The Sciences of the Artificial.* He argues that the fundamental problem of an organization as an artificial system is one of design to ensure appropriate adaptation to the external environment. Design, in turn, is concerned with what ought to be (prescription) in devising artificial systems to attain goals.[118] Simon seems to adopt a prescriptive stance in discussing design elements, such as the establishment of hierarchical control structures, the assignment of design and innovation responsibilities to top executives, the establishment of hierarchically prescribed decision premises, and the development of communication processes.

Finally, in the case of the employment contract, Simon's treatment appears to be neither descriptive nor prescriptive in nature. The concept of the employment contract is more a simplifying assumption than a description of, or a prescription for, organizational behavior. As Simon himself points out, his notion of the employment contract is "highly abstract and oversimplified, and leaves out of account numerous important aspects of the real situation."[119]

The problem is not so much that Simon is sometimes descriptive, sometimes prescriptive, and sometimes neither. The problem is determining when he is which. In the absence of clearer guidelines regarding his intent, the reader is hard pressed to distinguish one intent from the others.

The preceding statements are not meant to detract from the significance of Simon's contributions to the fields of public administration and organization theory. If there are shortcomings in Simon's analysis, they should be adjudged as such only by comparison to his ambitions—the construction of a science of administration and a unified explanation of human cognition in all its manifestations. Simon has proven to be a remarkably insightful and innovative theorist, and his esteemed position in the social sciences is both assured and well deserved.

Notes

1. Basic data on Simon's life is taken from *Who's Who in America*, vol. 2 (Chicago: Marquis Who's Who, 1976, 1977), 2889.

2. Herbert Simon, "Rationality as Process and as Product of Thought," *American Economic Review* 68, no. 2 (May 1978): 1.

3. Apparently, Simon also developed an early interest in decision making, since, as a high school student, he worked out a decision-tree analysis to prove that, if played properly, a game of Tic-Tac-Toe would always end in a draw. See Herbert Simon, *Administrative Behavior: A Study of Decision-Making Processes in Administrative Organization*, 2d ed. (New York: Free Press, 1945), xxviii.

4. Interestingly, given his research concerns, Simon's formal training in mathematics stopped short of calculus. He later taught himself calculus by reading through a textbook and working the problems. See Herbert Simon, *Models of Man: Social and Rational* (New York: Wiley, 1957), ix.

5. Ibid., vii.

6. Simon, *Administrative Behavior*.

7. Herbert Simon, Donald W. Smithburg, and Victor A. Thompson, *Public Administration* (New York: Knopf, 1950).

8. James G. March and Herbert A. Simon, *Organizations* (New York: Wiley, 1958).

9. Simon, *Models of Man*.

10. Herbert Simon, *The New Science of Management Decision*, rev. ed. (Englewood Cliffs, N.J.: Prentice-Hall, 1977).

11. Herbert A. Simon, *The Sciences of the Artificial* (Cambridge, Mass.: MIT Press, 1969).

12. Herbert A. Simon, *Models of Thought* (New Haven: Yale University Press, 1979), xi.

13. Simon, *Administrative Behavior*, xii.

14. Woodrow Wilson, "The Study of Administration," in *Classics of Public Administration*, eds. Jay M. Shafritz and Albert C. Hyde (Oak Park, Ill.: Moore Publishing, 1978), 10.

15. Ibid., 11.

16. Ibid., 12.

17. See Simon, *Administrative Behavior*, 58; and Herbert A. Simon, "The Changing Theory and Practice of Public Administration," in *Contemporary Political Science*, ed. Ithiel de Sola Pool (New York: McGraw-Hill, 1961), 87–88.

18. Simon, *Administrative Behavior*, 58–59.

19. Simon, "Changing Theory," 88.

20. Ibid., 89–91.

21. Ibid., 106.

22. Simon, *Administrative Behavior*, 47.

23. Ibid., 45–46.

24. Ibid., 5, 46, 48.

25. Simon, "Changing Theory," 99.

26. Ibid.

27. Simon, *Administrative Behavior*, 58.

28. Simon, "Changing Theory," 113.

29. Care should be taken to distinguish among Classical authors in drawing this difference. Simon approved of the techniques, if not the organizational *gestalt*, of the Scientific Management movement, which had emphasized systematic, empirical investigation. However, he had little use for the "principles" of the Departmentalists. Simon argues that those principles amount to little more than rules-of-thumb for organizational analysis and, like proverbs, tend to occur in contradictory pairs. See Simon, *Administrative Behavior*, 20–41.

30. Simon does not deny the utility of prescriptive analysis. Instead, Simon believes that description should precede prescription and that prescription should be based on a better understanding of how organizations actually operate. See ibid., 37.

31. Herbert A. Simon, "A Comment on 'The Science of Administration,'" in *Administrative Questions and Political Answers*, eds. Claude E. Hawley and Ruth G. Weintraub (New York: Van Nostrand, 1966), 34.

32. Simon, *Administrative Behavior*, 253.

33. Simon, Smithburg, and Thompson, *Public Administration*, 10–12.

34. Ibid., 8.

35. Simon, *Administrative Behavior*, xxiv.

36. Ibid., xxiii.

37. Ibid., xxx, xxxi.

38. Ibid., xxiii.

39. Simon, *Models of Man*, 200.

40. Ibid., 241; March and Simon, *Organizations*, 138; and Herbert Simon, "Rational Decision Making in Business Organizations," *American Economic Review* 69, no. 4 (September 1979): 500.

41. March and Simon, *Organizations*, 138; and Herbert Simon, "The Behavioral and Social Sciences," *Science* 209, no. 4 (July 1980): 75.

42. March and Simon, *Organizations*, 138.

43. Simon, "Rational Decision Making in Business Organizations," 495.

44. Ibid., 497.

45. Simon, "Rationality as Process and as Product of Thought," 2.

46. Simon, *Administrative Behavior*, xxiv.

47. Ibid., xxvi.

48. Ibid., 75.

49. Ibid., 76–77.

50. Simon cites some steps in mathematical invention as evidence of subconscious rationality. Ibid., 76.

51. Simon, "Behavioral and Social Sciences," 75.

52. Simon, *Sciences of the Artificial*, ix.

Herbert A. Simon

53. Ibid., 53.

54. March and Simon, *Organizations*, 10.

55. Ibid., 140.

56. Ibid., 10.

57. Ibid., 11.

58. Simon, *Sciences of the Artificial*, 53.

59. March and Simon, *Organizations*, 11.

60. Herbert Simon, "Information-Processing Theory of Human Problem Solving," in *Handbook of Learning and Cognitive Processes*, vol. 5, ed. W. K. Estes (Hillsdale, N.J.: Lawrence Erlbaum Associates, 1978), 272–73.

61. Indeed, Simon maintains that the distinguishing characteristic of humans is their ability to anticipate the consequences of alternative courses of action based on previously observed regularities. This is what Simon refers to as "docility," or the ability of individuals to observe the consequences of previous behavior and to adjust their behavior on the basis of those observations to achieve desired purposes. See Simon, *Administrative Behavior*, 85–86.

62. Simon, "Information-Processing Theory of Human Problem Solving," 283.

63. Ibid., 278.

64. Simon, *Models of Man*, 246–48, 250–52.

65. Simon acknowledges that, in contrast to the optimality criterion of Economic Man, the satisficing criterion of choice does not provide a unique solution to the problem of choice and thus reduces the utility of his model in regard to predicting decision-making behavior. However, he contends that if we learn enough about the dynamics of setting aspiration levels, a near-unique solution is possible. That enterprise has not yet been successfully completed. See ibid., 253.

66. Simon, *Administrative Behavior*, 220.

67. Ibid., 8.

68. Ibid., 102.

69. March and Simon, *Organizations*, 81–82.

70. Ibid., 85.

71. Simon, *Models of Man*, 183–95.

72. Ibid., 167.

73. Herbert Simon, "On the Concept of Organizational Goals," in *A Sociological Reader on Complex Organizations*, 2d ed., ed. Amitai Etzioni (New York: Holt, Rinehart, and Winston, 1969), 158–74.

74. Ibid., 174.

75. Ibid., 51.

76. Ibid., 85–86.

77. Ibid., 51.

78. Simon, *Administrative Behavior*, 126.

79. Simon, Smithburg, and Thompson, *Public Administration*, 188–201.

80. Herbert Simon, "Decision Making and Organizational Design," in *Organization Theory*, ed. D. S. Pugh (Baltimore: Penguin, 1971), 193.

81. Simon, *Administrative Behavior*, 9.

82. But Simon does not feel that unity of command is required to secure coordination. Decision premises may originate from a number of sources. It is

215

only necessary that these premises be satisfactorily synchronized. In this stance, Simon agrees with Taylor and departs from a fundamental "principle" of the Departmentalists. Ibid., 22–26, 140–47.

83. Simon, "Decision Making and Organizational Design," 204.

84. The degree of decentralization possible within the hierarchical structure varies with the decision-making needs of the organization. The question for Simon is not *whether* to decentralize (he says this is a laudable, and necessary, objective), but how far to decentralize. The permissible degree of decentralization in the organization is dependent on the level of interaction required for organizational decision making. An organizational division of labor that minimizes interdependencies permits the maximum amount of decentralization, since organizational subunits can then select their own decision premises with minimal impact on other parts of the organization. March and Simon, *Organizations*, 208.

85. Simon, Smithburg, and Thompson, *Public Administration*, 493. Opportunity costs are simply opportunities foregone by selection of a particular project as opposed to other possible projects.

86. Simon, *Administrative Behavior*, 172. The criterion of efficiency assumes that employees are neutral regarding the means employed to achieve organizational objectives. This assumption is consistent with the terms of the employment contract in which the employee becomes a neutral instrument of the organization. As such, the employee values not the act of production but the right to consumption, which that production entails. Simon does caution that employees will be neutral only to the extent that minimal standards have been reached in terms of the satisfaction of the employee. See Simon, Smithburg, and Thompson, *Public Administration*, 493–97.

87. March and Simon, *Organizations*, 150–51.

88. Simon, *Administrative Behavior*, 50.

89. Ibid., 50–51.

90. March and Simon, *Organizations*, 155–56.

91. Ibid., 192–93.

92. Ibid., 126.

93. Ibid., 140.

94. Ibid., 165.

95. Simon, *New Science of Management Decision*, 40–41.

96. March and Simon, *Organizations*, 141–42.

97. Simon, *New Science of Management Decision*, 50–51.

98. Ibid., 54–62.

99. March and Simon, *Organizations*, 182–83.

100. Ibid., 184.

101. Ibid., 180.

102. Ibid., 179–80.

103. Simon, *New Science of Management Decision*, 51–54.

104. Ibid., 62–77.

105. March and Simon, *Organizations*, 38–39.

106. Ibid., 152–53.

107. Simon, *Administrative Behavior*, 176.

108. Simon, Smithburg, and Thompson, *Public Administration*, 491.

109. For an interpretation of displacement of goals based on affective considerations, see Robert K. Merton, "Bureaucratic Structure and Personality," in *Reader in Bureaucracy*, Robert K. Merton, et al., eds. (New York: Free Press, 1952), 361–71.

110. Simon, Smithburg, and Thompson, *Public Administration*, 502.

111. March and Simon, *Organizations*, 112–35.

112. Simon, *New Science of Management Decision*, 98.

113. Ibid., 121.

114. Ibid., 119.

115. Ibid., 33.

116. Simon, *Administrative Behavior*, 37.

117. Ibid., 38.

118. Simon, *Sciences of the Artificial*, 59.

119. Simon, *Models of Man*, 192.

CHAPTER 8

Dwight Waldo: An Eclectic
View of Public Administration

The reasons for including the works of Dwight Waldo in this collection differ from those for the other authors chosen. Waldo is included as much for his observations on the contributions of others as for his own contributions to the field. Waldo is recognized as an astute critic and a knowledgeable chronicler of the history of the study of public administration. He is also representative of an approach to public administration—the Administration-as-Politics approach—that, combined with the Behavioral approach, constituted a devastating critique of the Classical paradigm of public administration. Waldo is thus included both because of his views on the development and current state of the field of public administration and as a representative of a particular perspective on the field.

As a commentator on, and critic of, public administration, Waldo came to his task with reservations, and he has approached his subject with a certain wariness ever since. Waldo's intellectual interests while a student centered on political philosophy, not public administration. His dissertation dealt with public administration, but was intended as an exposé. His intent was to expose the political theory he believed to be implicit in the Classical approach to public administration. Waldo argued that by concentrating on the technical aspects of public administration, the Classical approach embodied a philosophy and constituted an ideology that effectively supported the existing political order. The publication of *The Administrative State*, a book based on his dissertation, earned for Waldo, by his own estimation, the status of a pariah in the field. Waldo's views have softened over time, but there is still an element of the skeptic in him. He denies the possibility of constructing a science of public administration. He doubts the existence of "principles" of administration. He questions the plausibility of a unified theory of organizations. He is skeptical of those who would indiscriminately intermingle politics and administration. He even despairs of reaching common agreement on a definition of the field of public administration. Nonetheless, he believes that the fate of civilization may well rest on our ability to master the functions of administration.

218

Waldo is also representative of a perspective on public administration—the Administration-as-Politics approach—that emerged in the 1940s. Waldo's position was initially based on his response to the Classical approach, but his later writings extend elements of that critique to the Behavioral approach. Waldo denies that politics and policy considerations can be excluded from administration. Moreover, facts cannot be separated from values. Consequently, administration is inevitably both art and science, and perhaps more art than science. Also, since administration cannot be separated from politics, Waldo argues that public administration is different from private administration, being distinguished by the political environment in which the public administrator must operate. Our objective, Waldo argues, should not be to keep administrators out of policy and political matters but to encourage cooperation between the political and administrative domains and to discover ways in which we can benefit from the creative potential and substantive contributions of administrative officials.

Waldo's works serve as a fitting conclusion to this volume. He presents an overview of the field, offers a series of penetrating insights and criticisms, comments on some more recent developments, and speculates about the future of the enterprise of public administration. Perhaps more important, he reveals the implicit assumptions, the hidden premises, that underlie the various approaches to public administration. Although Waldo may not provide definitive answers, he certainly leads us to the right questions and provides some insights that better equip us to make more informed choices among difficult alternatives.

Life

Clifford Dwight Waldo was born in Dewitt, Nebraska, on 28 September 1913.[1] Waldo's father, Cliff Ford Waldo, owned a livery stable and raised hogs. His mother, Grace Gertrude (Lindley), managed the household. In commenting on his youth, Waldo says only that it was largely misspent for his future purposes (he cites his victory in a hog-calling contest as a major achievement) and that his ultimate career developed largely by accident.

Upon graduation from high school, Waldo entered Nebraska State Teachers College in Peru, Nebraska. Waldo received a B.A. degree from Nebraska State in 1935 and looked for a job as a teacher. In the depths of the Great Depression, however, he was unable to locate a position. In what he describes as more an act of desperation than choice, Waldo accepted a job reading papers at the University of Nebraska and enrolled in the master's program in political science.

In 1937 Waldo received his M.A. degree, married Gwen Payne (with whom he would eventually have three daughters), and accepted a Cowles Fellowship offer at Yale University. At Yale, Waldo studied political science with a specialization in the history of political thought. He served as an instructor in the Political Science Department in 1941–42 and received his Ph.D. in 1942.

Waldo's dissertation at Yale was initially entitled "Theories of Expertise in the Democratic Tradition" and was originally intended to address the question of how much democracy should be yielded to expertise.[2] Both the intent and scope of the dissertation, as is often the case, changed over time. Waldo's central concern remained political theory, but the final dissertation dealt with only one chapter of his original design and focused on public administration.[3] This change was prompted largely by Waldo's discovery that public administration had an underlying matrix of theory, and his intent became that of "exposing" the theory of public administration.

Waldo came to his newly defined task with a self-described "animus toward, even contempt for" public administration.[4] He viewed public administration as a "lower" field of endeavor preoccupied with such relatively mundane matters as counting manhole covers.[5] Although he thought public administration and political theory to be at opposite ends of the applied-theoretical continuum, Waldo's objective was to treat public administration as yet another chapter in political theory and thereby prove the usefulness and relevance of political theory itself.

Waldo's attitude and intent resulted in a dissertation, later to be published as *The Administrative State*, which he admits was "presumptuous, smart alec, and hostile."[6] In Waldo's words, "I savored over much the paradox and the irony. Occasionally the warranted critique tended toward the unwarranted exposé."[7] Although the book was toned down at the behest of his publisher, who advised that making unnecessary enemies would not help Waldo's career, Waldo observes that he was initially viewed as something of a pariah by those in public administration and that it took him nearly a decade after the publication of *The Administrative State* to achieve a measure of respectability in the field.[8]

In the eight years that intervened between the conception and publication of *The Administrative State*, Waldo's ideas and attitudes about public administration changed substantially. In the spring of 1942 Waldo was offered a university teaching position in political theory. He declined the offer and chose to go to Washington where he spent the next four years. Between 1942 and 1944, Waldo worked as a price analyst for the Office of Price Administration and, from 1944 through 1946, as an administrative analyst in the Bureau of the Budget. Though

Waldo considered himself a failure as a bureaucrat, his administrative experience started a process of resocialization that resulted in an identification with public administration rather than political theory. He reports that he emerged from governmental service with respect for the difficulties of administration, empathy with administrators, and a conviction that no one should be allowed to teach political science without experience in public affairs.[9]

After the war, Waldo was hired to teach political theory at the University of California at Berkeley. Waldo proceeded to teach courses in everything but political theory; and he found himself increasingly interested in, and identified with, public administration. Waldo participated in a movement to establish a graduate school of public affairs, he was involved in changing the University Bureau of Public Administration to the Institute of Governmental Studies, and he served as director of the institute from 1958 to 1967. Waldo's interests in public administration were also widening. An encounter with Weber's writings stimulated an interest in comparative administration, and, in the early 1950s, Waldo offered a course in Comparative National Administration. Later, he went to Italy on a project to improve Italian administration, an experience that, he reports, made him acutely aware of the limitations of "principles" of administration.[10] In the early 1960s Waldo became actively involved in the Comparative Administration Group of the American Society for Public Administration.

Having served his decade of "intellectual exile," Waldo also became centrally involved in the administration of his professions. Between 1957 and 1960, Waldo served on the Council and then the Executive Committee of the American Political Science Association, becoming vice-president in 1961. He also served on the editorial board of the *American Political Science Review* from 1959 to 1963. In public administration, Waldo served on the Council of the American Society for Public Administration (1963–66) and on the editorial board of the *Public Administration Review* (1958–66). In 1966 he became editor-in-chief of the *Review*. Since 1963, Waldo has been a member of the editorial board of the *International Review of Administrative Sciences*.

Waldo's stay at Berkeley was thus characterized by an increasing and expanding interest in public administration. This was accompanied by a similarly increasing disaffection with political science, either as a disciplinary "home" for public administration or as a supportive environment for those who wish to study it. Waldo states that, by 1967, his interests were running to sociology, business administration, and organization theory and that he found those subjects more germane to the agenda of public administration than political science.[11] Moreover, he felt that the political science environment was inhospitable to his interests. As a result, Waldo moved to Syracuse University to become professor of political science and Albert Schweitzer Professor of Humanities in the Maxwell School of Citizenship and Public Affairs. Waldo describes Syracuse and the Maxwell School as one of the few places where public administration is valued and viewed with respect.[12] While at Syracuse, Waldo served as vice-president and president of the National Association of Schools of Public Affairs and Administration. In 1979, Waldo retired as professor emertius from Syracuse. He spent the next two years at the Woodrow Wilson International Center for Scholars of the Smithsonian Institute and has remained professionally active since that time.

Over the course of his distinguished career, Waldo has received a number of awards including the Silver Medallion of the University of Bologna; an honorary Ph.D. from the University of Nebraska; an honorary life membership in the International City Managers Association; the William E. Mosher and Laverne Burchfield awards of the American Society for Public Administration; and the Berkeley Citation of the University of California at Berkeley. He has memberships in the National Academy of Public Administration, the American Society for Public Administration, the American Political Science Association, the American Society for the Advancement of Science, the International Institute of Administrative Sciences, and the International Political Science Association.

Waldo on the Classical Approach to Public Administration

Since so much of Waldo's writing has dealt with the history of public administration, I start with a review of Waldo's conception of, and commentary on, that history before proceeding to his own view of public administration.

Waldo emphasizes that public administration did not begin in the twentieth century. A stream of administrative technology has developed over the centuries to which, until recent times, the public sector has made the more important contributions. Waldo does credit the late nineteenth and early twentieth centuries with the development of the self-conscious study of public administration on a scale new in human history, and he identifies the United States as a major focal point of administrative studies. Although a number of forces were important in shaping the overall contours of the field, Waldo asserts that the proximate determinants of the specific content of public administration were the reform movement and the Progressive era, which emphasized executive leadership, civil service reform, and education for citizenship and sought to expose inefficiency through scientific investigations.[13] All these characteristics, to one degree or another, were incorporated in what has become known as the Classical approach to public administration.

General Characteristics of the Classical Approach

Waldo identified five basic characteristics of the Classical approach to public administration, which dominated the field until roughly 1940. These characteristics were acceptance of the politics-administration dichotomy, a generic management orientation, the search for principles of administration through scientific analysis, an emphasis on centralization of executive authority, and a commitment to democracy.

A fundamental premise of the Classical approach was that politics should be separated from administration. Despite some differences, Waldo argues that, on the whole, the authors of the Classical period accepted the distinction between politics and administration, asserted that administration is in the realm of expertise from which politics should be excluded, and argued for a strengthened chief executive to curb the centrifugal forces of the administrative branch.[14]

A second basic characteristic of the Classical approach was a generic management orientation that assumed that the techniques of private management were applicable in the public sector. Waldo argues that public administration accepted both business procedures and a business ideology as the business model was used to deprecate the balance of powers and aggrandize the role of the chief executive, as well as to justify hierarchical control mechanisms, merit appointment, and the adoption of businesslike budgetary procedures.[15]

A third characteristic of the Classical approach was the search for a science of administration. The Classical approach had a practical rather than an idealistic orientation. It was believed that the scientific study of administration could lead to the discovery of general "principles" of administration on which efficient government could be based.[16]

Next, the Classical approach emphasized the centralization of executive activities. The general prescription was centralization, simplification, and unification. The objectives of this emphasis were to centralize responsibility, to build the power of the chief executive by establishing stronger hierarchical controls within the executive branch, and to abolish superfluous offices in the name of efficiency.[17]

Finally, the Classical approach contained a basic commitment to "democracy." Democracy was defined substantively rather than procedurally, however. Democracy was to be achieved by establishing a strong, responsive, and responsible government designed to serve efficiently the needs of the people in an emergent "Great Society."[18]

223

Ideological and Philosophical Aspects of the Classical Approach

Although the authors of the period purportedly avoided value commitments, ideology, and philosophy, Waldo contends that strong elements of each were contained in the Classical approach to public administration. The value orientation of the Classical approach, according to Waldo, was embodied in a tacit commitment to individualism, materialism, and equality; a preference for harmony over conflict; a belief in the superiority of urban life; and a dedication to science as a primary instrument of progress.[19] In adopting these values and by concentrating on means and methodology, Waldo contends, the early authors on public administration effectively accepted and supported the existing political order.

Waldo also maintains that the Classical approach had an implicit ideological framework. This ideology embraced the idea of a democratic "mission of America," a belief in fundamental law, adherence to the doctrine of progress and progressivism, adoption of the "Gospel of Efficiency," and a faith in expertise on which a "democratic ruling class" could be founded. The "mission of America" was seen as "witnessing Democracy before mankind, bearing democracy's ideals of freedom and equality, and its material blessings to the nations of the world."[20] It was held that this mission could not be accomplished in competition with ethically inferior ideals unless greater efficiency in governmental operations could be achieved. The belief in fundamental law was expressed in the search for "principles" of administration that were to reflect a "higher law and a fundamental moral order." Waldo attributes a pervasive "aura of evangelical protestantism" in the reform movement to this belief in fundamental law.[21] Progress was to be achieved through a planned and administered society. The "Gospel of Efficiency" represented an attempt to reconcile traditional democratic institutions with the requirements of new administrative technology. More efficient organization and administration were seen as means of creating responsive and responsible government that would better serve the needs of the people. This requires both the assembling of scientific knowledge and the placement of experts in government, as the Classical authors sought to establish a governing class of expert administrators who would exercise governmental power to preserve democracy.[22] In sum, Waldo concludes that the early students of public administration were "part of a well-known company of political theorists, not removed from political theory," despite their protestations to the contrary.[23]

Finally, Waldo argues that the Classical approach to public administration had a recognizable philosophical component consisting of pragmatism, utilitarianism, and positivism.[24] Pragmatism was reflected in the concentration on the efficiency of means. Utilitarianism was reflected in the objective of achieving the "greatest happiness of the greatest number," presuming a practical equality of persons. Positivism was reflected in the opposition to intangible criteria and the attempt to, in Waldo's terms, "substitute measurement for metaphysics."[25]

Weber on Bureaucracy

Before leaving Waldo's description of the Classical period, it is probably appropriate to discuss his views on Max Weber. One must say "probably" because Waldo, as have others, has some difficulty in defining a suitable niche in the development of administrative thought for Weber. As Waldo puts it, Weber has been seen as a traditional systems builder, a seminal behavioralist, and even a disguised metaphysician.[26] Although he acknowledges some validity in each of these views, Waldo is primarily concerned with Weber's concept of bureaucracy, which he regards as the single most important statement on formal organization.

Waldo considers Weber's genius to lie in his ability to relate the concept of bureaucracy to history, economic life, technological development, political philosophy, and social structure and social processes. In short, Weber saw the development of bureaucracy as related to the development of civilization itself, a view that, as we shall see, Waldo shares. Waldo assesses Weber's formulation of bureaucracy as having a "plausible fit" for his time, but he has some reservations about the desirability of bureaucratic organizations, a point to which I return.[27]

Waldo's Critique and Comments on the Classical Approach

So much for Waldo's recounting of the Classical approach to public administration. What is his reaction to that approach? Characteristically, Waldo gives it a mixed review, some of which has been implied in the preceding pages.

On the politics-administration dichotomy, Waldo contends that the separation is inadequate, either as a description of reality or as a prescription for administrative behavior.[28] The dichotomy, according to Waldo, was intended to resolve the conflict between bureaucracy and democracy by making elected officials responsible for framing policy and restricting administrators to the execution of that policy. Democracy itself was then defined in terms of an efficient response to public needs that could best be accomplished by a cadre of experts. But Waldo argues that public administration in the Classical period was, in actuality, false to the ideal of democracy. Democracy was seen as desirable, but peripheral to the concerns of administration and hostile to the central principle of efficiency.[29] The Classical movement indicted "centrifugal democracy" and sought to implement its own version of "centripetal democracy" by proposing a separation between politics and administration and relying on what Waldo calls the "dogmas of centralization" and the "canons of integration" as a solution to the problem of efficiency.[30]

The politics-administration dichotomy was also intended to solve the value problem. Here it was asserted that the political system would establish values and set goals for administration. Waldo regards this as disingenuous, since it ignores the desire to extend the compass of the science of administration to an ever-larger complex of phenomena. As a result, public administration threatened to "overrun the realm of policy—as the British conquered India—not by intent and plan, but by a continuous process of tidying up the border."[31] Waldo contends that the real question raised by the Classical authors is not whether politics and policy should be separated from administration but how far the administrative function should extend in determining values and policies, a question for which they failed to provide a suitable answer. Waldo's own view is that we should move toward a philosophy that encourages cooperation among powers, be they administrative or political, not competition among separated powers.[32]

Waldo is similarly critical of the organizational paradigm of the Classical approach. He criticizes both the emphasis on supposed principles or commonalities among organizations and the rationalist bias of Classical organization theory. In regard to the search for commonalities, Waldo contends that Classical organization theory ignored the specificity that is the "stuff of administration." Organizations, Waldo maintains, should be defined and structured to meet purposes, not general principles, and the organization form and process actually adopted should be suited to the specific situation confronting the organization.[33] Waldo asserts that Classical organization theory prescribed general organizational forms and processes that were not readily adaptable to specific situations or changing circumstances.[34] Waldo also argues that the Classical "principles" were based on an idea of law (Waldo calls it "Cosmic Constitutionalism") that mixes a scientific, descriptive concept of the "natural order of things" (what is) with the notion of moral necessity (what ought to be). Waldo observes that even if the Classical "principles" were based on empirical observation and could tell us what exists, that does not necessarily constitute a prescription for the way things should be.[35] Finally, Waldo claims that the Classical approach ignores the irrational and informal aspects of organizations. A case in point is Weber's concept of bureaucracy. Waldo argues that Weber placed undue emphasis on the functional side of bureaucracy, ignored the informal and socioemotional aspects of organizations, and elevated position over knowledge as the basis for hierarchical authority.[36]

Waldo also chides the Classical authors about their "scientific" pretensions. Waldo says that the Classical "science" of public administration relied primarily on a "heaping up of facts," and its principles were little more than an extension of common sense.[37] Waldo is even more critical of the intent of the Classical authors than he is of the execution of that intent. In a theme that recurs throughout his writings, Waldo expresses reservations about the possibility of developing a science of administration. Waldo contends that public administration must deal with thinking and valuing human beings and that the techniques of science are inappropriate to such subjects. Values cannot be treated scientifically, and human free will means that the principles of mechanical cause and effect are inapplicable.[38] This does not mean that Waldo thinks that science is unnecessary. Even if an administrative science is not possible, Waldo believes that a scientific mentality might at least make common sense more sensible and that some parts of administration may well be amenable to scientific investigation. Nevertheless, Waldo warns that we should not try to force on a subject matter a method that is not suitable to it.

Finally, Waldo challenges the Classical emphasis on efficiency. This emphasis was originally intended to replace a moralistic approach to public administration. Waldo maintains that the idea of efficiency itself became imbued with a moral significance, however, as the pursuit of "technical efficiency" was transformed into the pursuit of "social efficiency."[39] Moreover, Waldo asserts that, although efficiency itself is not a value, efficiency is a useful concept only within a framework of consciously held values. That is, one must consider the object of efficiency, since it is not reasonable to assume that it is desirable to accomplish *any* end efficiently.[40]

Although, as is evidenced by the preceding comments, Waldo was initially highly critical of the Classical approach to public administration, time and exposure to proposed alternatives have served to temper his views. Waldo still considers the Classical approach to be an ideology, but, as he puts it, that "is not to imply that it is a myth that a sensible man must summarily reject."[41] In Waldo's judgment, the Classical approach contained much truth and represented an intelligent response to a historical situation. In particular, Waldo suggests that the politics-administration dichotomy served, and still serves, a useful purpose in stimulating political reform and improvement in administration.[42] Moreover, the Classical approach is still deeply engrained in our culture, and no consensus on an alternative has yet emerged to replace the Classical paradigm of public administration.[43]

Contemporary Public Administration

With the 1940s came a series of challenges to the Classical approach to public administration as, in Waldo's words, "heterodoxy replaced orthodoxy."[44] The Classical claim to having discovered a "science" of public administration was branded as, at best, premature. The Classical "principles" of administration were relegated to the status of proverbs. The Classical emphasis on economy and efficiency was denigrated as having been too narrowly conceived. The politics-administration dichotomy was questioned. The generic management approach was seen as overly simplistic.

Waldo contends that the field of public administration is now characterized by a diversity of perspectives in which the Classical approach has not been so much repudiated as absorbed, amended, extended, and joined by new perspectives. In the process, some of the ideological and philosophical underpinnings of the Classical approach have been rejected, and others have simply gone underground. The influence of the business mentality has diminished, the idea of "fundamental law" as a higher moral order has been largely abandoned, and there is increasing skepticism about the notion of "progress." Though pragmatism has declined as a "fashionable" philosophy, Waldo maintains that it continues to be the unarticulated working philosophy of public administration and is manifested in the effort to construct a new science of administration in a manner consistent with the tenets of Behavioralism.[45]

Concurrent with the Behavioral emphasis has been the assertion that administration is both art and science, and perhaps more art than science. This has been the result of the rejection of the politics-administration dichotomy and the consequent inclusion of both politics and policy within the legitimate purview of public administration. The concern with policy, Waldo notes, has raised normative questions previously excluded from the domain of public administration. Thus, contemporary public administration has witnessed both a continuing interest on the factual side in the form of the Behavioral approach and an awakening of interest on the value side in the form of renewed concern with the role of the administrator in political and policy processes.[46]

Waldo identifies four basic, though not entirely separate, currents of thought in contemporary public administration: organization theory, comparative public administration, a public policy orientation, and the "new public administration."

Organization Theory

Waldo divides the development of organization theory into three stages.[47] The first stage was the Classical period, epitomized by the works of authors such as Taylor, Gulick, Fayol, and Mooney. The Classical stage of organization theory was based on the "machine model" of the organization and emphasized the rational aspects of human behavior. This stage reached it zenith in the 1930s and culminated in the publication of the *Papers on the Science of Administration*.[48] Waldo labels the second stage in the development of organization theory the "neoclassical" approach. This stage began with the Hawthorne experiments in the 1920s and retained major importance through midcentury. In contrast to the Classical stage, the neoclassical approach emphasized the emotive and sociopsychological dimensions of human behavior in organizations. The final stage in the development of organization theory is modern organization theory, which, according to Waldo, began with the publication of March and Simon's *Organizations* in 1958.[49] Modern organization theory is based on an "organic" or "natural system" model of the organization and stresses organizational growth and survival. The modern approach endorses organizations that have less reliance on hierarchical controls, more recognized sources of authority, greater opportunity for personal mobility, and greater receptivity to organizational change. Modern organization theory is decidedly Behavioral in orientation, adopting the methods of the physical and biological sciences and seeking a value-free "general theory" of organizations true for all times and places.

Neoclassical Organization Theory

In Waldo's scheme of things, the neoclassical stage of organization theory was dominated by the Hawthorne studies and its intellectual progeny, the Human Relations movement. With its emphasis on the affective and social aspects of organizational behavior, the Human Relations movement focused on considerations such as morale, perceptions and attitudes, group relationships, informal groups, leadership, and the bases for cooperation in organizational behavior. Waldo considers the Human Relations movement to be simultaneously a repudiation of, and continuation of, the Classical approach.[50] In its concentration on social and psychological factors in organizational behavior, the Human Relations movement demonstrated the limitations of perspectives such as Scientific Management. According to Waldo, however, the Human Relations movement was originally seen as merely an extension of, and corrective to, Scientific Management with a continuing stress on the values of science, managerialism, and efficiency. The objective was to bring the newly discovered "nonrational" under the control of the "rational." Thus, Waldo contends, Human Relations represented more a refinement of means than a radical departure from the Classical approach in terms of either goals or methodology.

Modern Organization Theory

Waldo finds modern organization theory to be a more elusive subject matter. It is, he says, diverse and heterogeneous and highly subject to changing fashions.[51] Modern organization theory has drawn its ideas from such varied sources as management science (which Waldo considers to be the principal legatee of the Scientific Management movement), sociology, social psychology, economics, and anthropology. Modern organization theory is founded on a belief in the "universals" of organization behavior and, as a result, has shown little concern for public organizations as a potentially separable subject of analysis. Finally, Waldo contends that modern organization theory continues to be grounded in the values of twentieth-century Western culture, namely, science, rationality, effectiveness, efficiency, and productivity. This has eventuated in a perceptible shift from description to prescription, from theoretical to applied science. Waldo cites Simon's focus on organizational design, the productivity movement, and the pursuit of "softer" values such as humanism, job enrichment, and self-actualization as illustrative of this trend.[52]

Reflecting the diversity of the period, Waldo includes several perspectives under the rubric of modern organization theory. Simon's work on decision making is but one aspect of modern organization theory, albeit, in Waldo's opinion, a crucial aspect. Waldo considers Simon's work to be, in some respects, a radical departure from Classical organization theory, but in other respects a conservative approach and one that is only partial in perspective.[53] Simon's approach to organization theory constitutes a radical departure in its insistence on more rigorous scientific standards and its focus on administrative decision making. Waldo also sees Simon as a conservative in that he seeks to establish a science of administration, he retains efficiency as the criterion of organizational decisions, he attempts to salvage the Classical principles (if only as diagnostic criteria), and he maintains a twofold structuring of the universe by substituting the fact-value dichotomy for the old politics-administration dichotomy. This conservatism, Waldo contends, is the reason Simon's formulation has not been accepted as the solution to the identity crisis in public administration.

The second perspective of modern organization theory in Waldo's schema is organizational humanism, represented by works of authors such as Argyris, Bennis, and Likert. Waldo observes that organizational humanism focuses on much the same kinds of human concerns as the Human Relations movement. From the humanist perspective, according to Waldo, the objective is simultaneously to achieve organizational effectiveness and self-fulfillment under the assumption that the interests of the individual and the organization are compatible.[54] Thus, although organizational humanism has been proposed as a means for escaping the impersonality of bureaucracy, it is also a pragmatic attempt to develop more flexible, knowledge-based organizations that can achieve rationality and efficiency in changing circumstances.

The third major strand of modern organization theory is what Waldo terms the systems-based "scientific and managerial" literature. Waldo includes contingency theory in this literature, arguing that it is a natural outgrowth of the system perspective in that it addresses the problem of specifying appropriate managerial strategies in a changing and uncertain environment. Other components of the scientific and managerial literature include elements of decision theory, organizational development, computer technology, and organizational futurism.[55] In assessing the scientific and managerial literature, Waldo notes that, like organizational humanism, this literature does not so much repudiate the old values of rationality and efficiency as it seeks to realize those values under more difficult circumstances.[56]

Waldo's attitudes toward neoclassical and modern organization theory are mixed and, in his words, range from "unqualified admiration, through curiosity and hope, to indifference and annoyance stopping short of hostility."[57] Waldo's first concern is that the techniques of modern organization theory may be used by managers "only to more skillfully manipulate their 'human material.'"[58] In a colorful comment on Elton Mayo and the Human Relations movement, Waldo says: "I have a persistent vision of a modern dairy farm, managed to perfection, each cow in its gleaming stanchion, contentedly munching vitaminized food, milking machines barely audible through the piped-in Vienna waltzes."[59] Waldo also charges that much of modern organization theory is "anti-individual" and "dwarfs and de-humanizes man."[60] This is most vividly reflected, Waldo asserts, in Simon's concentration on the rational and logical aspects of the organization. Simon, Waldo contends, does not just demystify rationality, he dehumanizes it.

Second, Waldo notes that the authors dealing with organization theory are not very specific in defining their object of analysis. Using the fable of the blind man and the elephant as an analogy, Waldo states, "it is not clear that the [authors] are talking about the same elephant, or even members of the same species ... if they all concern the same elephant, it is a very large elephant with a generalized elephantiasis."[61] The absence of definitional delimitation is consistent with the objective of developing a universal and unified "theory of organization," but the assertion that such universals exist and, therefore, that a unified theory is possible, according to Waldo, is more hope than certainty. Waldo charges that modern organization theory despite its pretensions, presents no unified "theory of organization." By becoming everything, systems theory runs the danger of becoming nothing in particular.[62] Contingency theory's central point that "it all depends" is plausible enough, but little indication has been given of what to do beyond that point.[63] Waldo also notes that modern organization theory has given little attention to public organizations and that it is "ironical that an enterprise that aspires for universality in its fruits should be so parochial in its roots."[64]

Finally, Waldo contends that, like the Classical approach, the newer theory of organizations is value laden. He asserts that the shift from "administration" to "organization" was, at least in part, intended to counter the value problem. The concept *organization* suggests that there is something out there which can be dealt with on a descriptive basis.[65] But Waldo claims that organizations, like administration, inevitably mirror the values of the societies in which they reside. In twentieth-century America this means, among other things, an attachment to the values of rationality and efficiency. Waldo maintains that there is no way to study organizations apart from the values they embody and the aims toward which they are directed. Consequently, in Waldo's opinion, a value-free theory of organizations is unattainable.[66]

Comparative Public Administration

The second major focus of the contemporary period has been comparative public administration. According to Waldo, comparative public administration both resembles and differs from modern organization theory. It shares with modern organization theory a concern for methodological problems; a reliance on models such as the systems framework and structural functionalism; an interdisciplinary orientation; a search for universal concepts, formulas, and theories; and an emphasis on empirical description. Comparative public administration differs from modern organization theory, however, in its explicit comparative perspective, its focus on cultural diversity, and its fascination with Weberian bureaucracies.

Though it was at one time widely believed that comparative public administration was the "area of greatest promise" in contemporary public administration, Waldo feels that promise has yet to be fulfilled. Comparative public administration, according to Waldo, taught us much about the relationship between administration and social ends, the critical dependence of civilization on effective governmental administration, and the difficulties in transferring the Western model of administration to other cultures. But the basic problem of the comparative administration movement was the distance between the theoretical models employed and the evidence of field research.[67] And even with its strong theoretical bent, Waldo asserts, the movement failed to produce anything in the way of rigorous theory.[68]

The pressure for practical results led to a switch from comparative to "developmental" administration, a switch that Waldo at one time endorsed.[69] The results, according to Waldo, have not been much more encouraging. We have simply learned much about what will not work, and no general "science of development" has yet emerged. Waldo charges that the developmental perspective has assumed that to be developed is to be "Western." The result, he asserts, is that developmental administration has become a "powerful and subtle ideology" with the characteristics of a "world-girdling religion," and the effort to achieve development has amounted to little more than an effort to reproduce the Weberian model of bureaucracy.[70]

Public Policy

The third major focus of contemporary public administration has been public policy, which initially took the form of the case-study approach. Most centrally a teaching method, the case-study approach was designed to provide the student with a vicarious experience in administration by giving an account of actual administrative happenings as recounted by an interested but impartial observer. The case studies focused on decision making in a holistic manner and attempted to raise basic questions about both policy and ethics. The motives of the approach were "scientific" in that the cases were to be based on careful observation and were to result in the accumulation of empirical data on the administrative process. But the approach also constituted a rejoinder to both logical positivism and to Simon's fact-value dichotomy that was viewed as an overly simplistic cleavage all too reminiscent of the old politics-administration dichotomy. Waldo judges the case-study approach to be potentially useful, but not sufficient as a means to study and teach public administration.[71]

Other than the case-study approach, Waldo says, little has been done with public policy within the field of public administration. Authors such as Appleby, Long, and Redford have addressed questions of policy and politics. Until recently, however, policy as a focus has been largely ceded to other disciplines, especially economics, and those disciplines have been attending to matters that Waldo feels ought to have been addressed by public administration.[72]

The New Public Administration

The final major development in contemporary public administration is the New Public Administration movement. This movement, spawned by the social and political ferment of the late 1960s and early 1970s, was, according to Waldo, part of the rebellion of youth and the counterculture of the non-Marxian left.[73] The New Public Administration criticized the "old" public administration for its lack of an explicit ideological-philosophical framework and supported an activist role for the administrator in the pursuit of social equity. Waldo refers to the movement as a "New Romanticism," as it shares with that philosophical movement the assumption that man is inherently good but is corrupted by bad institutions, and it reacts to rationalism by emphasizing the role of feeling over reason, senses over the mind, and spontaneity, creativity, and self-fulfillment over convention and rules.[74]

The basic themes of the New Public Administration were participation, decentralization, and representative bureaucracy. Participation was supported both as a political process and as an organizational process. Political participation was seen as a means of dispersing power and increasing citizen involvement in government. The movement rejected both simple majoritarianism and pluralism in favor of alternatives described by Waldo as ranging from "organic communitarianism" to moral and political elitism.[75] Support for organizational participation was part of what Waldo sees as the movement's "massive hostility" to anything perceived as "bureaucratic." Organizational participation was to be a means for promoting change and dispersing power within the organization. Decentralization, like participation, was intended to disperse power and increase citizen involvement in governmental and organizational processes. Representative bureaucracy was meant to produce client-centered administration and representation of clientele interests by administrators.

Waldo confesses a "sympathetic interest" in the ideas of the New Public Administration movement. But he also expresses some substantial misgivings. On participation and representative bureaucracy, Waldo asserts that the arguments are often "*ad hoc* and inconsistent, if not indeed dishonest."[76] Supporters of participation, Waldo argues, seem to assume that some "invisible" hand will resolve the problems of coordination, order, and survival in the new system of highly dispersed power. Moreover, Waldo finds the movement to be inconsistent in its desire to have democracy while rejecting majoritarianism and pluralism and, in effect, supporting rule by the minority.[77] On decentralization, Waldo points out that a cogent case can also be made for centralization and that neither case is universally right or wrong.[78]

Waldo finds some validity in the antiorganizational stance of the New Public Administration, but he considers much of the indictment to be "unfair, spurious, and above all unrealistic."[79] Waldo notes that, although our administrative ethos has been oriented toward the rational end of the spectrum, this does not constitute a blind dedication to rigid organizational procedures and bureaucracy. Moreover, those very bureaucratic organizations have often proven to be a force for change. Waldo notes that most innovative techniques and technologies have been created in, or at least at the behest of, bureaucratic organizations and that the era of bureaucracy has been an era of rapid change. Furthermore, even if bureaucracy serves the status quo, the status quo itself is not a monolithic interest, but a diversity of interests, all of which must be served. Finally, in addressing the question of efficiency, Waldo charges that the critics attack a narrow conception of efficiency that had long been discarded. Even the critics do not support inefficiency, but Waldo says that he hopes that he will never have to "fly with an airplane, have surgery in a hospital, or even stay in a hotel run in the new 'ideal style.' "[80]

To the extent that the New Public Administration movement simply reflects a conflict of youth versus age, Waldo observes that "children's crusades and youth movements have not on the whole written happy, brilliant pages in the history of civilization."[81] Even more acidly, Waldo asserts that the young represent a "continuing barbarian invasion" that must be socialized and civilized if a return to barbarism is to be prevented.[82]

In regard to contemporary public administration as a whole, Waldo describes it as "like Poland, open to invasion from every side," as no new synthesis has emerged to replace the old Classical formulation.[83] The field is marked by an increasing perimeter, but no agreed-upon intellectual core or "public philosophy." Waldo maintains that the problem now is to find the boundaries of public administration.[84]

Waldo's World of Public Administration

To this point we have examined Waldo's "map" of the field of public administration and his reactions thereto. Waldo himself has been more a commentator and critic than a creative theorist, or even a synthesizer. Scattered throughout his voluminous writings, however, are a series of observations that while not constituting the elusive unified theory of public administration, at least provide some insight into Waldo's own perspectives on public administration.

History and Public Administration

If there is a single dominant theme in Waldo's work, it is probably the importance he attaches to history, or, as he puts it, a strong sense that "what is past in prologue."[85] Waldo believes that there is much to be learned from history, and he deplores the fact that much of the public administration literature has been antihistorical in nature. Waldo asserts that history does indeed repeat itself, though "in different keys and with endless variations of its themes," and that ignoring the past denies an important source of "insights, hypotheses, and scientific conclusions."[86]

An important lesson of history, Waldo argues, is that the techniques of administration are at the center of the political-governmental evolution. Indeed, he maintains that government and administration are substantially equivalent. In Waldo's phrase, administration "frames civilization" by giving it a foundation or stage and by providing a base for growth.[87] In short, government qua administration and civilization are always intimately joined.

Accordingly, Waldo considers government and its administration to be more than merely an artificially created intruder in a state of nature that would otherwise be serene and prosperous.[88] Government, Waldo argues, is no more a "creation" than markets or private enterprise; and the "sustaining, nurturing, and creative" role of government has been largely ignored. Waldo acknowledges that "government is always marginally oppressive and sometimes massively so" and that "there are things that government cannot do or can do only clumsily."[89] He argues, however, that government and its administrative apparatus have performed their functions with at least moderate success despite increases in the scale and complexity of their activities.

Bureaucracy and Democracy

As government and administration have been intimately joined, so too, Waldo says, has administration been joined with bureaucracy. And it is the potential conflict between bureaucracy and democracy that Waldo identifies as the central issue of our time.

In using the term *bureaucracy* Waldo takes care to distinguish his usage from both the common perjorative use of the term and Weber's ideal type, which identified bureaucracy with rationality. Instead, Waldo employs "bureaucracy" in a descriptive-analytical sense connoting simply large-scale, formal, complex, task-specialized, and goal-oriented organizations. Waldo does assert that bureaucratic organizations, so defined, have proven to be crucially important and that they perform unrecognized, or at least unappreciated, functions relating to order and stability by virtue of the very rigidity and permanence for which they are commonly condemned.

Democracy, according to Waldo, is a "striving toward equality and freedom."[90] By this definition, democracy is characterized by an ethic or a set of values rather than by its procedural trappings. Moreover, democracy is a term equally applicable to both political affairs and administrative-bureaucratic matters. Waldo notes that bureaucratic organization is not totally incompatible with the concept of democracy. Bureaucracies provide important support for democratic values, such as universalistic criteria and opportunity based on ability and expertise. There are also conflicting characteristics, such as the bureaucratic emphasis on the rule of hierarchy versus the democratic value of equality and the bureaucratic reliance on discipline and supervision versus the democratic principle of liberty.

Waldo sees the conflict between bureaucracy and democracy as a dilemma. On the one hand, power is viewed as a dangerous commodity that should be fragmented and dispersed. On the other hand, it is recognized that power, if properly channeled, can serve good purposes. In administrative terms, this means that bureaucratic power is seen as a possible force for immorality and that decentralization should be encouraged. At the same time, it is held that democracy is possible only if power is concentrated so that it can both act and be held accountable. The dilemma deepens as the activities and services democracy increasingly seeks from government are rendered more difficult to deliver by democratic restraints and expectations.

In Waldo's opinion, the clash between bureaucracy and democracy has elicited no little hypocrisy. Conservative authors brand public organizations as inferior while failing to acknowledge that bureaucracy is also the organizational mode of capitalism. Liberals want participatory administration, but not when the client is a defense contractor. The artist or the novelist "eagerly accepts with one hand the material goods of an organizational society he vigorously flogs with the other."[91] Waldo expresses his disdain for such hypocrisy in saying, "the reaction to [bureaucracy] (right, left, and center) is essentially Ludditist, high in emotion and low in social knowledge and skill, ignorant and confused, dishonest and misleading in suggesting that in some simple fashion we can have our cake and eat it, that we can return to the simple life, but retain the high standard of living which is the product of present scientific, technological-administrative skills."[92]

The solution to the problem, according to Waldo, is to seek an optimal mix between democracy and bureaucracy with the recognition that while democracy is desirable, bureaucracy is necessary. Waldo argues that we should accept the fact that we have an administrative culture and that we should use that culture to get as much as possible of the goods of life. We must also be concerned with the values of human equality and participation. Even though a considerable amount of authority, hierarchy, and even coercion is necessary and inevitable, the bureaucratic game should be played with everyone knowing the basic rules and being allowed to play to the extent that skill and inclination dictate.[93] Moreover, we should plan carefully to preserve areas of freedom and spontaneity. In short, Waldo would have us reform the world, not attempt to escape from it or abolish it, and seek a reasonable balance between accommodation to authority and rebellion.

Public Administration and Politics

Related to the question of bureaucracy and democracy is the role of administration in politics. Here, Waldo seeks some new formulation to replace the politics-administration dichotomy. Politics and administration, Waldo asserts, are not separable realms, but related realms and perhaps even a single realm.[94] Waldo does not pretend to have the solution to the problem of relating administration to politics. He does suggest that moving toward a professional perspective may be helpful.[95] That professional perspective should recognize that public administration is characterized by an interlocking set of values, not by a rigid paradigm or doctrine, and thus should be receptive to ideas and techniques from many sources. The professional perspective should have a moral component drawn from the values of democracy. Finally, the professional perspective should incorporate the concepts of political and social rationality, as well as economic rationality, with the idea of the "public interest" playing an important role lest public administration lose its ethical aura and thereby degenerate into mere "governmental administration."[96]

Morality and Public Administration

Waldo recognizes that rejecting the idea that the function of the administrator is simply efficiently to execute the will of the state raises a bewildering array of value problems. In its early decades, Waldo charges, public administration simply avoided questions of values and morality by focusing on technical and scientific matters in the pursuit of efficiency. This, Waldo claims, is both unrealistic and insufficient. Instead of being divorced from questions of values and morality, Waldo asserts that public administration is inevitably both a morality and an ideology. Consequently, administrative theory must embrace ethical theory, which, in turn, requires that values be treated as more than merely data. Waldo maintains that values should be studied consciously and should be used to give direction to empirical research. Waldo does not envisage a "set of hornbooks to give 'Easy Ethical Answers'" to complex ethical problems. But he does believe that the conscious study of values can assist in reducing confusion and stress and may lead to the development of a "moral creativeness" or "moral architecture" in administration matters.[97]

Waldo himself offers some tentative first steps in his proposed study of values and morality. History, Waldo tells us, presents two traditions concerning morality in public affairs—one public and one private.[98] In the Greek tradition, as reflected in the writings of Plato and Aristotle, the polity itself is seen as the source of morality. Accordingly, the good man and the good citizen are one and the same.[99] The Stoics, in contrast, maintained that above the political community there exists a community of mankind that should be governed by a "natural law." Thus, considerations of right and wrong rest on interests beyond those of the polity.[100] With the rise of the Christian church came the claim that the church has a right to govern spiritual concerns independent of the political regime. The emergence of the modern theory of the state signaled a return to the Classical position that there is a unity of public and private morality. It was maintained that the state has the authority to determine right and wrong, but based on a higher law, and that public morality transcends matters of private morality. This formulation reached its extreme in the doctrine Reason of State, which justifies actions that in private morality are immoral if they serve the objectives of creating, preserving, or enhancing governmental power.[101]

The political theory of liberal democracy, Waldo says, attempts to encompass both of these historical traditions. Consequently, "fortune, honor and life" may depend not only on a choice between morality and immorality but also on the choice among differing versions of morality.[102] Waldo asserts that "all decision and action in the public interest is inevitably morally complex," and, like a Greek tragedy, is apt to be not so much a conflict between good and evil, but a conflict among competing goods.[103] That is, the individual is likely to have to weigh the moral claims of the state against the competing claims both of other collectivities (e.g., family, organization, or profession) and the claims of higher law or conscience.

Waldo maintains that all governments are conceived in sin and survive by at least occasional and moderate sinning. As Waldo puts it, "Those in government who decide and act on behalf of the public will from time to time, of necessity ... be lying, stealing, cheating, and killing."[104] Furthermore, Waldo contends that some cost in immorality is the price of any substantial act of public morality and that governmental actions are inevitably a mixture of morality and immorality. Waldo does not attempt to resolve the dilemmas posed by moral complexity in public affairs. Indeed, he feels that the problems are insoluble. Instead, he would call attention to the problems, suggest that they deserve serious study, and warn against facile moral judgments. Self-righteousness, Waldo notes, is equally distributed, and, under its influence, "thinking about public morality is likely to be partial and circumstantial no matter what universals are enunciated as the basis of judgment."[105]

Logical Positivism and Public Administration

Waldo's insistence on the inclusion of values in the study and practice of public administration leads him to question the utility of logical positivism as an analytical perspective. Waldo considers logical positivism to be an important and respectable viewpoint, but one that dismisses "ought" questions "with a wave of the hand."[106] Waldo argues that logical positivism takes a distinction in logic, that is, the distinction between facts and values, and employs it as a distinction in life. In reality, Waldo contends, facts and values are joined organically and cannot be separated, even in a "pure" science, as long as that science is social. He admits that facts and values *can* be logically separated and that values *can* be treated merely as data. But Waldo maintains that logical positivism goes beyond that in dismissing the consideration of values qua values as a useless pursuit that Waldo considers to be a "dogmatic and intolerant evasion of value problems."[107]

A larger, but related, problem of the logical-positivist perspective is that logical positivism leads to a premature technological orientation in which public administration is seen as simply a tool for the achievement of externally determined goals. This means that wide areas of human experience—namely the aesthetic, moral, and metaphysical—are abandoned, and the "rational" is thus put at the service of the "irrational," or at least matters judged to be beyond rational inquiry.[108] Waldo concludes that we need to be self-aware and self-critical of values, warns that we should not seek rigor at the price of relevance, and expresses the hope that we may be reaching a modus vivendi between the "scientific" and the normative.

Science and Public Administration

Waldo also raises the question whether a "science" of public administration has been achieved, is being achieved, or can be achieved. His response to that question is equivocal. In part, Waldo asserts, the response depends on how one defines "science." In its broadest sense, science is simply knowledge that leads to the control of "concrete transformations."[109] Waldo adjudges the social sciences, including public administration, to be scientific by this definition. He observes that social science has achieved a large degree of control over human behavior and is capable of making many accurate predictions. Indeed, he argues that, since the progress of social science technology and physical science technology are so intimately related, all science is, in an important sense, social science.[110]

However, Waldo concedes that the foregoing is a rather generous definition of science. If science is defined in the stricter sense of "highly abstract and systematized concepts which 'order' empirical reality" with hypotheses and laws, and knowledge obtained and legitimated according to the canons of a specified methodology, Waldo doubts the existence, or even the possibility, of a science of public administration.[111] He asserts that although there may be universal "principles" of administration, we do not know whether this is true or what they might be. Moreover, he questions whether "management science" is anything more than a covert, class-based ideology seeking to control in the interests of the managers.[112] Waldo's view, based on what he describes as a "mild commitment" to the proposition that, through study, administration can become more scientific, if not "a science," is that there are lawful regularities in organizational phenomena about which we can learn more through science.[113]

Public Administration: Discipline, Profession, Enterprise
If public administration is not a "pure" science, what is it? Waldo asserts that public administration can, at best, be considered an applied science, and is probably better thought of as an art, a profession, or something else. Waldo has wrestled with several alternatives in trying to arrive at an acceptable characterization of public administration.

Whether or not, for instance, public administration should be considered a *discipline* depends on how that term is defined, and, in any case, Waldo considers it preferable to think of public administration as being composed of the many disciplines required in preparation for a career in the public service.[114] Waldo is emphatic in rejecting the idea that public administration is merely a subdiscipline, particularly a subdiscipline of political science. Political science, Waldo maintains, has been too much influenced by logical positivism with the result that it now focuses on "what is interesting, but inconsequential, what is quantifiable, but trivial."[115] Waldo views the traditional relationship between public administration and political science as part convention, part inertia, and with a problematic future, since political science has failed to provide an understanding and nurturing environment for public administration. Nor, Waldo asserts, should public administration be subsumed in business schools or "generic" schools of management. Waldo argues that neither the values nor the techniques of administration can be universalized and that public administration requires both a differentiated technology and a distinctive philosophy. Moreover, as with political science, Waldo warns that public administration programs in business or generic schools are likely to face "slow death from lack of nutrition or atrophy from a lack of attention and affection."[116]

Waldo is more sympathetic to a "professional" orientation in public administration. Waldo acknowledges that public administration is not a profession in a strict sense, is not about to become one, and perhaps should not even be one. Nevertheless, he considers professionalism to be a good attitude or strategy and asserts that public administration should move from a disciplinary to a professional perspective with a separate professional school status in the university.[117] Waldo's favorite analogy in this regard is medicine, which, he says, is both science and art, both theory and practice, has a multidisciplinary focus rather than single theory, and is given direction by a broad social purpose. Thinking of public administration as a profession, Waldo maintains, frees public administration from its second-class status in colleges of liberal arts, frees it from a sense of guilt about not having a distinctive paradigm, and gives it license to seek whatever is needed, wherever it is located. Thus, Waldo suggests that public administration might act as a profession without being one, or even hoping to become one.

Waldo's ultimate judgment is that public administration is not a single thing but a focus of interest best characterized as an "enterprise." That enterprise contains many facets, perspectives, interests, and methodologies, and is eclectic, experimental, and open-ended in addressing the problems of an untidy, swiftly changing world. The enterprise of public administration should have "a solid center as well as an active circumference" and an emphasis on expanding its range of professional concerns.[118]

Public Administration and the Future

Where do we go from here? Waldo, a self-described "amateur futurist," sees the future as a world of turbulence and change. A major force for change is the current transition from an industrial to a postindustrial society. Although Waldo notes that many of the prophesies for the 1970s failed to come to pass, there is still validity to the notion that the postindustrial society will see the emergence of knowledge as a crucial factor in productivity, the creation of new technologies for processing information, the decline of the factory, the establishment of new power elites and power centers based on scientific-technological knowledge, and a shift in emphasis from production to distribution and service occupations.[119] All of this will result in an accelerated pace of economic-social-political change that will generate institutional and psychological-social crises.

These forces raise an array of problems that must, at least in part, be addressed by public administration. A particular problem for public administration, Waldo observes, will be dealing with new forms of organization and management and calls for the assumption of new responsibilities. Waldo predicts that organizations of the future will be less bureaucratic; increasingly of a mixed public-private nature; more "chains, complexes, or systems of organizations" than unitary organizations; and more international or multinational in their operations.[120] These new organizational styles raise questions about how to develop less bureaucratic organizations without encouraging chaos (i.e., with "adaptive" organizations, what happens to such matters as stability, predictability, and responsibility?), how to deal with increasing ethical complexity, and how to cope with the increasing likelihood of conflict and crisis. Moreover, public administration is apt to be called on to perform even more functions. This raises the danger of overload in a system that, according to Waldo, already has responsibility beyond the authority it can command or the virtue it can summon.[121]

The implications of this future for public administration are manifold. Public administration, Waldo contends, is government's primary mechanism for dealing with the forces noted above. It will thus be centrally involved in change and transformation. The decisions of public administrators will necessarily be a combination of policy judgments, instrumental judgments, legal judgments, and moral judgments. The enterprise of public administration will be marked by philosophical, disciplinary, and methodological pluralism as we attempt to survive, adapt, and control change.

In looking to the future, Waldo observes that there are two major scenarios: the totalitarian and the anarchist.[122] The totalitarian scenario reconciles public and private morality by definition as government totally integrates and controls. The anarchist scenario, which Waldo sees as preferable, or at least less undesirable, sees the future as characterized by a multiplicity of diffuse and complex economic-social-political institutions with considerable ambiguity in the concept of public morality. In reaction to the anarchist scenario, Waldo asserts that he feels as if he is watching a film run backward as the sovereign state is dissolved and its clear vertical structure of authority is replaced by complicated, contractual, and informal horizontal relationships. This does not mean that he thinks history will repeat itself. Waldo believes that the future must be created, it cannot be copied, and he expresses the hope that "reciprocal learning, mutual adjustment, and institutional intervention may now be speeded; that a world unified, but not unitary, harmonious, but not homogenized, may develop."[123]

Conclusion

As stated previously, Waldo has been more a critic and commentator on the field of public administration than a creator. He has thus played a different role than that of the other authors considered in this book.

It is possible to quibble with the particulars of Waldo's approach to the history of public administration, but the larger problem with Waldo's work is his essential ambivalence. Waldo insists that public administration is necessarily involved in politics, but he sees some continuing value in the politics-administration dichotomy. He states that public administration is both art and science, but he fails to specify an area in which each might be applicable. He argues that public administration is both different from, and the same as, private administration without specifying in any detail the similarities and differences, or their consequences. He thinks we should have both democracy and bureaucracy, but he does not tell us either how the conflicts between those forces can be resolved or what the optimal balance between them is. He says that public administration is not, and perhaps should not be, a profession, but he urges that it act like one. Perhaps Waldo best expresses his own ambivalence in stating, "I am skeptical of all faiths and philosophies. This includes, emphatically, skepticism."[124]

This does not mean that Waldo is necessarily wrong. He admits to the problem but finds his position defensible. In addressing the applicability of physical science methods to the social sciences, he says, "I must confess (on the evidence I could not do otherwise) to a certain indecisiveness and ambivalence. . . . But I don't find this posture, this attempt to find a middle ground, as 'error.'"[125] Perhaps so, but that posture does lead to a problem. Waldo's curious mixture of intellectual promiscuity and skepticism, in which he sees all perspectives as flawed but with each having something to contribute, makes him subject to his own criticism of systems analysis; that is, by attempting to include everything, public administration, in his hands, becomes nothing in particular. Nor can the problem simply be passed off with such felicitous phrases as this: "as the island of knowledge has expanded, the shoreline of mystery has lengthened."[126] It may be fair to say that public administration should have an active periphery, but Waldo ignores his own pronouncement that it should also have a recognizable core. At least, he does not define such a core.

Having defined public administration as broadly as he does, Waldo seems to be overwhelmed by the enormity of the task facing the study and practice of public administration. If that task is overwhelming, it is one of Waldo's own construction. Despite his call for the recognition of the limits of administration and the circumscription of administrative responsibilities, Waldo seems to see almost all problems as problems of administration.[127] This is, in large part, a product of Waldo's view that administration and civilization are intimately linked and that administration is government's central mechanism for dealing with change. Once again, his ambivalence appears. Waldo seems torn between his desire to confine public administration to some appropriate sphere that he feels has already been overreached and his belief that public administration will inevitably be involved in addressing most of the major problems of the present and the future.

Wallace Sayre once chided Waldo about his "youthful pessimism" regarding a perceived "identity crisis" in contemporary public administration.[128] Waldo has not so much resolved the problem as he apparently has learned to live with it. Waldo poses heroic demands on public administration, even if he does not necessarily see a heroic future for the enterprise. In this conception of public administration and his call to action, Waldo has already provided what he says is needed in public administration, namely, an "inspirational literature." In characteristic fashion, however, Waldo's "inspiration" is liberally sprinkled with pessimism and doubt.

Dwight Waldo

Notes

1. Information on Waldo's early life is taken from information provided by Professor Waldo and from *Who's Who in America,* 42d ed., vol. 2 (Chicago: Marquis Who's Who, 1982), 3451.

2. "Introduction" (unpublished manuscript) to the 2d ed. of *The Administrative State,* 1.

3. The final dissertation was entitled *Theoretical Aspects of the American Literature in Public Administration.*

4. Dwight Waldo, "The Administrative State Revisited," *Public Administration Review* 25, no. 1 (March 1965): 6.

5. Waldo, "Introduction," 3.

6. Waldo, "Administrative State Revisited," 7.

7. Waldo, "Introduction," 3.

8. Waldo, "Administrative State Revisited," 7.

9. Ibid., 6-7.

10. Dwight Waldo, *The Enterprise of Public Administration* (Novato, Calif.: Chandler and Sharp, 1980), 119.

11. Ibid., 6.

12. Ibid., xii.

13. Dwight Waldo, "Public Administration," *Journal of Politics* 30, no. 2 (May 1968): 447-48.

14. Dwight Waldo, *The Administrative State: A Study of the Political Theory of American Public Administration* (New York: Ronald Press, 1948), 114-15.

15. Ibid., 44.

16. Dwight Waldo, *The Study of Public Administration* (New York: Random House, 1955), 41; and idem, "Public Administration," in *International Encyclopedia of the Social Sciences,* ed. David Sills (New York: Macmillan and Free Press, 1968), 148.

17. Waldo, *Administrative State,* 133-34.

18. Dwight Waldo, "Public Administration," in *The Dimensions of Public Administration: Introductory Readings,* ed. Joseph A. Uveges, Jr. (Boston: Holbrook Press, 1971), 26.

19. Ibid., 71-73, 4.

20. Ibid., 12.

21. Ibid., 15.

22. Waldo, *Administrative State,* 19-20, 91.

23. Ibid., 21.

24. Ibid., 77-85.

25. Ibid., 80.

26. Waldo, "Public Administration," 456.

27. Dwight Waldo, "The Future of Management," *Bureaucrat* 6, no. 3 (Fall 1977): 109-10.

28. Dwight Waldo, *Democracy, Bureaucracy, and Hypocrisy* (Berkeley: Institute of Governmental Studies, 1977), 9.

29. Dwight Waldo, "Development of the Theory of Democratic Administration," *American Political Science Review* 46 (March 1952): 87.

30. Waldo, *Administrative State*, 133.

31. Ibid., 57.

32. Ibid., 128.

33. Ibid., 175.

34. Waldo, "Future of Management," 105.

35. Waldo, *Administrative State*, 159–61.

36. Dwight Waldo, *The Novelist on Organization and Administration: An Inquiry into the Relationship between Two Worlds* (Berkeley: Institute of Government Studies, 1968), 40.

37. Waldo, *Administrative State*, 181, 177.

38. Ibid., 181–82.

39. Ibid., 193–97.

40. Ibid., 202. Waldo suggests that a hierarchy-of-purpose approach may be useful in assessing the utility of the concept of efficiency with efficiency being an appropriate framework at the lower levels of the hierarchy where purpose can be taken as a given. See ibid., 204–5.

41. Waldo, "Public Administration," in Uveges, *Dimensions of Public Administration*, 27.

42. Waldo, *Enterprise of Public Administration*, 69.

43. Ibid.

44. Waldo, "Public Administration," in Sills, *Encyclopedia of the Social Sciences*, 148.

45. Dwight Waldo, "The Administrative State Revisited," 11. Waldo describes Behavioralism as a "mood" or "persuasion" that adopts most of the elements of logical positivism, particularly the view that values are unverifiable and thus removed from the realm of scientific investigation. In general, Behavioralism involves a movement from the philosophical to the positive (i.e., a focus on observable behavior), the separation of facts and values, the use of "proper" scientific methodology, and the search for a more unified empirical theory of human behavior. See Dwight Waldo, *Comparative Public Administration: Prologue, Problems, and Promise*, Papers in Comparative Administration, Special Series no. 5 (Washington, D.C.: Comparative Public Administration Group, American Society for Public Administration, 1964), 7.

46. Waldo, *Study of Public Administration*, 47.

47. Dwight Waldo, "Organization Theory: Revisiting the Elephant," *Public Administration Review* 38, no. 6 (November/December 1978): 589–90.

48. Luther Gulick and L. Urwick eds., *Papers on the Science of Administration* (New York: Institute of Public Administration, 1937).

49. James G. March and Herbert A. Simon, *Organizations* (New York: Wiley, 1958).

50. Waldo, "Public Administration," in Sills, *Encyclopedia of the Social Sciences*, 150; and Dwight Waldo, "Theory of Organization: Status and Problems," in *The Study of Organizational Behavior: Status, Problems, and Trends*, Papers in Comparative Administration, Special Series no. 8 (Washington, D.C.: Comparative Administration Group, American Society for Public Administration, 1966), 6.

51. Waldo, "Organization Theory," 590.

52. Ibid., 592.

53. Waldo, "Public Administration," in Sills, *Encyclopedia of the Social Sciences*, 149; idem, "Public Administration," in Uveges, *Dimensions of Public Administration*, 28–29; and Dwight Waldo, "Scope of the Theory of Public Administration," in *Theory and Practice of Public Administration: Scope, Objectives, and Methods*, ed. James C. Charlesworth (Philadelphia: American Academy of Political and Social Science, 1968), 6.

54. Waldo, "Future of Management," 111.

55. Ibid.

56. Waldo, *Enterprise of Public Administration*, 146.

57. Waldo, "Theory of Organization," 1.

58. Dwight Waldo, "Administrative Theory in the United States: A Survey and Prospect," *Political Studies* 2 (1954): 72.

59. Waldo, "Development of the Theory of Democratic Administration," 89. Also see *American Political Science Review* 46, no. 2 (June 1952): 494–503, for a rather acid exchange between Waldo and Simon.

60. Waldo, *Novelist on Organization and Administration*, 43–44.

61. Dwight Waldo, "Organization Theory: An Elephantine Problem," *Public Administration Review* 21, no. 4 (Autumn 1961): 216.

62. Waldo, "Organization Theory," 592.

63. Ibid.

64. Waldo, "Organization Theory," 211.

65. Ibid., 217.

66. Waldo, "Theory of Organization," 16.

67. Waldo, *Comparative Public Administration*, 27.

68. Waldo, *Enterprise of Public Administration*, 127.

69. Waldo, *Comparative Public Administration*, 29.

70. Dwight Waldo, "Reflections on Public Administration and National Development," *International Social Science Journal* 21, no. 2 (1969): 298, 304.

71. Waldo, "Public Administration," *Journal of Politics*, 466–69.

72. Waldo, *Enterprise of Public Administration*, 73.

73. Dwight Waldo, "Developments in Public Administration," in *Current Issues in Public Administration*, ed. Frederick S. Lane (New York: St. Martin's Press, 1978), 554.

74. Dwight Waldo, *Some Issues in Preparing Science Administration Leadership for Tomorrow*, Program of Policy Studies in Science and Technology, Occasional Paper no. 6 (Washington, D. C.: George Washington University, 1969), 6–7.

75. Dwight Waldo, "Some Thoughts on Alternatives, Dilemmas, and Paradoxes in a Time of Turbulence," in *Public Administration in a Time of Turbulence*, ed. Dwight Waldo (Scranton: Chandler, 1971), 271.

76. Ibid., 263.

77. Ibid., 267.

78. Ibid., 259–60.

79. Ibid., 273.

80. Ibid., 280–81.

81. Ibid., 268.

82. Ibid., 281.

83. Waldo, "Public Administration," *Journal of Politics*, 454.

84. Ibid. ; and Dwight Waldo, "Education for Public Administration in the Seventies," in *American Public Administration: Past, Present, and Future,* ed. Frederick C. Mosher (University, Ala.: University of Alabama Press, 1975), 107.

85. Waldo, *Enterprise of Public Administration,* 34.

86. Dwight Waldo, "Toward World 'Development,'" *African Administrative Studies* 16 (1976): 100; idem, "Organization Theory," 225.

87. Waldo, *Enterprise of Public Administration,* 18.

88. Ibid., 19.

89. Ibid., 29.

90. Ibid., 86.

91. Waldo, *Novelist on Organization and Administration,* 66.

92. Dwight Waldo, "Public Administration and Culture," in *Public Administration and Democracy,* ed. Roscoe C. Martin (Syracuse: Syracuse University Press, 1965), 61.

93. Ibid., 45.

94. Waldo, *Enterprise of Public Administration,* 80.

95. Ibid., 78.

96. Ibid.

97. Waldo, "Administrative Theory in the United States," 85.

98. Dwight Waldo, "Reflections on Public Morality," *Administration and Society* 6, no. 3 (November 1974): 273.

99. Waldo, *Enterprise of Public Administration,* 101.

100. Ibid., 102.

101. Waldo, "Reflections on Public Morality," 272.

102. Ibid., 273.

103. Ibid., 271.

104. Waldo, *Enterprise of Public Administration,* 100–101.

105. Waldo, "Reflections on Public Morality," 269.

106. Waldo, "The Administrative State Revisited," 13, 23.

107. Waldo, "Administrative Theory in the United States," 86.

108. Waldo, *Study of Public Administration,* 62–65.

109. Waldo, *Enterprise of Public Administration,* 21.

110. Ibid., 24.

111. Waldo, "Administrative Theory in the United States," 81; and Dwight Waldo, "Political Science: Tradition, Discipline, Profession, Science, Enterprise," in *Handbook of Political Science,* vol. 1, eds. Fred I. Greenstein and Nelson W. Polsby (Reading, Mass.: Addison-Wesley, 1975), 1–2.

112. Waldo, "Future of Management," 104.

113. Waldo, "Reflections on Public Administration and National Development," 306.

114. Waldo, "Education for Public Administration in the Seventies," 223.

115. Waldo, *Enterprise of Public Administration,* 6.

116. Waldo, "Administrative State Revisited," 29.

117. Ibid., 28.

118. Dwight Waldo, *Perspectives on Administration* (University, Ala.: University of Alabama Press, 1956), 137.

119. Waldo, *Enterprise of Public Administration,* 158–60.

120. Waldo, "Developments in Public Administration," 538–42: idem, *Enterprise of Public Administration*, 167–68.

121. Ibid., 187.

122. Waldo, "Reflections on Public Morality," 277.

123. Waldo, *Enterprise of Public Administration*, 134.

124. Waldo, "Introduction," note 39.

125. Ibid., 48.

126. Ibid., 45.

127. Waldo, *Enterprise of Public Administration*, 47.

128. Wallace S. Sayre, "Comment on Waldo's Paper," in Waldo, *Theory and Practice of Public Administration*, 27.

Index

Index

Adaptive society 133
Administration-as-Politics 2, 4, 10–12, 16, 218–219
Administrative responsibility 11, 187
American Society of Mechanical Engineers (ASME) 51, 64–65, 67
Authority 7–8
—Barnard 156–157, 164–165, 168–169, 176
—Follett 99, 105–106, 110–113, 115
—Gulick 86, 91–92
—Mayo 121, 132
—Simon 181–182, 198–201, 210, 226, 229, 237, 239, 242–243
—Taylor 54, 58–59, 62
—Weber 23, 26–28, 30, 39
Avocational administration 32

Behavioral approach 2, 4–9, 13, 16, 157, 219, 228–229
Blau, Peter 10
Bounded rationality 191, 206
Brandeis, Louis 65
Bureau of Municipal Research 66, 76
Bureaucracy 4
—Simon 186–187
—Waldo 225, 227, 234, 236–237
—Weber 15–16, 20, 29–34, 37–42

Calvinism 25
Capitalism 20, 23–25, 29, 32–33, 36–41, 52, 237
Chain of command 3, 99, 173, 177
Charisma 26, 28, 35, 39
Circular response 103, 105, 111, 114–115
Class 20, 34–36, 38, 127, 129–130, 145
Classical approach 2–13, 16, 181, 185–188, 196, 212, 218, 222–230, 235, 238
Clemenceau, Georges 66
Collegial administration 32–33, 38

Communication
—Barnard 157, 162, 164–165, 168, 170–173, 176–177
—Follett 99, 110
—Gulick 92
—Mayo 133
—Simon 185, 201, 204, 207
Comparative public administration 232
Compromise 98, 102, 116
Conflict 98, 102
Contingency theory 5, 10, 231
Contributions 156–157, 163, 165–166, 176, 196–197, 199
Control
—Barnard 173–174
—Follett 99, 102, 105–106, 109, 111–115
—Gulick 78–80, 86, 91–93
—Mayo 132–133, 145, 147, 151
—Simon 9, 186–187, 196, 200–201, 212
—Taylor 54, 58, 62
—Waldo 223, 229
—Weber 30–32, 38
Cooperation
—Barnard 160–161, 163–165, 172, 174, 177–178
—Follett 98, 102–103, 114
—Gulick 90
—Mayo 9, 121–122, 125, 133–134, 142–143, 145–146
—Taylor 54, 61–62, 68
—Waldo 229
Coordination 3–5
—Barnard 175, 177
—Follett 7, 106, 110–111, 113, 115
—Gulick 80, 85–87, 92
—Simon 9, 181, 200
—Taylor 62
—Waldo 234
—Weber 32
Culture 34

About the Author

Brian R. Fry was born in Chicago, Illinois, and raised in Indiana. He earned an undergraduate degree in political science from Wabash College, an MPA at Cornell University, and a Ph.D. in political science at Stanford University. Professor Fry has served on the faculties of Stanford University and the University of South Carolina; he has also taught at the University of Victoria and the College of Charleston. He is currently a professor of political science and director of the MPA program at the University of South Carolina.

Professor Fry's published works have appeared in some of the leading journals in the field, including the *American Political Science Review,* the *Journal of Politics,* the *American Journal of Political Science, Presidential Studies Quarterly,* and *Policy Studies Journal.* His research has been recognized by an award from the American Political Science Association and a listing in *Citation Classics.* Professor Fry has been nominated to serve on the Executive Council of the National Association of Schools of Public Affairs and Administration; he currently is the vice chair of the association's section on political science-based public administration programs and a member of the board for the international section.

Professor Fry has served with state governments in Indiana, California, and South Carolina. He is at present a member of the State Reorganization Commission in South Carolina and secretary of the board of the Council on Aging of the Midlands. He has received the Outstanding Public Service award for his work with the public sector in South Carolina.